Language Textbooks in the Era of Neoliberalism

This book examines how neoliberalism finds expression in foreign language textbooks. Moving beyond the usual focus on English, Pau Bori explores the impact of neoliberal ideology on Catalan textbooks. By comparing Catalan textbooks to English textbooks, this book interrogates the similarities and differences between a minor and a global language in the age of neoliberalism. Drawing on insights from critical theory and critical pedagogy, this study provides a fresh perspective on foreign language textbooks and second language education more broadly. *Language Textbooks in the Era of Neoliberalism* paves the way for new critical perspectives in language education that will challenge the current hegemony of neoliberalism.

Pau Bori is Lecturer in Catalan Studies at the University of Belgrade. He is interested in language education and language teaching materials, examining both from a political economy perspective. He has published papers in various journals and contributed chapters to books of collected articles.

Language, Society and Political Economy
Series editor: David Block, Institució Catalana de Recerca i Estudis Avançats, Universitat de Lleida.

For more information on any of these and other titles, or to order, please go to www.routledge.com/Language-Society-and-Political-Economy/book-series/LSPE

Additional resources for Language and Communication are available on the Routledge Language and Communication Portal: www.routledgetextbooks.com/textbooks/languageandcommunication/

This series aims to publish broadly accessible monographs which directly address how theoretical frameworks in political economy can directly inform the critical analysis and discussion of language in society issues. Contributions to the series include extensive theoretical background, dealing with an aspect or area of political economy, before moving to an application of this theoretical discussion to a particular language in society issue. The series takes up the challenge of interdisciplinarity, linking scholarship in the social sciences in general (and political economy in particular) with the kinds of issues which language in society researchers have traditionally focused on. The series also aims to publish books by authors whose ideas fall outside the mainstream of language in society scholarship and by authors in parts of the world which have traditionally been underrepresented in relevant international journals and book series.

Titles in the series:

Language Textbooks in the Era of Neoliberalism
Pau Bori

The Discourses of Capitalism
Christian W. Chun

Language and Neoliberalism
Marnie Holborow

Language Textbooks in the Era of Neoliberalism

Pau Bori

LONDON AND NEW YORK

First published 2018
by Routledge
2 Park Square, Milton Park, Abingdon, Oxon OX14 4RN

and by Routledge
711 Third Avenue, New York, NY 10017

Routledge is an imprint of the Taylor & Francis Group, an informa business

© 2018 Pau Bori

The right of Pau Bori to be identified as author of this work has
been asserted by him in accordance with sections 77 and 78 of the
Copyright, Designs and Patents Act 1988.

All rights reserved. No part of this book may be reprinted or
reproduced or utilised in any form or by any electronic, mechanical,
or other means, now known or hereafter invented, including
photocopying and recording, or in any information storage or
retrieval system, without permission in writing from the publishers.

Trademark notice: Product or corporate names may be trademarks
or registered trademarks, and are used only for identification and
explanation without intent to infringe.

British Library Cataloguing-in-Publication Data
A catalogue record for this book is available from the British Library

Library of Congress Cataloging-in-Publication Data
Names: Bori, Pau, author.
Title: Language textbooks in the era of neoliberalism / Pau Bori.
Description: Milton Park, Abingdon, Oxon ; New York, NY :
    Routledge, [2018] | Includes bibliographical references and index.
Identifiers: LCCN 2017050946 | ISBN 9781138223196 (hardback) |
    ISBN 9781315405544 (ebk)
Subjects: LCSH: Language and languages—Study and teaching—
    Political aspects. | Neoliberalism—Political aspects. | Languages,
    Modern—Textbooks. | Catalan language—Textbooks for foreign
    speakers—English. | English language—Textbooks for foreign
    speakers—Catalan. | Applied linguistics.
Classification: LCC P53.6128 .B67 2018 | DDC 410—dc23
LC record available at https://lccn.loc.gov/2017050946

ISBN: 978-1-138-22319-6 (hbk)
ISBN: 978-1-315-40554-4 (ebk)

Typeset in Sabon
by Apex CoVantage, LLC

To Jelena, my great love and inspiration.

Contents

Acknowledgements viii

1 Introduction 1

2 A short history of foreign language education
in Europe 19

3 Critical research on language textbooks 41

4 Analyzing textbooks from a political economy
perspective 66

5 The Catalan context 83

6 Social class in textbooks 102

7 The world of work: constructing an entrepreneurial
identity 120

8 The world of housing: creating a neoliberal fairytale 142

9 Conclusions 162

References 170
Index 193

Acknowledgements

I would like to express my appreciation to all of those who have contributed to this book. Here I mention those who have been especially helpful.

First of all, I thank my editor, David Block, for having given me the opportunity to write this book and for having helped me throughout the process of completing it. I deeply appreciate the many hours he spent carefully reading all the drafts of this manuscript and his incredible amount of valuable feedback that has greatly improved my book.

I also want to thank the scholars who read and commented on parts of the book or even the entire book. Thank you to Marnie Holborow for commenting on Chapter 1. Thank you to Nigel Harwood and Scott Thornbury for commenting on Chapters 1 to 8. And thank you to Christian Chun and John Gray for commenting on Chapters 1 to 9. All their comments, suggestions and criticisms have been very helpful to me. I am also deeply grateful to Chris Prickett for her proofreading of this book and her valuable assistance with issues linked to the English language. I also wish to thank the participants of the 7th *International Conference on Critical Education* in Athens, where the first draft of Chapter 8 was presented, for their comments.

I thank my PhD supervisor, Daniel Cassany, for providing guidance and support with the writing of my dissertation, which is the basis of this book. I would also like to extend special appreciation to my colleagues in the Department of Iberian Studies at the University of Belgrade for their support, and particularly to Jelena Filipović for her encouragement and advice during my research. I am also very grateful to the Faculty of Philology at the University of Belgrade for giving me the opportunity to work there and a chance to gain an invaluable professional and personal experience. Obviously, this book would not have been possible without the input and assistance of Routledge staff. I would especially like to thank Hannah Rowe, Laura Sandford and Louisa Semlyen, for their patience through the entire book writing process.

Finally, my wholehearted gratitude goes to my family for their love and understanding, and especially to my wife, Jelena Petanović, to whom this book is dedicated. Without all the love, readings, working hours and wonderful conversations that we shared together, this book would never have been possible.

1 Introduction

This book is about textbooks, political economy and ideology. More precisely, it is about connections between language textbooks and the latest form of the capitalist project, neoliberalism. This book will examine the ways in which neoliberalism, transformed into the new common sense of our times (Peck and Tickell 2002; Harvey 2005; Hall and O'Shea 2013), finds expression in foreign and second language teaching materials. The overall aims are to advance our knowledge about materials development, to illustrate different kinds of critical textbook analysis and uncover new important issues that need to be contemplated in more detail for critical research on language textbooks in an era of neoliberal globalization. The ultimate goal is to pave the way for new critical perspectives in language education that will counter the current hegemonic ideology of neoliberalism.

Three main arguments provide the rationale for this volume: the enduring centrality of language textbooks in most classrooms around the world (Gray 2015), the ubiquity of neoliberalism in our contemporary societies and above all the need for further and deeper investigations about the relations between language education and neoliberalism. Thus, I strongly agree with the critical education scholar Carlos Alberto Torres (2011: 183) when he suggests that now more than ever it is imperative

> to challenge the growing presence of instrumental rationality and neoliberalism's common sense in the way we live, practice, work, teach, provide advice to our students, conduct research, work in committees and even profess our most cherished values in our professional work as academics.

This first chapter provides the theoretical basis for the discussion and analysis that follows. It starts with insights from the political and economic philosophy of Karl Marx and ends with new approaches in applied linguistics devoted to the relations between language and political economy. First of all, I discuss our understanding of textbooks through the ideas of classical Marxism, the Frankfurt school and critical pedagogy. I then define neoliberalism as a global class project that shapes political economy and ideology

2 Introduction

worldwide (Harvey 2005) and also as the norm of our existence (Dardot and Laval 2013). This is followed by a presentation of relevant studies about real-world language problems from an interdisciplinary perspective that place neoliberalism at the center of the research. The chapter concludes with a call to make a 'turn to political economy' (Block *et al.* 2012a; Block 2017a) in studying phenomena related to language teaching.

Understanding textbooks

The textbook is a central element in the language teaching and learning process. It has been said that it is the "visible heart of any ELT [English Language Teaching] program" (Sheldon 1988: 237); "an almost universal element of ELT teaching" (Hutchinson and Torres 1994: 315); and "a guide for a teacher, a memory aid for the pupils, a permanent record or measure of what has been learnt" (Awasthi 2006: 1). Furthermore, language textbooks seem to "have a magical hold on both teachers and learners most of whom just can not do without them" (Kumaravadivelu 2012: 21). This is why I consider it essential to study and discuss language teaching textbooks in detail. The approach of this book is based upon the idea that textbooks are cultural artifacts of their time, like any other human creation or activity. They are not born in a vacuum. Textbooks are situated in a determinate moment in time and in a concrete place. As a consequence, they are influenced by the political, economic and historical context where they were created. As Andrew Littlejohn (2012: 287) explains, language teaching materials include "perspectives, attitudes, values, concepts, social and political relations – call them what you will – which will be current in the wider society".

This understanding of textbooks has its roots in the political and economic philosophy of Marx, known as historic materialism. In his base/superstructure model, Marx argues that human beings are subject to the social and economic circumstances of their existence that influence their particular class system, political organizations, thoughts and culture. The base refers to the economic conditions of the reality and involves the productive forces (labor-power, raw materials and machines) and the relations of production (the relationship between those who own the means of production and those who do not). From the base arises the superstructure, that is, "the social, political and spiritual processes of life" (Marx 1904 [1859]: 11). The superstructure involves the ideology and the political and legal organization that governs a society. In classical Marxism, the superstructure is shaped by the class division of the society between capitalists (or bourgeoisie) and workers (or proletariat). Hence, the ideas, values and beliefs which achieve dominance in any particular age are the ones of those in power, as noted in a famous quote from *The German Ideology*: "The ideas of the ruling class are in every epoch the ruling ideas: i.e., the class which is the ruling *material* force of society is at the same time its ruling *intellectual* force" (Marx and Engels 1998 [1845]: 67).

Introduction 3

From a Marxist perspective, capitalism is a socioeconomic system based on private property and the exploitation of the labor force. Its main motion is profit-making. The means for producing goods are owned by a small group of people, the capitalist class. The majority of people, the working classes, sell their labor to a capitalist for a wage in order to earn a living. Exploitation is the result of the uncompensated labor of the working classes, which is used by the capitalist members of society to increase their profit in the market.

The Marxist claim that the ideological superstructure is determined by the economic base has been often attacked for being much too mechanical or reductive. However, the Marxist tradition had repeatedly addressed this criticism. It has been argued that the economic base is a crucial element to understanding the evolution of history, but other factors belonging to the superstructure also influence changes in society (see Chris Harman 1986 for a discussion about the base and superstructure debate in Marxist scholarship). Indeed, as David Block (2014) argues, the relationship between base and superstructure could be interpreted in a nuanced way: "one can appropriate the idea that economic activity is the base for all social activity and development while arguing for a more dialectical approach to how the economic base interacts with Marx's 'social, political and intellectual life' " (30). In my study, base and superstructure are understood essentially as a starting point to explain how a cultural artifact as the textbook is shaped by the material conditions of capitalism.

The legacy of Marx has led to a tremendous variety of schools and movements that examine social phenomena in their dynamic relation to wider historical, political and economic realities in capitalist societies. For the approach of this book, particularly relevant is the notion of hegemony used by Antonio Gramsci to explain the ways in which the dominant ideology is disseminated and accepted as commonsensical and normal. Hegemony in Gramsci's terms is seen as the:

> 'spontaneous' consent given by the great masses of the population to the general direction imposed on social life by the dominant fundamental group; this consent is 'historically' caused by the prestige (and consequent confidence) which the dominant group enjoys because of its position and function in the world of production.
>
> (Gramsci 1971: 12)

Gramsci sees that the ruling class expresses its power not only by physical force or economic control, but also through cultural institutions such as the media, the school or the church, which are capable of presenting a particular ideology as 'common sense', or the natural way of thinking and acting. Of course, hegemonic consent is not always total and complete since "people may accept some aspects but reject others" (Holborow 2012b: 41). Indeed, Gramsci (1971) himself offers the prospect to turn the situation

4   Introduction

around by encouraging the subaltern classes to develop their own alternative hegemonic 'collective will' as a first phase to the revolution.

In order to understand a cultural product such as a language textbook, it is also very important to have in mind the Marxist critical theory of the Frankfurt School, and especially its studies of mass culture. Frankfurt scholars examined mass-mediated cultural products (music, cinema, soap operas, magazines, etc.) within the context of the consumer and industrial society of the mid-twentieth century in Western capitalist countries. In their *Dialectic of Enlightenment*, Max Horkheimer and Theodor Adorno (2002 [1944]) coin the term 'culture industry' to signify the process of industrialization of culture created by the commercial imperatives that guide capitalism. These two authors argue that cultural products have the same characteristics as the rest of goods in mass capitalist production: commodification, standardization and massification. However, unlike other goods such as clothes or food, cultural products are not directed to human material needs, but to people's thoughts (Dant 2003: 110). Hence, cultural products have the specific function of legitimizing capitalism penetrating people's minds: "Capitalism has an interest in the state of those minds: it needs workers who are happy enough to accept uncritically their position within the system" (Dant 2003: 110). In a similar way, Herbert Marcuse (1964 [1954]) explains that art in advanced capitalist societies became simple entertainment, commercialized according to its value as a commodity in the market. These new artistic manifestations, instead of awakening people's critical thinking, encourage conformism with the status quo or, in the words of Marcuse, a 'happy consciousness': "the belief that the real is rational and that the system delivers the goods" (Marcuse 1964: 84). In sum, for Frankfurt scholars, the culture industry of their time provides "amusement, distraction, relief" to the people and, in that way, "ameliorates the violence that capitalism performs" (Taylor and Harris 2008: 71). As Marnie Holborow (personal communication) reminds me, it is worth noting that the Frankfurt school thesis was developed in a period of capitalist expansion which may explain some the school's tendency to present the masses as passive victims. They rather wrote off the working class's ability to resist as they believed that increased material consumption had dulled working-class anger.

In the field of education, the works of Marx, Gramsci and the Frankfurt school are the roots of critical pedagogy, an approach which aims to show how formal and informal education are transformed by relations of inequality and power (Apple et al. 2010). Critical pedagogy is also "a practical approach to teaching, learning, and research that emphasizes teaching through critical dialogue and a dialectical analysis of everyday experience" (Macrine et al. 2010: 2). This movement has been developed mainly in North America with key figures such as Peter McLaren and Henry Giroux, but its genesis can be traced to Paulo Freire's literacy campaigns with working-class and peasant students in Brazil, in a struggle against oppressive social structures. Freire's work, especially his *Pedagogy of the Oppressed* (Freire

1970), has inspired many critical educators and theoreticians who viewed his work as "a new synthesis for a humanist and libertarian pedagogy, which aimed through its praxis at transforming oppression and the culture of domination" (Peters 2005: 35). For our understanding of textbooks, the research carried out by critical pedagogues on the ideological character of curriculum and textbooks is especially interesting. Michael Apple, in his widely influential book *Ideology and Curriculum*, first published in 1979, argues that curriculum is not neutral knowledge, but is always the result of a process of 'selective tradition':

> the way in which from a whole possible area of past and present, certain meanings and practices are chosen for emphasis, certain other meanings and practices are neglected and excluded. Even more crucially, some of these meanings are reinterpreted, diluted, or put into forms which support or at least do not contradict other elements within the effective dominant culture.
>
> (Apple 1990: 6)

The selective tradition disseminated in schools reflects the interest and the beliefs of the ruling class in society. Thus, schools have the function to reproduce the hegemonic ideology and, in that way, reinforce and natural-ize the current socioeconomic system (Apple 1990; Giroux 1997). In this vein, critical educators agree that textbooks embody particular ideologies and present an officially sanctioned knowledge (Luke 1988; De Castell et al. 1989; Apple and Christian-Smith 1991). For example, in *The Poli-tics of the Textbook*, Apple and Linda Christian-Smith (1991) contend that school textbooks "are not simple 'delivery system' of 'facts' " (1), but "they signify – through their content *and* form – particular constructions of real-ity, particular ways of selecting and organizing that vast universe of possible knowledge" (3–4). In that way, as an educational tool in general, textbooks have an important ideological and reproduction role in society:

> As part of a curriculum they participate in no less than the organized knowledge system of society. They participate in creating what a society has recognized as legitimate and truthful. They help set the canons of truthfulness and, as such, also help re-create a major reference point for what knowledge, culture, belief, and morality really are.
>
> (Apple and Christian-Smith 1991: 4)

What knowledge is relevant, accurate and worthy of transmitting to future generations will vary depending on each historic context (Choppin 2000). More precisely, according to Marxism, it will depend on the dominant ideol-ogy at a given moment in history. The dominant ideology coincides with the interests of the ruling classes, and it is conditioned by the material activity of people in the society at large (Marx and Engels 1998 [1845]). Following

6 *Introduction*

Holborow (2012a, 2015), in my study, the term ideology is understood as "a one-sided representation, articulated from a particular social class but constructed as a world view, part-believed and part rejected, influenced by real-world events and coextensive with language, but distinct from it" (2015: 130). The purpose of my book is to analyze the underpinnings of neoliberal ideology in current textbooks in capitalist societies. Evidently, though, other textbooks instantiate ideologies other than a capitalist or neo-liberal one. For example, textbooks from other contexts and periods may endorse a socialist ideological paradigm or a particular system of religious values in line with the guiding principles of the social, political and economic system where they are created.

Besides being an ideological artifact, the textbook is also seen by critical education scholars as a commercial product, that is, an economic commodity that should compete in the market to achieve profits for the publishing industry (Apple 1985). In other words, the content and the form of textbooks are determined by political and ideological conditions outside the classroom, which also include the economic imperatives of the market, meaning the need to augment its sales and accomplish corporate goals. The seminal work of critical pedagogy in the analysis of education materials in relation to the political and economic climate has subsequently inspired many critical studies of textbooks, including also foreign and second language textbooks such as *The Hidden Curriculum of Survival ESL* (Auerbach and Burgess 1985), the studies of John Gray (2010b, 2013b) and Christian Chun (2009) about English textbooks, or a recent edited collection about the politics of language textbooks (Curdt-Christiansen and Weninger 2015a), as I will explain in detail in Chapter 3. Finally, in the particular field of applied linguistics, Marxism has also influenced the emerging interest to put neoliberalism at the center of the research from the perspective of political economy. Before considering the studies of neoliberalism and applied linguistics, however, it is necessary first to define our understanding of neoliberalism.

What is neoliberalism?

Neoliberalism is a term used today mainly by its critics[1] to designate the latest phase of capitalism which began in the late 1970s and early 1980s. In the first instance, neoliberalism is an economic policy paradigm based on a theory which holds "that human well-being can best be advanced by liberating individual entrepreneurial freedoms and skills within an institutional framework characterized by strong private property rights, free markets, and free trade" (Harvey 2005: 2). For Pierre Bourdieu (1998: npn), one of the first critical scholars to use this term, neoliberalism is a political "programme for destroying collective structures which may impede the pure market logic". Its theoretical roots can be found in the works of the Austrian political philosopher Friedrich Hayek in the 1940s and of the Chicago School of

Economics in the 1950s with Milton Friedman as its key figure.[2] Neoliberal thinking was first put into practice in Chile after the US-backed Pinochet coup in 1973 under the direction of many economists who had graduated from Friedman's University of Chicago, and which imposed drastic economic changes on the country (Klein 2007). The characteristics of neoliberal economic policy are free trade and deregulation of financial markets, privatization of state enterprises (including energy, water, health, education, housing and transport services), reduction of public spending on welfare, and tax cuts for the rich. It promotes a flexible work market, the decline of worker unions and consumption through debt. Another key feature of neoliberalism is the "extension of market-based competition and commodification processes into previously insulated realms of political-economic life" (Brenner et al. 2010: 329), such as education and health.

In the 1980s, neoliberal policies began to be implemented at the center of the capitalist system under the governments of Ronald Reagan in the United States and Margaret Thatcher in Britain. According to David Harvey (2005), this neoliberal recipe came in response to the mid-1970s international crisis of the capitalist system that had dominated from the end of World War II. That approach had followed Keynesian economic prescriptions that advocate for state planning to reduce unemployment and stimulate economic growth, and which had led to the development of a welfare system in most Western capitalist societies. Especially after the collapse of state socialism in Eastern Europe in 1989 and the disappearance of this strong alternative to capitalism, neoliberalism became the dominant economic doctrine around the world. US-dominated financial bodies such as the International Monetary Fund and the World Bank played a highly active role in the spread of neoliberalism globally through the imposition of the dictates of what was known as the 'Washington Consensus' in developing countries that received the loans they issued. The Washington Consensus, a term first used in 1989, is a set of ten economic prescriptions promoted by US-based institutions such as the International Monetary Fund, the World Bank and the US Treasury Department. These prescriptions comprising the new global economic policy include the decrease of government spending to control inflation and reduce the public deficit, trade liberalization with the abolition of state restrictions on imports and exports, the deregulation of markets, the privatization of state enterprises and the protection of property rights (Williamson 1990).

Since then, neoliberal economic policy has been adopted by the great majority of governments, from those led by conservative parties to those led by social-democratic forces (Holborow 2012a; Dardot and Laval 2013). The spread of neoliberalism was accompanied by a further process of globalization and a new technological revolution. The move towards a post-industrial economy[3] in the West allowed its corporations to outsource and offshore production to countries with lower labor costs, fewer workers' rights and little environmental regulation (Block 2018c). Apart from the

8 *Introduction*

massive environmental destruction, the implementation of neoliberal policies worldwide in the last decades have brought greater socioeconomic inequalities, a greater concentration of wealth and increasing levels of poverty (Harvey 2005). Class inequalities have further increased since the current global economic crisis began in 2007–2008. An illustrative example can be found in Ken Loach's highly acclaimed 2016 film *I, Daniel Blake*. Loach illustrates the struggles to survive that working-class people experience in the United Kingdom, especially since the crisis and the implementation of austerity measures. The main character in the film is a working-class man who is about to retire. After suffering a heart attack, he attempts in vain to receive some support of the inhuman and uncaring UK benefit system. With this story, Loach captures the cruel way in which capitalist states treat many of their citizens, and especially those more vulnerable. At the global level, wealth inequalities have grown larger in recent years and poverty has continued to threaten the lives of millions of people. The richest 1 percent of the world's population now owns more wealth than the rest of the world combined, according to a recent Oxfam (2016) report: "In 2015, just 62 individuals had the same wealth as 3.6 billion people – the bottom half of humanity. This figure is down from 388 individuals as recently as 2010" (Oxfam 2016: 2).

The official neoliberal doctrine advocates for minimal government, while at the same time insisting that strong states are necessary "for the operation of ostensibly free markets and to deal with the consequences of 'market failure'" (Price 2014: 569). One recent example of the active intervention of the state into the market can be found in the aftermath of the great economic crash of 2008 with "the unimaginably huge sums of government money injected into the financial system across the US, the UK and the Eurozone" (Holborow 2012a: 18) to rescue a deregulated and speculative capitalist system from its own collapse. After the 2008 meltdown, neoliberalism returned with even greater force (Morgan 2013). In the Eurozone, for example, austerity policies imposed by the European Commission meant more cuts of public spending, wage reductions and new labor reforms that led to a radical degradation of living standards, especially in southern countries such as Greece, Spain, Portugal and Italy. At the same time, "[a]usterity measures, selectively applied, became the means of recreating the conditions under which the market, and those who gained from it, could flourish again" (Holborow 2015: 35). For Harvey (2005), this increasing economic inequality testifies that neoliberalism was from the very beginning a class project from above for "the restoration or reconstruction of the power of economic elites" (19) that felt threatened by the international economic capitalist crisis of the 1970s.

From the Marxist standpoint, neoliberalism should also be understood as an ideology: "This understanding maintains that elite actors and dominant groups organized around transnational class-based alliances have the capacity to project and circulate a coherent program of interpretations and images of the world onto others" (Springer 2012: 136). One of the key concepts of the neoliberal ideology is that (free) markets are the answer for all human and societal issues. For neoliberals, "the market is the most efficient and moral institution for the organization of human affairs" (Springer et al. 2016: 3). Neoliberal ideology presents the market as a natural system, like gravity. Marnie Holborow (2015: 34) synthesizes the central role that the market has in neoliberal ideology as follows:

> the market captures a basic truth about human nature and social organization. It redefines the relationship between the individual and society with social behaviour being guided, not by collective institutions and interaction, but by supply and demand, by entrepreneurs and consumer choice, by individual companies and individual people.

One of the most appealing features of neoliberal ideology for some people is its promise of greater personal freedoms. As explained by Harvey (2005: 41–3) and Matthew Morgan (2013), capitalism showed its capacity to adapt to new circumstances and absorbed in its own discourse demands from the social movements of the 1960s for civil, cultural, sexual and reproductive rights that reclaimed more individual freedom to overcome the restraints of a bureaucratic and intrusive state and of the dominant morality in order to be able to make one's own decisions. In practice, freedom in neoliberalism is mainly understood as "the liberty of consumer choice, not only with respect to particular products but also with respect to lifestyles, modes of expression, and a wide range of cultural practices" (Harvey 2005: 42), and above all as the freedom of capital to move without barriers.

Drawing on the Gramscian notion of hegemony, Harvey (2005) suggests that neoliberalism "has become incorporated into the common-sense way many of us interpret, live in, and understand the world" (3). In a similar vein, Holborow (2012a: 14) asserts that neoliberalism is 'the stamp of our age': "In less than a generation, neoliberal principles have spread across every continent and become so integral to public and private life that thinking outside their parameters is almost unthinkable". However, the hegemony of neoliberal ideology does not mean that its acceptance is complete (Holborow 2015). Chun (2017) illustrates this point in his book about how everyday people understand what capitalism means to them. This author examines the responses of ordinary people from the United States and the UK to a street installation entitled *Capitalism Works for Me!* The results show very different understandings of capitalism, from those that are in line with the dominant neoliberal discourse to those that challenge the narratives of neoliberal ideology and, indeed, present counter-hegemonic views of capitalism.

Finally, at a deeper level, neoliberalism has also involved a sharp reversal in the ways we conduct ourselves in our public and private lives, in the sense that competition and entrepreneurial mindsets now govern the

10 *Introduction*

behavior of many people and institutions. This vision is indebted to the concept of 'governmentality' developed by Michel Foucault in the late 1970s to explore how the practices of knowledge are produced through their relations to power. It is a neologism that combines 'government' and 'mentality' to study the links between the ways governments manage people's actions through techniques of domination and the ways people conduct their own behavior through techniques of the self. As Foucault (1993: 204) suggested, the governing of people is a "versatile equilibrium" between the way people coerce and dominate each other and the way the techniques of the self are integrated into the structures of coercion and domination. In this regard, Foucault (2008) understood neoliberalism as a rationality that determines both the ways governments manage people's actions and the ways people conduct themselves. With this in mind, Pierre Dardot and Christian Laval (2013: 8) explain that neoliberalism has become "the form of our existence". According to these two authors, neoliberalism is the norm that shapes the mode of our living, our relations with others and even the ways we represent ourselves:

> This norm enjoins everyone to live in a world of generalized competition; it calls upon wage-earning classes and populations to engage in economic struggle against one another; it aligns social relations with the model of the market; it promotes the justification of ever greater inequalities; it even transforms the individual, now called on to conceive and conduct him- or herself as an enterprise.
>
> (Dardot and Laval 2013: 8)

To think of ourselves as enterprises implies to live in constant risk. People should now take individual responsibilities in all spheres of their lives and constantly attempt to improve themselves in a competitive climate. As a result, if people do not have a job or are evicted from their houses, it is because they are not enterprising and have not worked enough to develop their abilities to fit in the new order governed by competition. In other words, the structural inequalities of the capitalist system, such as labor exploitation, inheritance or class, are no longer relevant to explain poverty, since the individuals are the only ones responsible for their own economic failure.

In sum, neoliberalism in this book is understood as the ruling global political economic paradigm and the dominant ideology of the last four decades, and also as the rationality that shapes people's behavior in Western societies and even beyond. It is worth noting here that, at the time of writing this book in 2017, it has become evident to many people around the world that capitalism in its neoliberal form is an economic system that does not work satisfactorily anymore. Chun (2017: 50) emphasizes this point for the case of the United States, but his consideration could be easily extrapolated to any other Western capitalist society: "[I]t is clear that the majority of the general public in the US clearly knows, or at the very least feels, something is very wrong with the economy". Indeed, before the 2007–2008 economic crisis, many people believed that capitalism might be the best (or the only) viable system in the world's history, as it seemed to ensure the well-being of the majority of its citizens, at least in Western countries. However, the harsh consequences of the 2007–2008 crisis have made many people aware that something is wrong with neoliberalism since they have been severely affected by cuts in spending in public health and education, increasing unemployment, declining wage salaries and difficulties accessing decent housing. The political crisis of neoliberalism has recently arrived at the centers of the global capitalist system. In 2015, Jeremy Corbin became the leader of the Labour Party in the United Kingdom, with a discourse against neo-liberalism diametrically opposed to the ideas of his predecessors Tony Blair or Gordon Brown. Although from a contradictory perspective, the victories of Brexit and Donald Trump in United States presidential elections in 2016 might also be interpreted as a revolt against neoliberalism. All these developments make even more relevant in the current conjuncture of the history the critical research about language and neoliberalism.[4] In what follows, I will review selected works in applied linguistics that have recently dealt with the political economy in general and with neoliberalism in particular.

Applied linguistics and political economy

My book belongs to a body of research which seeks to contribute to an emergent approach in applied linguistics which proposes a reorientation of the interdisciplinarity in applied linguistics towards a Marxist-oriented frame that focuses on the economic and material conditions of human existence to study phenomena related to language use. Block, Gray and Holborow expound this new approach in the introductory chapter of their book *Neoliberalism and Applied Linguistics*:

> to reorient interdisciplinarianism in applied linguistics in such a way that these economic and material bases of human activity and social life not only get a look-in, but they become central to discussions of a range of language related issues. For applied linguistics to be truly socially constituted, it must take full account of the political economy of contemporary capitalism – a political economy which encompasses both social classes and their ideologies.
>
> (Block et al. 2012b: 4)

These three authors make this call to correct a "blind spot" in the interdisciplinarity of applied linguistics to include the "political economy and in particular a detailed critique of neoliberalism as the ideology driving the practice of economics by governments and international organisations today" (Block et al. 2012b: 1). Indeed, in these last decades of globalization

12 Introduction

under a neoliberal economic system, interdisciplinary approaches in applied linguistics have focused on concepts such as interculturalism, gender or identity, but omitted an analysis and discussion of the economic organization of societies and related key constructs such as ideology or social class. In a chapter of the same book dedicated to globalization and social class, Block (2012a: 73) explains this process in the following words:

> during the neoliberal era – from the late 1970s to the present – there has been a remarkable increase in debates and discussions around multiculturalism and identity politics. These have occurred both inside academia (including in applied linguistics) and outside and they have been framed in terms of gender, race, ethnicity, nationality and sexuality, while celebrating difference and diversity. Meanwhile, class has disappeared off the radar or has been invoked only to make clear its irrelevance in the new global village.

However, the situation is slowly changing with an increasing number of scholars introducing questions of political economy and references to neoliberalism in their applied and sociolinguistics research, (see Block 2017a for broader review of research on language and political economy). As mentioned above, one of the main features of neoliberal ideology is to "subsume all aspects of social life into the frame of free-market economics" (Holborow 2012b: 46) and language, of course, is not an exception. The global spread of capitalism, the increasing labor flexibility and mobility of businesses and workers, and the growth of the service industry where language plays a central role have involved important transformations of language that have been examined from a variety of perspectives.

In the new knowledge economy, in which the central role is not played by physical labor but by "knowledge, information, affect and communication" (Hardt and Negri 2001: 285), what is valued above all is the use of the language as an effective communication tool (Cameron 2002) to make people economically competitive. Relying on the *McDonaldization* thesis by George Ritzer (1996), Block (2002) coins the term *McCommunication* to refer to "the framing of communication as a rational activity devoted to the transfer of information between and among individuals in an efficient, calculable, predictable and controllable manner via the use of language" (121). The spread of *McCommunication*, as Block (2002: 120) argues, leads to a "depressing" hypothesis:

> not only will consumption soon be globalized to such an extent that eating, shopping, and holidaying come to be very similar across different geographical locations, but that our ways of communicating in institutional contexts and our personal lives, will also come to be similar as we all follow the same recommendations on how we should and shouldn't talk.

McCommunication could be related to what Norman Fairclough (1992) calls the 'technologization of discourse'. It refers to the effort to design the discourse (or the language) in order to be implemented in a controlled way to achieve calculated purposes in particular settings such as the service industries, advertising or political campaigns (Fairclough 1995). This phenomenon has been widely studied, particularly through the linguistic rituals predominant in call centers (Cameron 2000, 2002; Heller 2003; Holborow 2007), which have become a paradigmatic example of the shift from a national industrialized economy to a global, post-industrial, offshore production, characterized by high levels of precarious work. Call centers encourage their workers to feel they are a constituting part of the business, to adapt their behavior to the image of the corporation and to show empathy for the customers (Heller 2003). In order to sell products and services, call centers provide employees with strict norms to regulate their telephone conversations, such as smiling, never arguing, showing understanding towards the customer, apologizing sincerely and so on (Holborow 2007: 66).

Fairclough (1995, 2002) also highlights how there has been a 'colonization' of public domains such as education or health by the discursive practices of market domains like business and advertising. Holborow (2012a: 22–4) maintains a critical distance from Fairclough's discourse driven understanding of neoliberalism because she believes that it minimizes the part played by the economic base and the ruling ideology. However, her research over the last decade about language and ideology may be seen as a continuation of Fairclough's work on the market colonization of public discourse. Drawing on Raymond Williams's (1985) notion of key words, Holborow (2007, 2012b, 2013, 2015) shows the ways in which neoliberal meanings such as *customer, entrepreneur, deregulation, human capital, market, commercialization* and *intellectual property* have come to dominate the language of social settings previously independent of the economy, such as in the case in higher education. These key words have been promoted in the education field by think tanks such as the Organization for Economic Cooperation and Development (OECD) with the purpose of spreading a particular ideology – the neoliberal one. Yet, as Holborow (2013) points out, the ideology of this market-speak is contested in some cases, which shows that neoliberal hegemony is not complete. Closely related to the spread of a corporate language in public domains, Allan Luke et al. (2007: 4) refer to a new "planetary 'newspeak'" that saturates "the pages of newspapers, blogs, and screens with the language of the 'market', and with its images and discourses of competitive and possessive individualism", which promotes the neoliberal hegemony within our contemporary societies.

Within the studies on language and political economy, social class has recently become a focus. As Block (2014) recounts, this construct intimately associated with Marx was a central concept at the beginning of sociolinguistics, especially in the works of variationist research (Labov 1966; Bernstein 1971; Trudgill 1974). However, from the 1980s onwards, interest in social

14 *Introduction*

class waned, not only in applied linguistics and in the social sciences in general, but also "in society at large" (Block 2014: 169). This lack of interest in social class went hand in hand with the rise of neoliberalism and a less class-consciousness-oriented or collective identity (known in Marxian terms as 'class for itself') among working-class people in the West. In a world characterized by individualism, political apathy and the society of the spectacle, the working class has often failed to recognize the assault that the neoliberal project represents to them and to organize collectively to fight against it. On the other hand, as Dave Hill (2010: 121–2) notes, the capitalist ruling elites are the only ones that have a clear class consciousness:

> They are rich. They are powerful. And they are transnational as well as national. [. . .] [T]hey survive precisely because they do know they are a class. They have class consciousness, they are 'a class for themselves' (a class with a consciousness that they are a class), as well as a 'class in themselves' (a class or group of people with shared economic conditions of existence and interests). The capitalist class does not tear itself to pieces negating or suborning its class identity [. . .]. And they govern in their own interests, [. . .] in enriching and empowering themselves – while disempowering and impoverishing others – the (white and black and other minority, male and female) working class.

Nevertheless, especially after the 2007–2008 crash, social class is again entering into the discussions about society. Guy Standing (2011) famously coined the term *precariat* to refer to an emerging global class, "consisting of many millions around the world without an anchor of stability" (1), which faces different kinds of labor insecurities, such as part-time jobs or unemployment. From a Marxist perspective, however, precariat should not be considered a 'new' social class because, in fact, precariousness is "quite simply the condition of the working class under capitalism" (Di Bernardo 2016: 14). In the field of applied linguistics, Block (2012a, 2014, 2015a) is the author who has most recently developed the construct of social class to understand a wide range of language-related phenomena in the era of neoliberalism. Block, for example, shows the relevance of social class to study issues related to second language acquisition (2012b), language teacher education (2015b), language and identity (2016a), language and migration (2017b) or language policy and planning (2018c). In the particular realm of ELT, social class has also been discussed as a key factor in China (Gao 2014) and in Mexico (López-Godar and Sughrua 2014), where only those students who can pay private schools have access to quality English language instruction. This situation, of course, is not unique for China and Mexico, and we would probably find similar cases in other geographical locations around the world. In South Korea, for example, the most affluent families can easily afford various English learning opportunities for their children, including study abroad programs, while "the working class must rely on limited English language learning offered by the public education system" (Park 2016: 462).

Another area of research in language and political economy has been the work about language commodification (Heller 2010; Tan and Rudby 2008) or the ways in which languages are dealt with as an economic currency that can be exchanged in the market for profit. According to the language commodification approach, languages are no longer just the expressions of national identity but are treated as commodities and have their specific value in the global economy (Block 2008). To put it in another way, languages are increasingly associated with 'profit' and terms such as 'added value' or 'economic development' rather than with 'pride', that is, cultural and national belonging (Duchêne and Heller 2012). Monica Heller (2002, 2003) examines this new paradigm in francophone Canada. In these regions, the bilingual practices in the workplace, in education and in francophone associations demonstrate a shift "from an ideology of authentic nationhood to an ideology of commodification" (Heller 2002: 47). French is treated less as a marker of ethnicity as it was some decades ago, and striving to learn both French and English is mainly valued as an individual investment to profit in a globalized economy (Heller 2002). Under this process of commodification, languages (and especially English) are presented as 'soft skills' that should result in better employment in the new knowledge economy (Urciuoli 2008; Park 2011; Kubota 2013). According to neoliberal rhetoric, the English language has become a key skill that opens the doors to a better education and to a competitive labor market (Park and Wee 2012; Price 2014). On the whole, the body of research dedicated to language commodification examines the ways in which language becomes an economic value and plays a key role in different spheres of society, such as in the workplace, education, marketing or tourism. Alfonso Del Percio et al. (2017: 58) summarize in the following way the thesis of the studies interested in language commodification:

> [C]urrent political- economic conditions produce a particularly fruitful terrain for language to act as a key tool in the reproduction of capital [. . .]. [T]his key role of language is due to its believed capability to fulfill a dual role: acting as a semiotic marker for a specific quality that is projected onto a specific product, knowledge, or service, and acting as a source of added value.

Language commodification as a concept has been recently criticized by various authors (McGill 2013; Holborow 2015; Block 2018b) who consider that it is ill-defined and that language skills cannot be separated from the wider process of work in capitalism. Block (2018b), for example, argues that far too much weight has been placed on language commodification without providing a comprehensive definition of this concept, and without addressing Marx's crucial notion of commodity. In his opinion, what many

16   *Introduction*

researchers have meant by language commodification could more consistently be called 'skilling' or 'branding'.

Finally, in the particular field of second and foreign language education, there has recently been an increasing interest to show the ways neoliberalism impacts the content, the approaches and the organization of language teaching. According to Katie Bernstein et al. (2015: 6), "[s]econd/foreign language education, like education more broadly, has not only been influenced by neoliberalism; it has been responsible for reproducing many of its discourses". These authors argue that language education contributes to the understanding of language only as a job skill and to the conception of culture as a commodity. On the other hand, neoliberalism has also involved the conversion of language teachers into "expendable and replaceable knowledge workers" and of language learners into "entrepreneurs and consumers" (Bernstein et al. 2015: 6–7). I will return to the impact of neoliberalism on foreign language teaching in Chapter 2, which is dedicated specifically to language education. What all the studies reviewed above show is the increasing awareness within the academy of the need to include issues related to political economy in applied linguistics studies in the neoliberal age.

Conclusion

This chapter has highlighted that the economic and political philosophy of Marx and the later insights of those working within the broad parameters of Marxist tradition, such as the Frankfurt School and the critical pedagogy and new approaches in applied linguistics regarding neoliberalism, are relevant when studying a cultural product such as a language textbook in an era of continuing spread of capitalism around the world and the increasing importance of the economy in all dimensions of human existence. Following Block et al. (2012a), my thesis is that the time has arrived for a 'political economic turn' in applied linguistics to challenge the hegemony of neoliberal ideology, especially now that the political crisis of neoliberalism has become evident to many people around the world. With this in mind, my book attempts to show how the economic base of current capitalist societies conditions language education, and particularly foreign or second language textbooks. However, I will not address the reception of textbooks by teachers and students in the classrooms, since this question would require another kind of analysis to the one proposed in this book. Instead, following a Marxist approach, my core focus is on the historical process in which these textbooks are situated. By doing so, I aim to understand current language textbooks in the light of an examination of today's capitalism as a whole.

The theoretical framework for a critical understanding of language education in the twenty-first century described here will be applied throughout this book. The eight chapters that follow are organized in two parts. The first part presents an international overview of foreign language teaching and language textbook studies, and a framework to analyze textbooks in relation to neoliberalism. Chapter 2 starts from the idea that education depends on economic conditions and dominant ideology. I explain the evolution of foreign language teaching in relation to capitalism and its political institutions, with a special emphasis on the key role of the Council of Europe in the spread of Communicative Language Teaching. Chapter 3 provides a survey of research in critical language textbook analysis and comments on the need for more studies that take into account the socioeconomic transformations engendered by capitalism in recent decades. To respond to this exigency, Chapter 4 presents the methodological approach of analysis of this book which begins with a quantitative approach to the topics of language textbooks and is followed by a qualitative content analysis through social class dimensions and neoliberal values and practices.

The second part of the book is dedicated to Catalan textbooks. The Catalan case is important to study for several reasons. Since the research published in English is centered principally on ELT (and to a less extent in Spanish or French language teaching), my book will explore an entirely new field in language research in English. The study of Catalan textbooks will allow comparisons with ELT textbooks. This question promises to be especially interesting because the sociopolitical differences between English as a global language and Catalan are immense. Furthermore, while the majority of ELT students do not live in Anglophone countries, most of Catalan language students live in areas where Catalan is spoken. In order to address the Catalan case, I will first present the economic, political and social context of Catalan language textbooks. Later, the proposed analytical model is applied to a sample of Catalan language textbooks. Chapter 5 deals with the Catalan case in connection to wider economic and political transformations in Western capitalist countries. In Chapter 6 the results of the quantitative analysis confirm the relevance of topics such as work and housing, and the content of Catalan textbooks is analyzed from a social class perspective. Chapter 7 presents and discusses the results of the analysis of content that focuses on the world of work, particularly in relation to neoliberal features such as flexibility, lifelong learning, self-branding or risk management. Subsequently, Chapter 8 deals with the content related to housing and links it to the broader socioeconomic transformations in this sphere of life in the neoliberal era. The book ends with Chapter 9, which discusses why textbooks of a relatively small language like Catalan constantly associate content with the same neoliberal worldview adopted by global English textbooks.

Notes

1 Although today the term *neoliberalism* is mainly used by its critics, the name was first coined by its proponents. The origins of this term are often situated at the Walter Lippman Colloquium, a conference of intellectuals organized in Paris in 1938 that devised a new political and economic project against communism, fascism and the 'old' liberalism. The name *neoliberalism* was finally chosen over

18 Introduction

other terms such as *néo-capitalisme, libéralisme positif* or *libéralisme social* (Plehwe 2009: 13).

2 Both Hayek and Friedman were prominent members of the Mont Pèlerin Society, an elite international organization mainly comprised of Western economists founded in 1947 with the aim to combat the state's intervention in the economy and to establish the principles of the future neoliberal societies.

3 The post-industrial economy refers to the departure of the Fordist model of production dominant in capitalist countries after World War II, which was based on the mass production of standardized goods, and also on mass consumption. The new mode of production implies the predominance of the services sector over manufacturing, the growing importance of new information and communication technologies, and a more flexible and networked world economy. This term applies to the more established and advanced capitalist economies in the world and not to the so-called developing countries, which are now homes to the world's industries. It is also known as the *knowledge economy, information capitalism* or the *Toyotist* mode of production.

4 My thanks to Marnie Holborow (personal communication) for reminding me of this.

2 A short history of foreign language education in Europe

Introduction

> The politics of language teaching (e.g., the shifts in enrollments due to geo-political factors, the relationship of language teachers to the target country's political regime, the prestige differential among languages, and the academic pecking order between literature and language) have been shaped by the historical outcomes of military conflicts, colonial wars, ethnic conflicts and tensions, and by the economic conditions that have grown out of such tensions (Pennycook 1998).
>
> (Kramsch 2000: 322)

In this quote, Claire Kramsch (2000) makes reference to one of Alaistair Pennycook's (1998) key theses, that is, the ways in which language policy is shaped by historical, political and economic events. In my view, Pennycook's arguments were persuasive some two decades ago and in this chapter my aim is to critically examine the evolution of foreign language education in Europe over the past five decades in relationship to its political, social and economic context. In other words, I will link the larger socioeconomic and political forces and processes to applied linguistics theory which has led to the development of methods and approaches to language learning reflected in materials used in language learning environments in the age of neoliberalism.

In Chapter 1, I suggested that language textbooks are conditioned by their specific historical, political, economic and social background. For this reason, I consider it necessary to address now the most immediate context of language textbooks, that is, the main trends of language education in Europe. As we shall see throughout this study, the dominant approaches in teaching languages have a great impact on the form and the content of language textbooks. Although other studies have already addressed the history of language teaching (e.g. Howatt 1984; Richards and Rodgers 2001; Howatt and Smith 2014), I would like to come back to this issue from a somewhat different perspective. My aim here, inspired by Littlejohn (2012, 2013), is to situate the political economy at the center of this short history

20 *History of foreign language education*

of foreign language education in order to highlight and understand the relevance of the capitalist economic transformations in the evolution of language teaching and learning and, ultimately, also in language textbooks.

This chapter will focus on the enormous impact on how languages are learned today by the Council of Europe and especially by two documents created and published by this institution, namely *The Threshold Level* (van Ek 1975) and the *Common European Framework of Reference for Languages* (Council of Europe 2001). This overview will include a discussion of how English Language Teaching (ELT), for a number of reasons, gained the status of a pace setter for all other languages and has influenced and still continues to influence foreign language teaching around the world. Finally, I will present the main reasons given for learning languages in the twenty-first century and I will relate them to neoliberalism, which undergirds this book as a whole.

Early developments

For what is today still considered the modern way of learning and teaching languages by many in the field, the years between 1950 and 1980 were of great importance. It was then that the audiolingual method and later the communicative language approach were developed. After WWII, the world itself was rapidly changing. The world's population grew, there was a long period of economic growth and relative stability, and new inventions in technology and mass media brought the world closer together. As the historian Geoffrey Jones (2005: 33) puts it:

> Technology made it easier than ever before for companies to move people, knowledge, and goods around the world. There were new waves of innovations in transport and communications. In 1958 the first commercial jet made an Atlantic crossing. This was followed by a phenomenal increase in air traffic. The development of telex was a considerable advance over telephones in facilitating international communications and coordinating multinational business. In 1965 the first satellite for commercial telecommunications was launched. During the 1970s the use of the facsimile machine took off. The movement of goods across the world was facilitated by the development of larger ocean-going ships, or super-freighters, and the growth of containerization.
>
> (Jones 2005: 33)

With faster movement of goods, capital and people, the need for a more instrumental language learning approach, whether for business or everyday purposes, was slowly rising. This was a period in which the global view on languages changed and for the first time in history since the spread of Latin and Arabic in the Middle Ages, there was a language used for communication worldwide, English. As Jack Richards and Theodore Rodgers have

History of foreign language education 21

noted, it was the beginning of North American supremacy as the world's number one economy and that country's interest was focused on the spread of English as a *lingua franca*:

> America had now emerged as a major international power. There was a growing demand in foreign expertise in the teaching of English. Thousands of foreign students entered the United States to study in universities, and many of these students required training in English before they could begin their studies.
>
> (Richards and Rodgers 2001: 51)

In order to establish a system of ELT which would cater for such a large public it was essential to have substantial funding. In the period between 1950 and 1980 government and private foundations such as Ford or Rockefeller invested in English language programs (Howatt 1984: 269; Phillipson 1997: 202). It was a large sum of money – "perhaps the most ever spent in history in support of a propagation of a language" (Troike1977: 2; cited in Phillipson 2009: 335). Interestingly enough, when the USSR launched the first artificial satellite and soon after that organized the first journey to space by a human being, this triggered the United States' desire to work faster on technological developments, which implied that foreign language teaching should take on a particular priority: "The 1958 National Defense (Foreign Language) Act was swiftly ushered in, providing massive funds for the development of language programs" (Littlejohn 2012: 286). The foci was not only on English programs but also on "the teaching of uncommonly taught languages, the training of language teachers, and the development of teaching materials and tests" (Kramsch 2005: 554) in order to meet the national security needs of the United States. Linguists, supported by the American government, were intent upon establishing a scientific, efficient method of language learning, which resulted in a method which became known as Audiolingualism. The origins of this approach can be found in the foreign language program developed for military personnel during WWII in the United States, the so-called Army Specialized Training Program (ASTP), which "changed the approach to language teaching in the USA in a radical way" (Stern 1991: 102). The American army's program drew the attention of linguists especially because it made clear that languages can be learned faster and more efficiently and for a much larger population of "ordinary learners, servicemen" than with the conventional methods such as the grammar-translation ones used in schools at the time (Stern 1991: 102). With structural linguistics as its core and highly influenced by behaviorist theory in psychology, which emerged in the United States in the 1950s, the audiolingual method saw learning languages as a habit formation in which the oral language was emphasized over the written. The correct way of teaching and learning languages was in memorizing dialogues and organizing pattern drills and in that way minimizing possible errors.

22 *History of foreign language education*

In Europe the application of new methods and theories of second languages education took a similar path. British linguists were also proponents of structural grammar used together with contextual situations. This is why the British structural approach is sometimes called Situational Language Teaching (SLT). France, in the 1950s, developed another version of this structural approach (promoted initially for the teaching of French as a foreign language) with a greater emphasis on visual content, which is known as the audio-visual method (Howatt and Smith 2014: 88). Ministers of education of various countries in Europe agreed in 1963 that priority should be given to research on spoken and specialized language and to teacher training that would make it easier for inexperienced teachers to be introduced to these new methods.

Communicative language teaching (CLT), the most commonly used method for learning foreign languages today (at least in Western countries), was developed in the 1970s and the 1980s by British and American linguists as a reaction against grammar-based methods such as Audiolingualism and SLT that tended to ignore communicative competence (Hymes 1972), which refers to the human ability to communicate effectively and appropriately. CLT emphasizes communication in real-life situations and focuses on the language needed for everyday life. It is language use, rather than the rules of grammar, that now became the focus of teaching: "The focus shifts away from the language and towards the user, emphasizing the effectiveness with which communication takes place and the skills which the user can muster in order to maintain and promote it" (Howatt 1984: 278–9). For these reasons, CLT encourages the development of autonomous learners, group and pair work, and the use of authentic materials.

Scott Thornbury (2016) reminds us that CLT was born and developed from a mixture of contributions of theories belonging to different disciplines (linguistics, education, psychology, philosophy) such as Dell Hymes's sociolinguistics, Michael Halliday's Systemic Functional Linguistics, discourse analysis, Jürgen Habermas's theory of communicative action and even the educational philosophy of John Dewey, among others. Littlejohn (2012) sees the origins of CLT in "social moves towards greater democratisation and a more popular (in the sense of 'of the people') recognition of cultures" since "CLT championed not the way language *should* be but rather how ordinary people *use* it" (289; italics in the original). Similarly, Kramsch (2005: 548–9) argues that CLT was in part "born out of the idealism of the 1960s" and it represented "a first attempt to democratize language learning by wresting it from the exclusive control of philologist and literature scholars. It brought language down to the functional level of streets and supermarkets".

The development of CLT was also a product of a specific historical and economic context of the capitalist system. As Kramsch (2005) notes, CLT "was also in part the outcome of an expanding market place, which was seen as the prototypical site for communicative transaction and negotiation" (548). Indeed, CLT was born in a moment of a great transformation

History of foreign language education 23

in capitalist societies from the industrial to a post-industrial economic order, based on the production and distribution of goods globally, the expansion of the service industry, flexibility in job markets, the mobility of workers and the application of new technologies. This great economic transformation meant an even bigger increase in international exchange (through business, tourism and migration) that required the ability to communicate with people from different origins. Communication, interaction and an individual culture of self entrepreneurship became increasingly important values in this new capitalist model of production, especially in the work order (Virno 2004). The emphasis of CLT on everyday interaction rather than on grammar or literature fitted perfectly with the imperatives of this new capitalist system. CLT strived to promote communicative competence and 'about me' activities, and, in many occasions, limited the learning of languages to individual practical abilities that were required by post-industrial capitalism that then was just beginning to emerge. Of course, CLT has the potential to include 'deep' discussions about social and political issues, but it is usually linked only to topics like service transactions in shops or proposals of spending leisure time, at least in the world of language teaching materials.

CLT was initially developed for English as a foreign language and helped to increase the spread of this language worldwide. Critical scholars, such as Robert Phillipson (1992, 2009), argue that the expansion of English was a result of the efforts of Anglo-Saxon countries to maintain their supremacy (political, economic, cultural and linguistic) over their former colonies (in the case of Britain) and other developing countries. Europe was then going through a process of greater economic and political multinational integration, and English became the main language of communication among the various countries. It was precisely in Europe that "the shift toward communicative language teaching arose the earliest and most prominently", especially thanks to the works of the Council of Europe (Warschauer 2000: 512). As the next sections detail, the Council of Europe played a key role in the development and the spread of CLT through multiple second language education projects.

The Council of Europe

With its headquarters in Strasbourg, the Council of Europe is a political organization devoted mainly to the defense of human rights and to the cultural and educational fields that today comprises 47 states, including not only all the members of the European Union, but also countries such as Russia and Turkey, among others. It was founded in 1949 by 10 Western European countries to promote European unity, protect human rights and facilitate the social and economic progress of the continent. Significant information that forms part of this chapter is based on a document published by the Council of Europe, called *Modern Languages in the Council of Europe 1954–1997* (Trim 2007). This document was written by the British

24 *History of foreign language education*

linguist, John Trim. He was, together with Jan Ate van Ek, one of the driving forces behind the most important projects carried out by this institution in the field of second language learning. Trim was the director of the Council of Europe's Modern Languages Projects for almost 30 years. Since 1954, the Council of Europe has launched a number of projects concerned with improving linguistic policies inside the then European Community. The aim has been to develop better mutual understandings between neighboring states and to preserve cultural and linguistic diversity while also "facilitating the movement and exchange of persons and objects of cultural value" (Trim 2007: 5). Making the communication between the neighboring states as easy as possible was mostly needed for commerce and trade. It was also required for the labor market which was expanding with numerous immigrants coming from the dissolved European colonies, and for the purposes of educating future generations.

In its first efforts to make a unified system for foreign language education in European countries in the 1960s, the Council of Europe was a promoter of projects concerning modern language learning which used audio-visual methods. At the beginning of the 1970s, the idea to create the so-called unit/credit system[1] for learning languages was reinforced with the initiation of numerous projects, conferences and publications involving groups of experts. The most important projects that dealt with language teaching were the *Unit/Credit Scheme* (1971–1977), Project 4 (1977–1981) and *The Threshold Level* (van Ek 1975). The publication of the latter document and its subsequent translation and adaptation with reference to more than 20 languages would have a great impact on the unification of language teaching and the spread of CLT, as I will show in the next section.

The threshold level

The Threshold Level was first published in the mid-1970s (van Ek 1975) and a new edition came out in 1980 under the title *Threshold Level English* (van Ek and Alexander 1980). The document was re-published with some modifications at the beginning of the 1990s (van Ek and Trim 1991) and reprinted several years later (van Ek and Trim 1998). The document's enormous importance for the development and change in the way modern languages are still learned is, however, rarely mentioned. The main objective of *The Threshold Level* was to capture "what a language learner needed to be able to do to communicate independently in the target language, with the emphasis firmly on social situations and interaction" (Fulcher 2004: 255). According to its authors, the point of this document was that communication on everyday matters and everyday life is to be the goal of modern language learning:

> By far the largest single group of language learners everywhere consists of people who want to prepare themselves to communicate socially with

History of foreign language education 25

people from other countries, exchanging information and opinions on everyday matters in a relatively straightforward way, and to conduct the necessary business of everyday living when abroad with a reasonable degree of independence.

(van Ek and Trim 1998: 1)

This 'largest single group of learners' consisted at that time especially of migrant workers and their families, and part-time workers such as au-pairs, hairdressers or people from the tourist industry. Needs analyses were carried out on some of these target groups by the Council of Europe's Project 4 (Trim 2007). So, at least a part of the broader considerations that led to the birth of what was to become CLT were "the language needs of a rapidly increasing group of immigrants and guest workers" to Europe (Savignon 1991: 263). A new approach for language teaching was also needed to support the spread of the English language worldwide, as the authors of *The Threshold Level* explain:

Spread all over the world, there are hundreds of millions of people for whom English is the key that may unlock the door of the space assigned to them by birth and upbringing. A command of this language will enable them to extend their mental horizons beyond almost any geographical or cultural limitations, and, if so desired, also physically to cross the threshold into the world outside. [. . .] It is for this target group that *Threshold Level 1990* has been developed.

(van Ek and Trim 1998: 4)

The 1970s was a period in which many in the emergent field of applied linguistic eminences felt that it was time for a paradigm shift. Languages were no longer considered the preserve of the educated elite, but were now considered a subject for everybody (Kramsch 2005). In the words of *The Threshold Level*'s authors, the purpose was to "convert language teaching from structure dominated scholastic sterility into a vital medium for the freer movement of people and ideas" (van Ek and Trim 1998: 1). The reasons behind a language paradigm shift lay, in part, in the new socioeconomic situation in which Europe had found itself at the beginning of the 1970s:

The accelerating internationalization of life was at its point of take-off, as technical developments in the communications and information industries massively transformed social life in many interconnected aspects. Multinational industries; global financial markets; mass tourism and entertainment; science and medicine were creating a mass demand for practical proficiency in modern languages, particularly for English.

(Trim 2007: 16)

26   *History of foreign language education*

This need for a more 'practical proficiency in modern languages' meant the shift from structural approaches to more communicative ones in syllabus design, which began with the introduction of the notional-functional syllabus, which "organize[d] language teaching in terms of content rather than the form of the language" (Wilkins 1976: 18). *The Threshold Level* is the first document of its kind to follow the language learning imperatives in which the social function of a language is considered above the form. It gives an exhaustive list of various functions and notions, or according to its authors, "what people do by the means of language" (van Ek and Trim 1998: 27). Some of the typical examples of a function could be 'asking for directions' or 'request permission'. Notions were divided in general notions (such as existential, spatial, temporal, etc.) and specific notions which were arranged under 14 themes that are maintained in foreign language curriculums today (such as personal identification, daily life, travel, shopping, etc.).[2]

The application of a new methodology required new school curriculums, new materials and teacher training programs. But above all, it required a wide public and academic acceptance. The idea to incorporate what the Council of Europe called the 'unit/credit system' for language teaching began first with adult education as it was a suitable environment for experimentation which would not create much noise in national educational systems:

> Fundamental changes were needed, but to make them in an established system of national education is a long-term process fraught with practical difficulties and certain to encounter both active and passive resistance from those at all levels set in their existing ways. In this respect, the marginal position of adult education in national systems was actually an advantage. Away from the spotlight, the Expert Group was able to develop a new approach without the political constraints to be expected in a large intergovernmental organisation, but was, hopefully, in a position to exert considerable influence should its ideas gain the support of the Council's decision-making bodies.
>
> (Trim 2007: 16)

It would not take long before *The Threshold Level* and above all CLT were introduced to formal and informal education in Europe.[3] Such changes were "very warmly received by the field" (Trim 2007: 20). The shift from form to function was soon to be followed by ELT syllabus designs, textbooks and public examinations (Trim 2007). After its initial problems (*The Threshold Level* was considered too high to reach at the beginners' levels), a new level, *Waystage* (van Ek et al. 1980), was developed. Using similar notional-functional syllabus design, the BBC produced its highly influential multimedia course *Follow Me* which was followed by 500 million viewers in over 60 countries in the world (Trim 2007). The British Council, together with Cambridge University and BBC English, obviously sensing the potential of *The Threshold Level* and *Waystage* for the future of ELT, decided to make an "important financial contribution" (van Ek and Trim 1998: 3) and lent professional support in revising these two documents in the 1990s. The task conducted in this period by the experts from the Council of Europe is recognized as a milestone in the field of language learning, something which never before happened in the history of language teaching (Sánchez 1992: 337). Nevertheless, as I will explain in the following section, in 2001, the Council of Europe published another document, the Common European Framework of Reference for Languages (CEFR) which would have an even greater impact in the way languages were taught and in the spread of the unit/credit system in Europe and beyond.

The Common European Framework of Reference for Languages (CEFR)

Antecedents

The 1970s ended with the introduction in Western Europe of the Threshold and Waystage levels to adult education for learning languages and to some extent to formal educational institutions. However, the work of the Council of Europe regarding the making of a unitary system for language learning had still not gained total acceptance. Indeed, in the late 1970s, when the Council of Europe first tried to introduce this idea, many countries, especially in Scandinavia, were skeptical about European centralism (Saville 2005). The idea would revive in a somewhat different form two decades later with the publication of the *Common European Framework of Reference for Languages: Learning, Teaching, Assessment* (CEFR). Nevertheless, the years in between were not wasted. The Council of Europe engaged in at least two very important projects: Project 12, subtitled *Learning and Teaching Modern Languages for Communication* (1982–1987); and *Language Learning for European Citizenship* (1990–1997).

One of the aims of Project 12 was to help national governments reform language teaching in lower-secondary education (Trim 2007: 30). In a period of just three years (1984–1987) 37 conferences were held in 15 countries for about 2,000 teacher trainers who were later able to spread what they had learned to other teachers in their countries. The estimation was that a thousand teacher trainers would be able to directly influence 100,000 teachers and even more indirectly (Trim 2007). It was "the largest and most intensive project of international co-operation in the teacher training field so far undertaken" (Trim 2007: 34). Once again, the Council of Europe was doing pioneering work in terms of changing the way languages were learned and influencing the method and speed of this change. One of the fruits of Project 12 was also the book *Communication in the Modern Languages Classroom* by Joe Sheils (1988), written with the intention of helping teachers understand how the communicative approach worked with a special focus on language materials produced in the years prior to its publication. It is a book

28 History of foreign language education

which provides a wide range of examples from textbooks published in the 1980s using the communicative approach in English, German, Spanish and Italian as second languages. It is a very valuable resource for the way communicative activities were presented in various textbooks, but also a clear example of a successful strategy to unify the teaching of the represented European languages. It is a book which offers the rare occasion to compare the way various languages are presented in textbooks, and we can see that they were all tailored according to the same principles promoted by the Council of Europe. The final Council of Europe project prior to the CEFR was *Language Learning for European Citizenship*, which lasted from 1990 to 1997. It placed priority on some of the sectors that had not been the primary focus of the previous project such as primary education or topics such as the sociocultural dimension of language teaching, new technologies such as Computer Assisted Language Learning (CALL) or the interest in bilingual education, which would be the basis for the development of Content and Language Integrated Learning (CLIL).

The 1990s were years in which the ideas promoted by the Council of Europe were introduced and became more familiar to the countries of the former Eastern Bloc, some of which would later enter the European Union. The countries formerly under Soviet influence were now in need of teachers of languages like English, French or German. The Council of Europe would offer them help, not just in switching from Russian to English, but in changing their entire idea about the teaching process: "the adoption of the aims and objectives advocated by the Council of Europe meant a far-reaching reorientation of teachers' values, attitudes and beliefs" (Trim 2007: 35). The Council of Europe was consulted regarding questions of changing the national language policies of the Baltic states in areas such as employment and citizenship, and *The Threshold Level* was being adopted and translated in countries such as the Czech Republic, Slovenia, Estonia, Hungary, Lithuania and Russia (Trim 2007: 35).

At the same time, after the fall of the Soviet bloc, the English language industry saw the potential to expand its market into Eastern Europe (Gray 2012b). Private organizations, such as the Open Society Foundation of the billionaire financier George Soros, contributed to opening the way for the English industry to enter into the former socialist countries in Eastern Europe (Gray 2012b). Soros spent more than 5 billion dollars between 1993 and 2009 on the so called 'democracy-building initiatives' in Eastern countries and beyond (Minett 2009). The aim of Soros was to lead former socialist countries towards integration into global capitalism, and the implementation of ELT was acknowledged by his organization as a key element in this process (Minett 2009).

The document and its influence

The CEFR has been a major point of reference in foreign language education since its publication in 2001[4] and has already been translated into 40 languages worldwide. Its main aim is to provide "a common basis for the elaboration of language syllabuses, curriculum guidelines, examinations, textbooks, etc. across Europe" (Council of Europe 2001: 1), but its influence has gone beyond this continent, to the Americas and the Asia-Pacific region (Byram and Parmenter 2012). According to a survey carried out in 2006 with responses from 30 Council of Europe member states, the CEFR "is used – often as the exclusive neutral reference – in all educational sectors" (Martyniuk and Noijons 2007: 7). From the first introductory lines of the CEFR, it can be seen that it is a logical continuation of all previously mentioned documents authored by the Council of Europe. As early as the second sentences of Chapter 1, similar to *The Threshold Level*, it is stated that it is a document which "describes in a comprehensive way what learners have to learn to do in order to use the language for communication" (Council of Europe 2001:1).

According to Trim (2007), its name was mentioned for the first time at a symposium held in Rüschlikon, Switzerland, together with another Council of Europe document, also to become famous as early as 1991, named *European Language Portfolio*. It therefore took exactly 10 years for the idea to become reality. At this symposium, it was decided to create a common framework in order to promote easier communication among educational institutions, to assist teachers and learners, and to coordinate the process of language learning, but most importantly "to provide the sound basis for mutual recognition of language qualifications" (Trim 2007: 38). The CEFR's second draft, which was written in 1996 after consulting experts in the field, members of governments and NGOs, stated that the CEFR provided:

a) a descriptive scheme, presenting and exemplifying the parameters and categories needed to describe, first, what a language user has to do in order to communicate in its situational context, then the role of the texts, which carry the message from producer to receiver, then the underlying competences which enable a language user to perform acts of communication and finally the strategies which enable the language user to bring those competences to bear in action;
b) a survey of approaches to language learning and teaching, providing options for users to consider in relation to their existing practice;
c) a set of scales for describing proficiency in language use, both globally and in relation to the categories of the descriptive scheme at a series of levels;
d) a discussion of the issues raised for curricular design in different educational contexts, with particular reference to the development of **plurilingualism** in the learner, and for the assessment of language proficiency and achievement.

(Trim 2007: 39; underlines and bold in the original)

This draft, with minor 'presentational' modifications, was to become the CEFR, published in 2001 simultaneously in English and French by

30 *History of foreign language education*

Cambridge University Press and Didier, respectively (Trim 2007). Its original version has never been changed. The Council of Europe's idea established in the 1970s to create a unit/credit system of language learning in order to centralize syllabus and curriculum design, testing and assessment, and systems of qualification, as well as to greatly influence national language policies inside and outside of Europe, was finally becoming a reality. With its intensified mobility, Europe was finally ready to support what in the 1970s seemed impossible (Trim 2007: 41).

The CEFR itself contains a definition of communicative proficiency at six levels (from A1 to C2), proposals about communicative language use (context, themes, tasks, activities, strategies and processes) and a descriptive scheme which embraces general competences (declarative knowledge, skills and know-how, existential competence and ability to learn) and communicative language competences (linguistic, sociolinguistic and pragmatic). It is 264 pages long, complex, at times ambiguous, and not an easy document to follow. For this reason, additional documents were required to help users read it more easily. A series of *User Guides* were produced at the same time as the CEFR with the following objectives:

> to deal with aspects of provision specific to a particular class of user, and to assist such users (e.g. educational administrators, adult education providers, inspectors, examiners, textbook writers, teacher trainers, teachers and learners) to make effective use of the Framework in their particular sphere of activity.
>
> (Trim 2007: 41)

Later, many guides were substituted by *A Guide for Users* (Trim 2003), in which various experts explain the document in yet another 236 pages. Since then, various documents commenting on the CEFR have appeared, such as the *Reference Level Descriptions for National and Regional Languages* or a toolkit for using the CEFR in language examinations.[5]

Neus Figueras (2012) argues that there are two main factors behind the general acceptance of the CEFR. The first was both geopolitical and scientific in the sense that governments together with applied linguists worked on linking language learning, teaching and assessment to a "more real-life oriented approach" (478). In order to accomplish this, an effort was made to establish common levels of proficiency and common terminology which would be offered for everyone willing to use them. The second factor, according to Figueras (2012: 479), lies in the very characteristics of the approach which the document represented: "the positive wording" behind the level descriptors and it being non-compulsory in nature, i.e., being open to adaptation and change. A third factor that might also explain the enormous impact of this document is the development at that time of the European Higher Education Area, "which included – alongside other initiatives such as the so-called Bologna process – the CEFR" (Hu 2012: 69). Similar

History of foreign language education   31

to the CEFR in the field of second language education, the Bologna Declaration of 1999 "initiated an important and irreversible process of harmonizing the various European systems of higher education" (Muñoz 2015: 30).

As Figueras (2012) argues, the two features of CEFR that have gained most attention in practice are the reference levels (from A1 to C2) and reference level descriptors. And indeed, these reference levels and descriptors are an inevitable feature of the materials offered by any publishing or second language learning business. These levels also seem to reassure learners, teachers and parents that the course of study is following the recommendations given by the Council of Europe, although they may not be particularly familiar with the document or have little to no knowledge of what the CEFR is actually all about. Despite the CEFR's wide acceptance among professionals and the public, the document itself has been, however, even since its draft version, heavily attacked and criticized on various grounds, as I will discuss in the next section.

Critics of the CEFR

Philippe Valax (2011) critically analyzes the CEFR, quoting references from the document itself as well as fellow researchers who have raised issues about the uncritical application of this document in schools and other institutions over the past years. According to Valax (2011: 82), almost every aspect of this document (and he mentions many) could demand the scrutiny of "serious criticism", but until now very few authors have dared to engage. One major criticism of the CEFR concerns its content. Its authors proclaim that it is an easy to read, user friendly and coherent piece of writing, but several studies have shown that this is far from the truth. Charles Alderson (2007:661) considers the document is "not easy to understand, often vague, undefined and imprecise". Some of the difficulties in interpreting the CEFR are related to wording, due to its lack of detail and explanation of common terms used. For example, "*simple* is frequently used in the scales, but how is one to decide what is *simple* compared to what is *less simple* and, especially, what is *very simple* is not clear" (Alderson et al. 2006: 12; cited in Valax 2011: 58; emphasis in the original). Apart from *simple*, Alderson et al. (2006: 12) also indicate "definitional problems with expressions such as *the most common, everyday, familiar, concrete, predictable, straightforward, factual, complex, short, long, specialized, highly colloquial*" (Valax 2011: 58; emphasis in the original). On the other hand, Valax (2011: 63) explains that the CEFR's content "has been the subject of increasing criticism in terms of its perceived lack of empirical evidence to confirm the validity of its levels, scales and descriptors". Discussing methodologies for developing reference level descriptors, Alderson (2007: 660) remarks: "It is far from clear how much attention has been paid, for example, to empirical findings from 30 years of research into second language acquisition". More recently Katrin Wisniewski (2013: 251) also casts doubt on the empirical validly of

32 *History of foreign language education*

the reference's scale and its descriptors assessing learners' language knowledge. Moreover, Brian North (2000) and Glenn Fulcher (2004) argue that the levels scale does not necessarily represent the knowledge of a language learner, but only the personal perception of evaluators or teachers about the learner's knowledge.

Another important criticism of the CEFR explained by Valax (2011) is about the nature of the document. Although it is stated in the CEFR that it serves to describe and not prescribe what language learners need to learn to do (Council of Europe 2001: 1), some declarations by its authors seem to tell a different story. While Trim says that "the CEFR gives no instructions or even recommendations to its users as to what they should or should not do" (Trim 2005: 18; cited in Valax 2011: 47), another Council of Europe expert engaged in language policy, Jean-Claude Beacco,[6] asserts that "the Framework is a referential work, in other words a common tool that defines norms and standards" (Beacco 2004; cited in Valax 2011: 48). What is clear now is that the CEFR is being used as a norm and a standard in many countries in Europe and beyond (Byram and Parmenter 2012). Perhaps the best summary of what the CEFR really stands for is a comment made by Spiros Papageorgiou (2006; cited in Valax 2011: 68) when talking about language testing:

> I . . . feel it is not just a political mandate issue here: it is a marketing one as well. . . . [If] you are 'CEFR-aligned' you are probably going to survive, and this is why there is a false interpretation that a 'CEFR-aligned' test is a good test.

This statement could be easily extended to the publishing industry, which usually mentions the CEFR's scales on the covers of language textbooks. The use of the CEFR as a brand to enhance textbook sales has been commented on even by those involved in the CEFR implementation process: Beacco notes that French textbooks, for example, use the Council of Europe's labels as a guarantee of quality without "checking the validity of such a self-granted certification" (Beacco 2004: par. 3; cited in Valax 2011: 72).

Finally, the CEFR has also been controversial because of its clear political agenda. One of the main objectives of the CEFR and its predecessors is the centralization (sometimes euphemistically called 'harmonization') of all formal language education within and outside of Europe, which could imply the uniformity of language teaching worldwide under a one-size-fits-all approach to curriculum, learning methods and assessment. As Fulcher (2004: 255) argues, the centralization visualized by the CEFR could mean "less diversity, and less choice, with one degree program looking very much like another".

More recently, various authors have pointed out the cultural standardization of language teaching that is promoted by the document and its relation to neoliberalism. On the one hand, Littlejohn (2012) shows the alliance

History of foreign language education   33

between the CEFR and market profit in language education in the era of neoliberalism. According to this author, the CEFR

> provides precisely the kind of atomisation that the neo-liberalist logic requires. With its systematic description of levels from 'basic' to 'proficient' (A1, A2, B1, B2 etc.), the CEF[R] has encouraged the development of countless 'language products' all matched to the various levels, all embracing the 'added value' that CEF[R] compatibility offers. Thus, we see most new language courses now carry CEF[R]-compatible branding.
> (Littlejohn 2012: 294)

On the other hand, Ryuko Kubota (2013: 17) indicates the CEFR's "instrumental focus aligned with the development of neoliberal human capital" with its emphasis on "the learners' attainment of communicative language competences" required for the proper transnational communication in a globally competitive economy. Elsewhere, Béatrice Boufoy-Bastick (2015) argues that the CEFR is "a neoliberal policy document for international business" (443). She identifies three parts in the CEFR that enforce compliance with neoliberal policy. First, the document opens with an introduction based on widely accepted values such as culture, identity and linguistic diversity, which seek to convince the users of the virtues of the proposal. Second, the document redefines and limits the meaning of diversity, in a way that is aligned with the neoliberal agenda:

> The second principle is that this **diversification is only possible,** particularly in schools, **if the cost efficiency of the system is considered,** so as to **avoid** unnecessary **repetition** and to **promote the economies of scale** and the **transfer of skills** which linguistic diversity facilitates.
> (Boufoy-Bastick 2015: 452; emphasis in the original)

Finally, in the chapter dedicated to assessment, words such as 'diversity', 'respect' or 'identity' have disappeared altogether. Instead, there are many references to 'test' and 'testing', 'standard' and 'performance', which reveal "the negation of diversity in the assessment of language at the end of the document" (Boufoy-Bastick 2015: 453). In that way, according to this author, "the framework seeks to misinform by spinning the high value that language educators place on cultural diversity, and it exposes the CEFR [. . .] as a document for promoting the standardised neoliberal cultural identity of employee-ment." (453). In other words, the diversity celebrated at the beginning of the document is replaced by the aim to achieve the identity of the ideal worker required for companies to compete globally in a neoliberal climate.

To sum up, the CEFR has implied a further standardization and centralization of the process of teaching foreign languages across Europe and beyond. Following a neoliberal logic, the document reduces language learning to bits

34 *History of foreign language education*

of knowledge, organized into skills and competences, which can be easily assessed, mainly through standardized tests. Obviously, language teaching has always been based on testing to a great extent. However, the novelty of the CEFR is to focus on the bits of knowledge that could help in the construction of the learners' identity as oriented towards individual survival in a highly competitive and market-driven society. With these thoughts in mind, in the next section I will comment on the ways language teaching today is connected to global market values.

Teaching languages in the twenty-first century

Learning a foreign language in the twenty-first century is an obvious necessity in education today, at least according to official documents on education policies and statements made by political leaders. Actually, it is impossible to find any school program or curriculum in which learning one or more foreign languages does not exist. Knowing foreign languages in the era of neoliberalism is seen as a life skill that will improve a nation's position in the competing world economy, as the European Commission (2012: 5) states in a communication called *Rethinking Education: Investing in Skills for Better Socio-Economic Outcomes*:

> In a world of international exchanges, the ability to speak foreign languages is a factor for competitiveness. Languages are more and more important to increase levels of employability and mobility of young people, and poor language skills are a major obstacle to free movement of workers. Businesses also require the language skills needed to function in the global marketplace.

In the United Kingdom, in July 2014, a member of the UK's All Member Party Group for Modern Languages, Baroness Coussins, concluded that the UK economy is already losing £50 billion a year "because of a lack of language skills in the workforce" (Richardson 2014: par. 10). According to the Baroness, the UK's foreign language skills are in need of an urgent upgrade:

> Otherwise, our young people will continue to fall behind their European and global peers in education and employability; our export growth will be stunted; our international reputation will suffer and our security, defense and diplomacy needs will be compromised.
>
> (Richardson 2014: par. 9)

From the Baroness's quote, learning foreign languages is widely seen as a process to improve employability and export growth, but also to reinforce the defense and diplomacy of a nation. Similarly, in the United States, after the events of 11 September 2001, there was a resurgence of interest in foreign language education in order to remain competitive economically and

History of foreign language education 35

guarantee national security (Kramsch 2005; Kubota 2006). Thus, the post-industrial globalized world today needs experts especially in English, the international lingua franca, but also in many more languages. These future language 'experts' are the people who will provide their nations with an impetus towards a better economic and market position.

As explained in Chapter 1, languages are now seen as commodities for general sale in the market. Thus, in the new hegemonic discourse that Kubota (2011: 248) calls "linguistic instrumentalism", languages are now valued as skills to achieve "utilitarian goals" such as economic benefits or social mobility. In particular, according to Deborah Cameron (2002), great importance is given to the 'communication skills' that should assure the proper functioning of the global market economy. As a result, language teaching is increasingly informed by the use of particular genres and styles of speaking so that languages become "maximally 'effective' for the purposes of 'communication'" (Cameron 2002: 69). In this regard, one of the main features of teaching foreign languages in the twenty-first century is the advanced process of standardization and centralization, encouraged in part by the implementation of the CEFR criteria, which has spread outside Europe, from Latin America to Asia. No matter which language is taught, and independent of the context in which it is taught, the approaches (and the materials) are always very similar (Littlejohn 2012).

CLT, promoted among others by the Council of Europe, has become a global method (Block 2008). Although it is linked to the spread of English as the international language, CLT approaches are now implemented in many foreign language programs worldwide. However, a cautionary note should be added here. The implementation of CLT has not always been successful everywhere. Indeed, there have been many constraints in the adoption of CLT principles in non-Western countries, where this approach is in contradiction with local cultures of learning and teaching (Holliday 1994; Hu 2002; Kustati 2013).

Although CLT initially embraced some of the principles of humanism back in the 1970s, it has more recently evolved to adapt to the objectives of the neoliberal agenda (Kramsch 2005; Kubota 2013). For example, while students' autonomy was initially related to the humanistic concept of freedom from external control, it is now primarily associated with the ability of individuals to conceive of themselves as entrepreneurial, self-conducting subjects motivated by competition and flexibility (Kramsch 2005: 549; Kaščák and Pupala 2011: 150). Apart from autonomy, Kramsch (2005: 549) also mentions the transformation of notions such as communication, negotiation and strategy: "communication has become synonymous with getting one's message across, negotiating meaning is now equivalent to problem solving, and strategies are meant to increase competitiveness". Task-based language teaching, one of the approaches of CLT, has also been associated with the instrumental and economic goals of neoliberalism to make learners adaptable to the needs of the market since it "brought language learning yet closer

36 *History of foreign language education*

to the real world of work and the economy" (Kramsch 2014: 301). In a similar vein, Thornbury (2016: 233–4) remarks that the changes of the socioeconomic context with their emphasis on accountability "have shifted the focus from communication to commodification" in language teaching. For example, "the measure of its success is less communicative competence than the results of high-stakes testing" (Thornbury 2016: 234), such as the results from the Cambridge English examinations or from other foreign language testing systems organized in line with the levels established by the CEFR.

I should emphasize here that the evolution of language teaching towards a more economic-driven approach goes hand in hand with the restructuring of education systems across the world to serve the new political and economic agenda. The neoliberal reorientation of education and schooling has been the subject of study by many authors in recent years (e.g. Luke 2006; Ross and Gibson 2007; Hill and Kumar 2009; Urciuoli 2010; Torres 2011; Muñoz 2015; among others). Synthesizing insights from these studies, neoliberal education policy is characterized by the marketization of education and its submission to the needs of capital and to the ideology of market fundamentalism. In the last 20 years or so, there have been cuts in financing public education, increasing partnerships between education services and private companies and the implementation of a business model for the management of schools and universities (Kumar and Hill 2009). This 'new public management' implies "the emergence of an emphasis on measured outputs: on strategic planning, performance indicators, quality assurance measures and academic audits" (Olssen and Peters 2005: 313). As a result, educational institutions have been transformed into flexible networks that are in competition with each other in order to improve quality within a globally competitive economy. But, as Nico Hirtt (2009: 214) argues, decentralization and deregulation in management is accompanied by "more centralized state control over certain specific achievements and the definition of educational objectives (skills, work-related learning, and preparation for lifelong learning)". One of the best-known tools of the external imposition of targets, performance criteria and quantifiable outcomes is the Programme for International Student Assessment (PISA), which is a relevant example of the impact of a transnational economic institution such as the OECD in national school systems worldwide (Paramenter 2014). Since its first edition in 2000, PISA results are used to justify changes in education policies on the basis of greater economic competitiveness. Michael Uljens (2007) argues that this international evaluation following a single measurement standard for all the participating countries promotes the neoliberal interests of the OECD, supporting the homogenization of education and the creation of "a competition oriented mentality" (299).

The main purpose of education now is "the seamless reproduction of job skills, needed by the economy, nation, and, the prospective worker/citizen" (Luke 2006: 127). In that way, education "becomes the crucial driver of the economy, a power-house of economic potentiality from which anything

History of foreign language education   37

non-functional, not measurable in monetary terms or not immediately economically useful, is expelled" (Holborow 2015: 16). Therefore, the emphasis is no longer on 'general culture' but increasingly on skills aimed to fit students into the workforce within neoliberalism:

> From now on, the most important activity at school is no longer learning, but "learning to learn," the ability to adapt quickly to a fast changing technological environment and to a rapid rotation of the labor force in industry and services.
>
> (Hirtt 2009: 219)

In this new paradigm, learners should take responsibility for their educational career to become entrepreneurs and to be adaptable through lifelong learning for their own successful integration into the new world of work (Urciuoli 2010; Patrick 2013). From a Foucauldian perspective, Mark Olssen (2008: 37) argues that lifelong learning "represents a model of governing individuals in their relation to the collective" or, more precisely, "a technology of control". In this sense, lifelong learning enables states to avoid direct responsibility for their citizens and, at the same time, facilitates the flexibility of workers to the ever-changing needs of the workforce (Olssen 2008: 39). Capitalist states and international organizations such as the OECD, the World Bank or the European Commission encourage this new conception of education which teaches students how to consume (Hirtt 2009) and "prepares and cultivates future workers to become both useful and productive and obedient and docile" (Hill et al. 2009: 120). In this way, the education system today has become an agency to reproduce the necessary economic and ideological conditions for the enduring hegemony of neoliberal capitalism:

> Education is understood as a way to legitimize the neoliberal economic model based on production, free trade, and consumption. [. . .] The objective is to consolidate and legitimize economic neoliberalism rather than promote democratic social values that are critical and participatory.
>
> (Muñoz 2015: 35–6)

In sum, education is of utmost importance for the dominant neoliberal agenda, not only as a means of introducing a corporative model of schooling, but also as "an important means of inculcating market values in future generations" (Block et al. 2012b: 7). Like education more generally, teaching foreign and second languages in the twenty-first century has been strongly determined by neoliberalism (Bernstein et al. 2015; Shin and Park 2016). In recent years, several authors have shown different ways in which neoliberalism finds expression in particular language teaching settings, especially through ethnographic studies in the field of ELT. Kubota (2011) points out the relationship between neoliberalism and English learning in Japan

38 *History of foreign language education*

with the construction of this language as a key skill for career or work success, reinforced by a language testing industry that uses this idea for profit-making. However, as the results of Kubota's ethnographic study indicate, the individual economic success at the workplace in reality depends largely on social stratifications according to gender, race or geographical origin rather than in a good command of English. In her study of an ELT program for adult refugees in the United States, Doris Warriner (2016) reaches somewhat similar conclusions. The viewpoints of the institution, the teachers and the learners of this program are influenced by the assumption that English proficiency opens the doors to future economic success. Following a neoliberal standpoint, all parties seem to believe in the fairness of the labor market and that the improvement of the economic situation of refugees depends mainly on their individual hard work and entrepreneurial spirit. Nevertheless, as Warriner concludes (2016: 506), the neoliberal promise of learning English as a mechanism for economic success does not concur with the lived experiences of the students. Elsewhere, Dina López (2015) shows how an English Literacy and Civics Education program for adult immigrants in New York City is also based on neoliberal discourses of flexibility, choice, entrepreneurship and, above all, the individual responsibility to work hard to learn English in order to improve students' economic situation and reach the so-called American dream. Yet, in classroom activities, learners, most of whom are unemployed or have low paid jobs, find ways to express counter-hegemonic perspectives to confront the neoliberal ideology:

> Though not prompted by the teacher or curriculum, students claimed interactional space in the classroom and brought up issues of racism, linguistic discrimination, and immigration status that challenged the notion that all they needed to do was work hard to learn English, and the American Dream would be within arm's reach.
>
> (López 2015: 119)

Elsewhere, Hyunjung Shin (2016) shifts the focus to a South Korean pre-college-aged study program in Canada to underline that English learning is associated with the neoliberal discourse of 'self-management' in which education is understood as the development of individual skills to improve one's employment opportunities. This author also highlights the important role of the transnational language education agencies that organize these kinds of programs abroad to spread a neoliberal conception of language learning:

> it is not just that neoliberalism has an impact on the language education industry, but the language education industry has also become an instantiation of the ideologies of neoliberalism by developing and selling packaged products that make the projects of self-management seem more achievable and desirable.
>
> (Shin 2016: 511)

History of foreign language education 39

In the realm of language teacher education, Block and Gray (2016) discuss the neoliberal approaches of two British second language teacher preparation programs. Both programs emphasize an instrumental notion of English detached from social, economic and political conditions outside the classroom. Based around a very limited view of teaching, these programs favor practice over theory or critical awareness, and student teachers are subject to a greater control over their training and future profession than was the case in the past. As a result, this kind of program reinforces "a model of professional activity which is highly instrumental and indeed, emblematic of the kind of de-skilling and discrediting which have occurred in many professional sectors in recent decades" (482). Finally, in the particular field of language teaching materials that is the main concern of this book, neoliberalism has also been analyzed in relation to global ELT textbooks, as I will explain in Chapter 3.

Conclusion

In this chapter I point out some of the major political decisions which have led to changes in foreign and second language teaching in the past half century, focusing especially on Europe. Through the analysis of the main projects for language education of the Council of Europe, such as *The Threshold Level*, the CEFR or the implantation of CLT, I have shown that the motivations behind their development are not only pedagogical or linguistic but also ideological. They are products of the capitalist political economy of their times, which requires a particular epistemological universe. In its latest phase, language teaching is experiencing a rapid process of standardization and centralization, which has been developed in accord with the mercantilist spirit of neoliberalism that extends to all spheres of contemporary life. The changes discussed in this chapter are very relevant for providing a wider picture into the reasons why materials for language teaching are the way they are, a point which will be discussed more broadly in the last chapter of this book. In the next chapter, I will provide a review of selected critical studies on language textbooks and I will call for a reorientation in this field towards an approach more centered on political and economic issues.

Notes

1 The 'unit/credit system' of the Council of Europe aimed to standardize the teaching of languages across Europe. It followed a similar scheme to the one which already operated in the United States. According to this system, "subjects should not be taught or examined globally, but broken down into constituent parts, which could be taken one by one as learners were ready to do so" (Trim 2007: 14). Therefore, the development of a unit-credit scheme "would enable learners to study 'units' of work (in specific notional-functional areas) and gain 'credit' for these" (Morrow 2004: 5).

40 History of foreign language education

2 The *Common European Framework of Reference for Languages* (Council of Europe 2001: 52) includes the same list of 'communication themes' proposed by *The Threshold Level*.

3 According to Graham Crookes (2009: 70–1), activity-based learning (a legacy of Dewey and experiential learning much like CLT) had already been introduced into British English as a Second Language primary systems in the 1970s, at the same time that the Council of Europe was just starting to promote CLT in language teaching,

4 Before the appearance of the CEFR in 2001, another stage in learning languages called *Vantage* (van Ek and Trim 2001) was introduced after *The Threshold Level* and *Waystage*. All of these levels were based on the same notional-functional syllabus put into circulation some 30 years before. *Threshold*, *Waystage* and *Vantage* dropped their semantically driven names for levels marked with only a letter and a number such as A1 or B2 in the CEFR probably because it was then easier to translate them into different languages.

5 All these documents are available online: www.coe.int/t/dg4/linguistic/Manuel1_EN.asp (accessed 27 January 2017).

6 Jean-Claude Beacco is one of the authors of the *Guide for the development of language education policies in Europe* (Beacco and Byram 2003) and the *Guide for the implementation of curricula for plurilingual and intercultural education* (Beacco et al. 2010), both published by the Council of Europe.

3 Critical research on language textbooks

Introduction

This chapter explores how critical studies related to foreign/second language textbooks have evolved during the past four decades. Critical approaches draw on the idea that we live in a world in which our circumstances are conditioned by aspects such as social class, race, ethnicity, gender, sexuality or economic and geopolitical situations (Canagarajah 2005). They aim to identify, analyze or subvert different kinds of discrimination. One of the key aspects of critical work is "turning a skeptical eye toward assumptions, ideas that have become 'naturalized', notions that are no longer questioned" (Pennycook 2001: 6). Critical movements in applied linguistics borrow conceptual frames from other disciplines such as anthropology, sociology, economics, psychology or cultural studies, and are primarily centered on the relationship between power and language use. Many different approaches in applied linguistics bear the name 'critical' such as *critical discourse analysis* (or more recently, *critical discourse studies*), *critical applied linguistics*, *critical literacy*, *critical sociolinguistics*, and so on (see Pennycook 2010 for a review). Others, however, do not include the prefix 'critical' in their names, but draw on insights from theories and movements such as feminism, antiracism or Marxism, that are critical by definition since they examine questions related to inequality or discrimination with the goal of transforming reality.

Generally speaking, when it comes to studies of language materials, the objective behind critical research is to identify, analyze and critique injustices or partial views generated by power structures in societies that appear in textbooks and in that way contribute to the battle to overcome social inequalities. Materials for learning additional languages first became the object of studies in the 1970s, at a time when English was gaining momentum as the international *lingua franca*. At first, these investigations mainly centered on didactics. Textbooks for learning languages have always been important pedagogical tools and the research conducted was focused on how materials could be developed to facilitate language acquisition, help practitioners to choose the best textbooks or analyze the materials according to

42 *Critical research on language textbooks*

methodological approaches to language teaching and learning. This area of study, which Brian Tomlinson (2012) called 'material development', covers a wide range of issues such as materials production, design, implementation, evaluation, adaptation and content analysis. Despite the importance of materials in language learning, Tomlinson (2012: 144) states that "it is surprising how little attention they have received until recently in the literature on applied linguistics". Although this assertion might be correct, recent books suggest an emergent academic interest in language materials (Gray 2013a; McGrath 2013; Tomlinson 2013; Garton and Graves 2014; Harwood 2014a; Curdt-Christiansen and Weninger 2015a). Indeed, it seems that research on language textbooks is "on the rise" in recent years, as pointed out by Nigel Harwood (2014b: 30) in the introductory chapter of an edited volume that focuses on English Language Teaching (ELT) textbooks at three different levels: content, consumption and production.

However, materials for second languages have rarely been analyzed from a critical perspective and if they have, the attention was not on the relations between textbooks and political economy. Instead, following the trends in the social sciences, critical researchers of language textbooks opted to focus on politics of recognition or identity politics, as we shall see throughout this chapter. Nancy Fraser (2003) argues that there are two kinds of critical frameworks for approaching social injustices: the redistribution paradigm and the recognition paradigm. The first places the focus on socioeconomic inequalities, sees the victims of injustices according to their economic position in society, and proposes to change the economic structure to overcome discrimination (Fraser 2003: 12–15). Those working within the redistribution paradigm are interested in questions related to social class and political economy. In contrast, the recognition paradigm understands injustices as 'cultural' and sees people who are discriminated against as those who "are distinguished by the lesser respect, esteem, and prestige they enjoy", and seeks the response to social injustice in a positive valorization and a greater recognition of marginalized groups (Fraser 2003: 12–15). This second approach targets concepts such as gender, sexuality, race and ethnicity. Fraser (2003: 9) asserts that the distinction between these two paradigms is a "false antitheses" and calls for a third paradigm that reconciles redistribution and recognition. However, she recognizes that over the last few decades the recognition paradigm has dominated and even replaced the redistribution approach. In the particular field of applied linguistics, Block (2015a: 6), following Fraser, also explains that academic research has focused more on issues of identity and recognition than on issues related to redistribution:

> Up to the year 1990, applied linguistics had followed trends in society at large, whereby the political and academic left had abandoned its traditional concern with the shortcomings of capitalism and the need for socialism/communism as a system better able to distribute the economic and other resources of society. Instead, activists and academics alike

had embraced 'identity politics' and the attack on inequality through a recognition and respect agenda as the only ways to achieve a more just society. The option of combining a concern with identity politics and distribution, made difficult by the fact that the former primed equality based on the differences between people while the latter primed equality based on what human beings have in common, did not seem to be on the table.

This has somewhat changed in the last few years, especially after the 2008 global economic crisis. Analyzing materials for learning languages as indispensable objects in the process of learning a language by placing them in relation to a wider social, political and economic context has been the focus of several investigations. The introductory chapters of two recently edited books dedicated to language materials adopt the critical perspective I follow in this book in the conception about what a language textbook is. Gray (2013b: 3), in his introduction to *Critical perspectives on language teaching materials*, defines textbooks as follows:

> [T]hey are cultural artefacts from which meanings emerge about the language being taught, associating it with particular ways of being, particular varieties of language and ways of using language, and particular sets of values. At the same time, they are also ideological (in the Marxist sense) in that the meanings they seek to create tend to endorse and reproduce (although not invariably) existing power relations.

Regarding what language textbooks are from a critical perspective, Xiao Lan Curdt-Christiansen and Csilla Weninger (2015b: 1), similarly to Gray, highlight the selection of reality that the materials represent and the fact that they are shaped by the macro context in which they are developed:

> As sociocultural materials, they are the products of complex selective processes reflecting political decisions, educational beliefs and priorities, cultural realities and language policies. As such, language teaching and learning are not ideologically neutral practices; they are located within complex webs of political and historical contexts and sociolinguistic practices, all of which is mediated through the textual and visual worlds of textbooks.

In this chapter, I shall first select some studies that I consider relevant to illustrate the main tendencies in the field, and later I shall concentrate in particular upon those studies that are closely related to the approach of my book. At the beginning of this literature review, I will explain the origins of critical approaches to textbooks which were at first centered on gender bias. Later, with the rise of the neoliberal capitalist economy, critical studies centered more on questions of culture, race or ethnicity. These issues served to

44 *Critical research on language textbooks*

highlight inequality and power relations that appear in textbooks and were studied together with concepts such as prejudices and stereotypes, inclusion and exclusion, beliefs about what is normal and correct, idealization and positive self-representation. Although they have treated the questions of inequality mainly through the differences between people according to gender, race or ethnicity, and their misrepresentation in textbooks, these studies have brought to the surface the questionable and idealized reality represented in language materials and started questioning the reasons and politics behind this reality. It is for this reason that I consider them important to mention as part of a critical research on language textbooks. In the second part of the chapter, I will review studies of language textbooks that engage in questions related to social class, consumerist practices and entrepreneurial values. These works are, in my view, part of a broader turn to the political economy in critical language textbook research in the era of neoliberalism.

Gender

In the 1970s and the 1980s, critical studies of language textbooks were centered on gender discrimination and sexism (Hartman and Judd 1978; Porreca 1984; Carroll and Kowitz 1994; Rifkin 1998). This approach was inspired by the second wave of feminism, which first began in the early 1960s in the United States and later spread to the rest of the Western world and beyond. This movement represented a challenge to the pervasive androcentrism in the Fordist industrial societies and fought discrimination against women in different spheres of life in the capitalist world. In the field of textbook analysis one of the representative studies of this kind is by Karen Porreca (1984), who analyzed 15 ELT textbooks used in the United States. Porreca concluded that male characters tend to occupy a greater range of occupations and more powerful jobs than women:

> For each working woman appearing in the text, there are six male workers. For every woman worker shown in an illustration, five more illustrations depict men at their jobs. Occupations for women are often restricted to the traditional service and entertainment jobs, such as waitress, nurse, secretary, and actress, occasionally including a token professional job such as teacher or doctor.
>
> (Porreca 1984: 719)

Nearly two decades later, Jane Sunderland (2000: 152) argued that there was no more interest in these kinds of investigations because the gender bias was less evident in contemporary materials, although some authors continued to detect it in ELT textbooks, especially outside of the global commercial context (Amini and Birjandi 2012; Ullah and Skelton 2013; Hall 2014). Gender bias analysis usually draws on the perspective of Western feminism and is sometimes cross-culturally insensitive with a tendency to universalize and homogenize the roles, rights and aspirations of women, which are very often closely related to changes in the new capitalist order.

In the case of global textbooks for English language teaching in the age of neoliberalism, Gray (2010a: 109) detects further feminization of the content. Female characters are usually independent, show initiative and are professionally successful, while male characters often appear doing housework, taking care of children and with less professional aspirations than women. This trend may be explained by the extraordinary success of feminism in the social mainstream in Western countries, above all in symbolic terms (in material terms, there has been less success), which has coincided with the rise of neoliberalism from the 1980s onwards.

Finally, related to gender and sexism, it is also interesting to mention the growing interest in applied linguistics in questions of sexuality and sexual identity (Nelson 1999, 2008; Liddicoat 2009). Many of these studies draw on queer theory[1] and focus on ways to make language classrooms more welcoming to gay and lesbian learners. Within this paradigm, Gray (2013c) examines lesbian, gay, bisexual and transgender (LGBT) representations in global English language textbooks. Influenced by a Marxist approach, Gray (2013c: 43–44) argues that capitalism has allowed "the emergence of homosexuality as an increasingly assumed identity", at least in Western countries. However, the LGBT population and concomitant issues are scarcely represented in ELT global textbooks:

> In the treatment of the family and in content on ideal partners, internet dating and relationships, socialising, travelling and meeting new people, there is a blanket avoidance of any representation of clearly identified LGBT characters. Occasional short texts about gay figures (who might be familiar to students in some settings) do feature [. . .]. However, these are all notable for their avoidance of any mention of homosexuality.
>
> (Gray 2013c: 49)

Gray attributes this phenomenon to a prevailing heteronormativity (in which heterosexuality is presented as a norm), and to commercial reasons, saying that publishers also like to sell their textbooks in countries that are more conservative regarding the LGBT population. From a political economic angle, it would be advisable to integrate these gender and sexuality approaches with those centered more on the economic system in order to get a clearer picture of the reality represented. It is fair to say that women are being given more and more space in pedagogic materials and that LGBT[2] characters should be included in language textbooks. What is rarely said, however, is that these once misrepresented groups in textbooks have something in common with men and heterosexuals and that is their class representation. Nearly all of the characters that appear in second language textbooks, whatever gender or sexual orientation they might have, belong

46 *Critical research on language textbooks*

to the middle class and are usually typical representatives of neoliberal consumers. In brief, the treatment of the role of women and the LGBT population in textbooks usually goes hand in hand with the increase in interest in the broader construct of identity in language learning, which will be the topic of the next section.

Identity

Since Bonnie Norton (1995) argued for the necessity of introducing identity and social context in second language learning, identity has transformed into one of the key concepts for critical authors in this field (Preece 2016). Identity refers to "who we are and who we know ourselves to be" (Moran 2014: 14) and it is a multidimensional concept that may refer to different aspects such as gender, sexuality, race, ethnicity, age, religion, culture and so on. According to Mario Moran (2014: 146), "the proliferation of 'identities' in contemporary capitalism masks an ultimate sameness at the heart of the logic of capitalism, which demands that all human needs and wants are met in the same way, by purchase on the market". In other words, the fragmented identity, derived from postmodern thought, may contribute to an omission of the economic bases of capitalist society. By postmodern thought, I have in mind a social theory that rejects the 'grand narratives' which aim to provide totalizing explanations of social and cultural developments, such as those provided by religions or political philosophies such as classical liberalism or Marxism. Postmodernism does not view the world as a totality and seeks to 'deconstruct' the reality with 'mini-narratives' of individuals or particular cultural groups. For postmodernists, there is not an objective and absolute truth and what is important is the relative interpretation of each individual.

Postmodernism has become a very influential theory in the humanities and social sciences since the late 1970s with the writings of French intellectuals such as Jean-Francois Lyotard, Jacques Derrida, Jacques Lacan and Michel Foucault. From a Marxist perspective, postmodernism has been identified as the ideology of late capitalism (Jameson 1991). Marxist authors criticize postmodern approaches for not taking into account broader social issues such as historic events, class conflict and the material and economic bases of societies (Callinicos 1990; Harvey 1991; Eagleton 1996). Postmodern theory, with its emphasis on individuality or cultural subgroups over the totality, is at the root of so-called identity or recognition politics (Fraser 2003), which focuses on issues relevant to specific groups such as the discrimination against women, people of color or homosexuals.

I will highlight two studies of textbooks that have focused on identity. Marya Shardakova and Aneta Pavlenko (2004) used tools from critical discourse analysis to investigate the identity of imaginary North American learners and their Russian interlocutors who appear in textbooks for learning Russian as a second language in the United States. In this analysis, these

Critical research on language textbooks   47

two authors take into consideration elements like social class, professional occupation, age, gender, sexuality, marital status, ethnicity and religious affiliations. Apart from detecting an exaggerated simplification in the reality and identities in textbooks, these authors warn of the dangers of stereotyping in textbooks. For example, the textbooks say that Russians are fascinated with the technological advantages of Americans and the supposed social and gender equality that exists in the United States. In this sense, the authors show that at times the textbooks present American culture as superior to Russian culture. Instead of portraying an idealized world, Shardakova and Pavlenko (2004) propose that the authors include in textbooks cultural misunderstandings that might be beneficial for students who have to learn to negotiate meanings in environments that can be indifferent or even hostile.

Another study centered on identity in textbooks is by John Kullman (2013). This author finds that the most notable change in the identity discourses in the global English textbooks from the 1970s onwards is the central role of the learner. Through activities and tasks, textbooks place an increasing emphasis on learners' lives, personal qualities, personal development, change and lifestyles. According to Kullman, textbooks encourage learners to talk about themselves in narrow ways, excluding certain issues and promoting "discourses of individualism, consumerism, the medicalisation of everyday life and psychotherapy" (36). In that way, textbooks seem to promote what a few years ago Frank Furedi (2004) defined as the ascendancy of a 'therapy culture' in Western countries that celebrates the individual feelings and languages of therapy. For Furedi (2004: 22), "therapeutic culture regards the management of emotion as the most effective way of guiding individual and collective behaviour" in society today. Kathryn Ecclestone and Dennis Hayes (2009), following Furedi, chart a 'dangerous' trend in the UK to turn education into a form of therapy that emphasizes the emotional aspects of learning such as 'self-esteem', 'self-confidence' or 'emotional intelligence' and thereby "creates a curriculum of the self that lowers educational and social aspirations in its quest to be more 'personally relevant'" (Ecclestone and Hayes 2009: xiii). Regarding the critique of neoliberalism that this book proposes, the prioritization of personal emotions and therapy identified by Kullman (2013) in language textbooks may work as an ideological mechanism to hide the structural social inequalities of capitalism and to make people feel solely responsible for their own economic failures (Silva 2010). As Jeff Sugarman (2015) reminds us, the focus of therapy culture is not on the broader socioeconomic circumstances of the society but on working on the self to attain personal fulfillment and, in that way, deal with one's own problems in a form that is aligned with neoliberalism:

> [T]he road to personal fulfillment is paved with the same stones as those leading to success for businesses and other institutions, namely, becoming more independent and self-sufficient, enterprising, competitive,

48   *Critical research on language textbooks*

flexible, adaptable, risk-seeking, less reliant on government support, and oriented toward pursuing self-interest in a society reconceived in the image of a market.

(Sugarman 2015: 109)

Within what Fraser calls the 'recognition paradigm', together with identity, culture is another concept that attracted wide interest in the area of second language education from the 1990s (Kramsch 1993; Hinkel 1999; Kumaravadivelu 2008). Among many definitions of culture in applied linguistics, one widely influential understanding is that of Kramsch who sees culture "as a membership in a discourse community that shares a common social space and history, and common imaginings" (1998: 10). I now turn to review some of the most relevant critical studies that focus on how culture is represented in language textbooks.

Culture

Culture remains a key concept in the language textbook analysis of the last 25 years (Alptekin 1993; Batteman and Mattos 2006; Santos 2007). Martin Cortazzi and Lixian Jin (1999) famously distinguished three types of cultural information that tend to appear in ELT textbooks: (a) target culture or the culture of the countries where English is spoken as an L1; (b) source culture, the learner's own culture; and (c) international culture, the various cultures of English and non-English speaking countries. Similarly to identity studies, the majority of cultural studies, derived from postmodern thought, have not focused on the circumstances or implications of the social, economic, political or historic context of textbooks. They have separated the concept of culture from the economic bases of society and forgotten to address the most important questions about socioeconomic redistribution. In general, these types of studies have been strongly influenced by the concept of 'intercultural competence' developed by Michael Byram (1997), which proposes an interaction between cultures and takes into consideration the target culture but also the culture of the learner and the international culture as well. At roughly the same time, Kramsch (1993) coined the metaphor the 'third place' to capture what happens when learners are becoming 'intercultural speakers'. According to this author, the third place "grows in the interstices between the cultures the learners grew up with and the new cultures he or she is being introduced to" (1993: 236).[3] Later, in a similar vein, Kumaravadivelu (2008) proposed development of language learners' global consciousness. This meant a critical and reflective approach that aimed "to identify and understand what is good and bad about our own culture, and what is good and bad about other cultures" (Kumaravadivelu 2008: 6).

In critical studies of cultural representation, the work of Arnulfo Ramirez and Joan Kelly Hall (1990) about Spanish textbooks in the United States

Critical research on language textbooks   49

should be mentioned. Within a sociocultural perspective, these two authors identify a limited representation of Latin-Americans in the United States and an under-representation of the majority of the countries in which Spanish is spoken. Moreover, these authors adopt an economically grounded approach in their critical position in denouncing the absence of issues like poverty or political conflict, and the under-representation of working-class people in the books analyzed:

> [T]he majority of Spanish-speaking countries are underrepresented in the textbooks examined. In addition, no text contains significant representation of the Spanish-speaking groups living in the United States. Within the cultural spheres, references to poverty, malnutrition, and political strife are omitted. [. . .] All but a few of the photographs of all five textbooks examined depict the middle to upper classes, a segment which represents, in reality, a very small percentage of the Spanish-speaking population.
>
> (Ramirez and Hall 1990: 63)

Elsewhere, Enrique Basabe (2006) shows that ELT textbooks in Argentina present a certain type of Anglo-American culture as both universal and a model to be imitated:

> The world constructed by these coursebooks still remains one in which the English-speaking countries are not only linguistic but also cultural "targets" the globe has to aspire to, imitate and follow. These aims, however, have been, in most cases, transformed into "universal" or "international" attitudes we all seek to share and identify with.
>
> (Basabe 2006: 68–9)

Although a certain effort to reflect cultural diversity exists, according to Basabe, these textbooks primarily represent an Anglo-American utopia, without proposing a critical reception of the culture of the target language. More recently, Simon Coffey (2013) discovered that France is preferred over other French-speaking countries in his analysis of which communicative contexts are presented in two current French language textbooks. According to this author, such an approach reflects

> both the traditional hold on the imagination of French as exclusively the language of France and reinforces the cultural and linguistic hegemony of native speakers as privileged custodians of the language. [. . .] Furthermore the tight, exclusive linking of French to France reinforces the centralising post-colonial power of metropolitan France, which is at odds with the internationalising aims of an inclusive Francophonie agenda.
>
> (Coffey 2013: 149)

50 *Critical research on language textbooks*

Similarly, Cristina Ros i Solé (2013) detected a different treatment of Latin American countries versus Spain in one Spanish textbook that she analyzed in order to evaluate the different ways in which cultural topics are addressed:

> The bias towards a Spanish peninsular voice is patent in the way Latin American cultures are not integrated fully in the coursebook and in the choice of topics, which present certain values about the culture(s). Whereas peninsular Spanish stands for modernity, rationality and the world of work, Latin America is associated with more exotic and backward practices.
>
> (Ros i Solé 2013: 175)

So far, we have seen how critical language textbook analyses have been engaged in issues of identity related to gender, sexuality or cultural diversity. Their aim is to assert group distinctiveness and to give power and recognition to marginalized or underrepresented collectives in textbooks. I now turn to similar works in applied linguistics concerning race and ethnicity, which emerged as other key categories of identity. These works, as I explain in the next section, identify the misrepresentation and stereotyping of particular groups such as non-white and immigrant characters in textbooks.

Race and ethnicity

Race and ethnicity have also recently become key categories in critical approaches to second language acquisition (Kubota and Lin 2009). In the realm of language textbooks studies, the analysis of ELT textbooks written for immigrants in the United States by Elavie Ndura (2004) should be particularly emphasized. Ndura found racial bias in materials through stereotypical stories about non-white characters, such as one about a poor African boy who lived in misery and was once attacked by a lion. He had to work in the marketplace but he improved his life by working hard and getting an education. According to Ndura (2004: 147):

> Getting a Western education is by no means the only way an African boy can improve his life. Traditional, non-formal education has worked as well for many African families. Being chased by a lion is a hyperbolic presumption since most Africans can live their entire life without ever running into one.

Furthermore, textbooks do not include any reference to current racism in the United States and, when they explain a historical fact related to racism, they do it from a white man's perspective (Ndura 2004). Related to the concepts of race and ethnicity, Teun Van Dijk's (2000) work on 'Us' and 'Them' has also been influential among researchers critically analyzing textbooks. According to Van Dijk, a positive self-presentation and a negative other representation appears in many discourses, in order to emphasize the positive aspects concerning the in-group ('Us') and the negative things about the out-group ('Them'). Trevor Gulliver (2010) applies this theory in his study of English textbooks for newcomers to Canada to demonstrate that stories about immigrants which appear in texts usually portray Canada as a promised land for newcomers. These stories follow similar structural narrative patterns: when newcomers arrive in Canada, there is a period of economic deprivation, exclusion and personal battle, after which the immigrant economically succeeds. This success is attributed to his/her good character or hard work. As Gulliver explains, with these stories textbooks do not portray the real experiences of the newcomers but are an example of legitimation of the state of Canada and its migration policies.

More recently, Paul Thomas (2017) critically analyzed the representation of non-Westerners in ELT textbooks in Norway. The results suggest that textbooks present a 'prejudiced' portrayal of characters from non-Western backgrounds, often from a Western, white perspective:

> There is a dearth of imagination when non-westerners are portrayed. Texts selected aim at reproducing and perpetuating the hackneyed representations of the "rest" (as opposed to the "West") spawned in the heyday of colonialism. Overt racism and denigration may have been ameliorated, but the gaze is still on that which makes the "rest" different from the "West".
>
> (Thomas 2017: 9)

Along similar lines, in one of my studies with Jelena Petanović dedicated to the representation of immigrants in Catalan language textbooks, we identified certain differences in the representation of Western and non-Western immigrant characters:

> Western newcomers are always portrayed as part of the upper/middle class while non-Westerners are represented as working class members. On the other hand, non-Western immigrants are characterized by physical or gender stereotypes, while Western immigrants have positive attributes. We also found an idyllic representation of reality, together with an absence of cultural comparisons or information about immigrant countries of origin.
>
> (Bori and Petanović 2017: 61)

Problematizing diversity

Regarding ethnicity and race, it is evident that there is a tendency in contemporary language textbooks to consistently include a wider variety of characters of different races and cultures, although sometimes in a stereotypical and biased manner. In that way, textbooks follow the theoretical

52   *Critical research on language textbooks*

trend of multiculturalism so popular in the neoliberal age. The enthusiastic celebration of racial and ethnical diversity often hides another and more determinant difference in our societies: the economic inequality between rich and poor people, as Walter Benn Michaels (2006) explains in his book *The Trouble with Diversity*. Michaels argues that the devotion to multiculturalism in the United States has created a false vision of social justice which omits the most important social differences, such as those of class and wealth.

Some time ago, Michael Halliday (1990) suggested that racial differences (like gender) are easily accommodated by the economic and political system because they do not pose a threat to the capitalist order. He further noted that "it is not acceptable to show up classism, especially by objective linguistics analysis [. . .] because capitalist society could not exist without discrimination between classes. Such work could, ultimately, threaten the order of society". A decade later, bell hooks (2000), a critical writer who has dealt extensively dealt with race and gender in American society, also made clear that critical studies should focus attention on social class and the economic system:

> To challenge racism or sexism or both without linking these systems to economic structures of exploitation and our collective participation in the upholding and maintenance of such structures, however marginal that engagement may be, is ultimately to betray a vision of justice for all.
> (161)

Similarly, from a Marxist perspective, critical educators Hill et al. (2009: 104) remind us that "[w] hereas the abolition of racism and sexism does not guarantee the abolition of capitalist social relations of production, the abolition of class inequalities, by definition, denotes the abolition of capitalism". Furthermore, these authors argue that analysis centered only on gender and racial oppression serves "to occlude the class-capital relation, the class struggle, and to obscure the essential and defining nature of capitalism, the labor-capital relation and its attendant class conflict" (105).

Apart from the promotion of cultural, racial or gender diversity in neoliberal times, it is also relevant to point out here the uncritical celebration of plurilingualism in language teaching, promoted among others by the Council of Europe. Nelson Flores (2013: 513) argues that are several similarities between the ideal subjects of plurilingualism and neoliberalism:

> Both subjects are characterized as dynamic and ever changing, and able to adapt to the increasing diversity of society through a lifelong development of cultural competence and a lifelong expansion of their linguistic repertoire. In addition, both subjects are depicted as emerging naturally from the changing global political economy and as the inevitable and desired outcome for all of the world's population.

Critical research on language textbooks   53

To avoid the current complicity between plurilingualism and neoliberalism, Flores highlights the need for a further critical engagement with the concept of plurilingualism that could be used as a tool to resist neoliberalism. In a similar vein, Kubota (2014) develops the concept of 'neoliberal multiculturalism' which is built upon the celebration of individualism, diversity, plurality, flexibility, mobility and cosmopolitanism and which neglects racism or other economical injustices. Similar to the approach that I propose in this book, this author calls for a shift in attention in critical applied linguistics from individual diversity and hybridity to a more political and economic critique devoted to neoliberalism.

On the other hand, Del Percio (2016) critically examines the celebration of intercultural communication as a key factor in the European Union's policy on the reception of migrants in recent years. Through an ethnographic study in two organizations of the migration infrastructure in Italy using Foucauldian governmentality, this author shows that the investment on intercultural communication serves to maintain a neoliberal rationality among the workers and volunteers of these organizations, but also to prepare immigrants for subservient roles in the host society. Del Percio argues that the investment in intercultural communication made by the European Union to receive immigrants could be seen as a neoliberal multicultural paradigm that "invests in politics of recognition and valorization of difference and contributes to the affective domestication and tranquilization of the subalterns" (96). In that regard, he concludes:

> While the commitment to intercultural communication and to discourses valorizing diversity more generally creates the illusion of equality and inclusion, it also tends to erase and bypass questions of power and structural domination, and lacks a commitment to material equality and social justice.
>
> (Del Percio 2016: 96)

The previous sections have offered a synopsis of the main interests of critical studies of language textbooks centered in identity politics. As I have argued, these approaches tend to focus on the differences within humankind. In their frameworks, they divide people between men and women, heterosexuals and homosexuals, black and white, natives and foreigners. In that way, even unwittingly, they may contribute to a fragmentation of humanity and to blocking the development of a class consciousness that could lead to its emancipation. As Tom Hickey (2006: 196) explains, the focus on gender and racial oppressions can easily help the maintenance of capitalism:

> Oppressions, in dividing the working class, operate to secure the reproduction of capital; they construct social conflict between men and women, or black and white, or skilled and unskilled, thereby tending to dissolve the conflict between capital and labour.

54 *Critical research on language textbooks*

In the next section, I turn to critical analysis that is centered on what people have in common, that is, the economic and material bases of human existence. I first review textbook analysis related to social class, and later I continue with works that focus on consumerist and entrepreneurial values and practices in language materials.

Social class

One of the first works adopting the critical economic approach that this book proposes dates from more than three decades ago. Elsa Auerbach and Denise Burgess (1985) studied the hidden curriculum of ELT materials designed for adults newly arrived to the United States, through the analysis of health, housing and work units. The two authors reported that language materials do not take into account the socioeconomic situation of the newcomers since they only reflect the values, the culture and the economic status of the middle class:

> A [. . .] serious limitation of many texts results from not taking into account the socioeconomic conditions of newcomers' lives. Middle class values, culture, and financial status are often reflected in lesson content; for example, a dialogue describing a student spending his one day off work playing golf fails to acknowledge that golf is a culture- and class-specific sport.
>
> (Auerbach and Burgess 1985: 478–9)

Furthermore, according to these authors, textbooks prepare the students for subordinate roles and reinforce hierarchical relations through the exclusion of concepts such as conflict or the development of the ability for critical thinking. Elsewhere, Karen Risager (1991) examined ELT textbooks in Scandinavian countries, even though her conclusions could be extended to textbooks for foreign languages throughout Western Europe (Cortazzi and Jin 1999). According to Risager (1991), the characters in textbooks are middle class, they are young, presented as isolated individuals (more than as members of a family) or as tourists often visiting urban centers. They engage in trivial linguistic interactions mostly related to consumerism and free time. Moreover, the characters in textbooks do not express their feelings or opinions and are never bothered with social, moral or philosophical problems. Similarly, another study by Bessie Dendrinos (1992) analyzed international ELT textbooks and detected an exaggerated representation of upper-middle class white men under the age of 40. Moreover, according to this author, textbooks have a tendency to present an idealized world similar to that of TV commercials. Phillipson (1992) goes a step further and sees the materials for English for foreigners as tools to promote the Western world (especially the British) with an economic and political agenda very well defined.

Critical research on language textbooks   55

Elsewhere, in her critical analysis of an ELT textbook published in the United States, Karen Grady (1997) argued that its socioeconomic content was trivial and irrelevant to the immigrant students' reality. Furthermore, the textbook concealed the economic inequalities in American society:

> An ideology that is blind to the economic realities of living in the United States pervades the text. Thinking about what one wants to do leads to being able to do it without overcoming any material or social constraints. Decisions are simply a matter of choice, with all options being possible and equally desirable.
>
> (Grady 1997: 8)

According to this author, the presentation and suggestions coming from the textbook could potentially perpetuate the economically, politically and socially unjust social organization. Several years later, Vivian Cook (2003) did not detect any substantial changes in his study of English, French and Italian textbooks for adult learners. He showed that textbooks emphasize infantilization and idealization of topics and situations that appear in them. In his study, the textbooks analyzed are aimed at young people without any kind of preoccupation in their lives, "without cares in the world or plans for the future, except tomorrow's party" (Cook 2003: 277).

In her study of Alice, a highly motivated French language student from a humble background in the United States, Celeste Kinginger (2004) shows that the implicit audience of the language textbook she examined is the upper-middle class, which can result in discrimination towards students from the working classes:

> The readers of this book were people who lived in 'mainsons', 'appartements', or 'pavillons,' – people who had the means to envisage France in the modern-day version of the Grand Tour, ordering wine at refined cafés, buying silk scarves from obsequious salespeople, and contemplating celebrated works of art.
>
> (Kinginger 2004: 225)

In a more recent study about global English textbooks in the last decades, Gray and Block (2014) detected a superficial treatment of the working class, and, above all, the progressive disappearance of characters, practices or topics related to the working class, which happened at the same time as the rise of neoliberalism in the 1990s. Even though materials in the 1970s at times mentioned themes such as industrial strike action, they did not address the reasons why the workers were on strike and did not comment on related matters such as a police presence at a factory where a strike was taking place. In the textbooks of the 1980s, the references to the working class became scarce and where working-class characters did appear, they did so "as anonymous participants in service encounters or as minor characters

56 *Critical research on language textbooks*

whose occupations are mentioned only in passing" (Gray and Block 2014: 61–2). From the 1990s onwards, the characters and topics related to the working class are even rarer and more insignificant in textbooks, with working-class characters presented mostly as entrepreneurs or self-entrepreneurs, a characteristic of the neoliberalism work order. As Gray and Block (2014: 64–5) further explain, "characters can be seen as entrepreneurs, both in the original sense of 'undertaker of a project' [. . .] but also in a more neoliberal, innovative, risk-taking, and wealth-generating sense". The authors conclude that this disappearance of the working class and the emphasis on the cosmopolitan characters of successful upper classes is not a unique phenomenon in commercial English textbooks, but should be considered in a wider context, that of neoliberalism, which aims to reconfigure society to make social class become a redundant concept.

In a similar vein, Keith Copley (2017) presents a comparison between current global English textbooks and earlier ELT materials published between 1975 and 1982. He examines the content in relation to the main tenets of neoliberal ideology, such as individualism, consumerism and the erasure of social class. One of the main insights of this study is the sharp contrast between the emphasis on collective problems and class solidarity in earlier textbooks and the individualization that appears in neoliberal textbooks today:

> In the neoliberal outlook foregrounded in commercial ELT products today, there is an obvious shift from the portrayal of social life as it is invariably seen from a working class perspective, as often burdensome, unsatisfying, and structurally rooted in antagonistic relations of exploitation, to one in which individual agency and personal satisfaction is foregrounded, cut loose from considerations of structural inequality and conflict.
>
> (Copley 2017: 6)

Unlike earlier materials in which working-class and social problems were addressed, the current English textbooks tend to portray only privileged characters, without social concerns, economic limitations or difficulties of subsistence. Actually, as Copley (2017: 13) puts it, "there is virtually no regard paid to even the possibility that working-class occupations might involve economic hardship, physical or emotional stress, unfair treatment, or even mild dissatisfaction". And if by any chance there is a problem, the solution in neoliberal textbooks is to be found in consumption, as in the story of an immigrant character who felt homesick but started to feel better after buying a car (Copley 2017: 14).

Another line of investigation developed by some critical researchers from a political economic perspective focuses on commercial textbooks as products of the global market, especially in the area of ELT textbooks. Authors like Littlejohn (1992), Pennycook (1994) or Gray (2002, 2010b) have pointed to the multi-billion-dollar profits that the publishing industry generates, and also to the way in which publishers' interests partially mark the form and the content of textbooks, in a way in which the publishers decide which topics are problematic for a particular group of students or what is to be done to make their product more attractive to a wider public. Littlejohn (1992) and Gray (2010a) interviewed publishers of ELT textbooks and concluded that their principal concerns were making the maximum economic profit. Similarly, Jack Richards (2001) asserts that some publishers strive to design their textbooks to out-do their competition, with major economic benefits as their primary concern. On the other hand, Tomlinson (2003) explains that many publishers (and authors) choose to copy syllabuses of ELT textbooks that sell well, such as the books in the *Headway* series. According to this author, the publisher assumes that the content that appears in the best-selling textbook is the one in which the students are most interested, but in reality the number of copies sold depends on the money spent on the textbook's publication and promotion, and not on the quality of the textbook's content.

Writing over a decade and half ago, Gray (2002) made the point, which still applies today, that ELT textbooks are all very similar, not only in design but also in their content which is designed with "inclusivity and inappropriacy" (157) in mind. Inclusivity refers to the necessity to include a non-sexist approach in the representation of men and women, whereas inappropiacy is related to a series of topics (politics, religion, drugs, sex, etc.) which the authors should omit in order not to offend the sensibility of different buyers or learners across the planet. More recently, Harwood (2014b: 7) also notes that "publishers avoid including materials which may provoke controversy since this can impact upon sales figures or even result in a textbook being excluded from a state-approved list". However, it is not just about omitting certain topics; the great majority of current language textbooks also tend to propose a kind of a language that Gray (2002), following Gillian Brown, qualifies as 'cosmopolitan' and which has one of the following characteristics:

> [It] assumes a materialistic set of values in which international travel, not being bored, positively being entertained, having leisure, and above all spending money casually and without consideration of the sum involved in the pursuit of these ends, are the norm.
>
> (Brown 1990: 13)

Gray (2002: 161) states that this model of language could serve to present the so-called 'aspirational content' which publishers and authors understand as the reality to which the students aspire, and for this reason, they are interested in it and find it motivating. The 'aspirational content' in textbooks, together with this concept of cosmopolitanism, also engages with concepts such as individualism, mobility and, above all, with the celebration of consumerism, as I discuss in the next section.

Consumerism

The promotion of consumerism has become one of the main features of the content of global ELT textbooks in the era of neoliberalism, associated with a particular understanding of cosmopolitanism. As Block (2010: 295) argues: "One lifestyle option which has become prevalent in recent years revolves around the idea of cosmopolitan global citizens who embody an ideology of global capitalism and consumerism in the different activities that textbooks show them engaging in". The exercises proposed by textbooks, especially those related to the topics of shopping and traveling, embody consumerist values, which are "ultimately conformist as regards the current version of demand-led capitalism, which dominates in most parts of the world today" (Block 2010: 298). Similarly, in his book covering ELT global textbooks from the 1970s until the first decade of the twenty-first century, Gray (2010a) argues that these materials present the English language (and culture) in a selective way, associating it with a series of values such as consumerism, cosmopolitism and individualism, that are in the line with the values proposed by neoliberalism. Based partly on interviews with the publishers of these materials, Gray (2010a) explains how students are seen mostly as consumers or clients that have to be entertained with nonproblematic content and through an attractive visual presentation.

In addition, according to Gray (2012a), the consumerist ideology in ELT global books is reinforced with the rising presence of celebrities. For Gray (2012a: 87), fame-related content serves to promote the 'aspirational content' which is centered on the following aspects: "spectacular personal and professional success, celebrity lifestyles, cosmopolitanism and travel". This author examines the changes brought to society by neoliberalism, "from one of producers to one of consumers [. . .] in which the wealth concomitant with celebrity is fetishised" (2012a: 96), with the growing presence of famous people in textbooks and the society of the spectacle. Gray also shows how the concept of celebrity radically changed in the ELT publishing industry from the 1990s onwards. While earlier famous characters appeared mainly in relation to their personal success (literary prizes, gold medals) or their character (bravery, dedication, intelligence), after the 1990s with neoliberal politics ever-more firmly ensconced in societies around the world, celebrities appear characterized mainly by their wealth or "by their business acumen or by professional success" (Gray 2012a: 99). For example, Joanna Hardy, a fictional writer characterized by her literary works and awards and who appeared in *Headway Intermediate* in the mid-1990s, is substituted in later editions by two other celebrities (Gray 2012a: 101–2):

> She is replaced in the 2003 edition by the equally successful if more glamorous and cosmopolitan Astrid Johnsson, a 42-year-old fictional Swedish cellist. The latter in turn is replaced by Calvin Klein in the 2009 edition, whose career high points are more entrepreneurial in flavour

Critical research on language textbooks   59

and feature the launch of his clothing company at age 26, a subsequent move into sportswear, followed by the creation of his trademark jeans, underwear, perfume and cosmetics ranges. The profile ends with the information that 'His company makes $6 billion every year'.

As Gray (2012a: 103–4) shows, textbooks encourage learners to make themselves famous and rich through activities such as one titled 'How to become an A-list celebrity' in which students learn different ways to become a celebrity. The promotion of a consuming culture detected by Gray in ELT global textbooks also appears in the French textbooks analyzed by Coffey (2013), where learners are encouraged to be consumers of goods, services and celebrity cultures, although sometimes in a particular way:

> [W]hat is offered is a quaint, French version of consumer choice, the shops included being la *boulangerie, pâtisserie, a boucherie, la charcuterie, le tabac* and so forth. What is *not* included is any invitation to problematise modes of shopping, for instance the phenomenon of clone towns and the disappearance of the *petit commerçants*, the rise of commercialism, the low wages of shopkeepers, the expansion of *grandes surfaces* (out-of-town retail markets) shopping in France.
>
> (Coffey 2013: 153)

The Spanish language textbook studied by Ros i Solé (2013) also features the promotion of consumerism to learners. Students are asked to simulate consuming different products and services, from furniture, clothing, and restaurants to holiday trips and cultural products:

> The readership of *AI* [*Aula Internacional*] is represented as being a social group who has a desire to consume popular culture such as music, food and holidays, and everyday hobbies and activities accessible to most Western Europeans. An example from the book, where students are asked to select a restaurant to go to from a selection after reading a brief description of what type of restaurant it is, illustrates this point.
>
> (Ros i Solé 2013: 172)

Kramsch and Kimberly Vinall (2015) present a similar view of the type of consumerism which appears in Spanish foreign language textbooks, discovering a discourse analogous to the one documented by Adam Jaworski and Crispin Thurlow (2010) in travel brochures, and other tourist materials. In the Spanish textbooks used in the United States they analyzed, the learners become tourists (consumers) looking for services and access to cultural experiences, developing instrumental skills to get things done, but always from an outsider's point of view without any kind of engagement with other people or cultures. In their conclusions, Kramsch and Vinall (2015: 25) assert that the "discourse of the foreign language textbook has largely become a

60 *Critical research on language textbooks*

tourism discourse that reinforces the neoliberal discourse of globalization in persistent and subtle ways".

Elsewhere, Vanderlei Zacchi (2016) also detects the promotion of aspirational content in ELT textbooks produced in Brazil through the focus on celebrity lifestyle, cosmopolitanism and travel. A paradigmatic example is a reading and writing activity accompanied by a picture of the Brazilian Formula One racing driver Felipe Massa, together with a picture of a boy who comments that Massa admires Ayrton Senna and Michael Schumacher and that the Brazilian racer is an inspiration to him (Zacchi 2016: 166):

> The writing portion of the activity prompts the students to write about their role models. So this activity is a clear example of the use of aspirational content in textbooks. It even sets up a lineage of F1 racers, beginning with Ayrton Senna and Michael Schumacher and going down to the boy character in the textbook. And the writing activity motivates the student to actually write about a celebrity of his/ her choice.

Drawing on critical discourse analysis, several Iranian authors have centered their studies of global ELT textbooks on the ways in which they promote the new capitalist economy and consumer society (Taki 2008; Keshavarz and Malek 2009; Baleghizadeh and Motahed 2010). Especially interesting is a study by Saeed Taki (2008) in which he compares ELT global textbooks to those produced and published in Iran. Taki (2008: 138) shows that locally produced textbooks contain no dialogues between members of the opposite sex, which could be a result of the influence and standards of the Islamic republic. On the other hand, this author stresses that global ELT textbooks represent a type of discourse dominant in the Western free-market economy. For example, characters are mostly depicted performing occupational and commercial roles. In that way, global textbooks give to students "the requisite skills and dispositions to compete efficiently and effectively" in a world that is "intensely competitive economically." (Taki 2008: 139).

From a similar perspective, other studies have analyzed the ways in which language textbooks promote a culture of entrepreneurism among learners. As explained in Chapter 1, neoliberalism proposes a new vision of society, consisting of self-entrepreneurs competing with each other to succeed economically (Dardot and Laval 2013). In this new paradigm, people should accept the increasing flexibility and mobility required from the markets and work on themselves to become self-branded individuals. As a continuation of the discussion about studies of language materials from a political economic point of view, the analysis centered on the neoliberal entrepreneurial culture is featured as follows.

Entrepreneurship

Chun (2009) explores the ways in which neoliberal discourses penetrate in an intensive university course of English for Academic Purposes (EAP) in

Critical research on language textbooks 61

the United States, including textbooks and the university's web page. Chun shows how the content of these materials promotes a neoliberal culture of representing oneself as a kind of an enterprise in constant transformation to be integrated into the global economy. This is done through the development of a particular communication skill centered on acquiring skills in emotional intelligence and the kind of language required by large corporations:

> The EAP content foregrounds this 'communication skill' as a necessary component in the neoliberal culture of seeing oneself as a project or enterprise to be continually worked on and improved. The content also serves to explicitly teach ways of communicating adopted by institutions, such as corporations, in their desire for productive workers in the burgeoning service sector, which includes telemarketing, customer relations, and so on. Students are thus taught a specific 'communicative skill' education that will hopefully equip them to better compete in the job market.
>
> (Chun 2009: 116)

In another of his studies of ELT global textbooks, Gray (2010b) focuses on representations of the world of work. He argues that representations of this world, associated with mobility, flexibility, freedom of choice, individuality and the full realization of the self, coincide with the values and practices of neoliberalism. Textbooks also celebrate entrepreneurship with the presentation of success stories of self-made entrepreneurs and activities to encourage learners to join this group of entrepreneurs. For example, in one of the course books:

> Vijay and Bhikhu Patel, the pharmaceutical company owners and joint winners of the 2001 Ernst & Young Entrepreneur of the Year award, are interviewed at length about how they built their multimillion pound business after arriving in the UK with just five pounds between them. The reading activity which introduces a series of listening and speaking exercises about the brothers carries an evaluative subheading 'The inspiring tale of two Asian brothers who fled to Britain from East Africa and made a fortune' [. . .], and in the speaking exercise which follows, students are asked to say in what ways the Patels are good role models for young people.
>
> (Gray 2010b: 726)

Gray also points out that the negative consequences of the neoliberal practices in the world of work such as labor insecurity and stress are not shown. The loss of a job, for example, is seen as an opportunity. Moreover, Gray (2010b) argues that the textbooks analyzed promote the transformation of the individual into a brand (like any other commodity) in order to survive and be visible in the new neoliberal society. To describe the main features of self-branding he identifies in textbooks, Gray refers to a book of Tom

62 *Critical research on language textbooks*

Peters (2008), a management guru who provides different key aspects to take into consideration in order to become a self-branded individual in the work order, such as distinction, commitment, and passion. One paradigmatic example of branding in textbooks noted by Gray (2010b: 724) is the story of the fictional character Linda Spelman:

> [S]he gave up her job as a lawyer to pursue a more fulfilling life as a trapeze artist. When asked for advice she says, 'I'd say to anyone with a dream 'Go for it! You only live once, so why stay in a boring job'.

In a later work, Block and Gray (2018) also examine the promotion of neoliberal entrepreneurship and particularly the construction of self-branding in two recent French language textbooks. The study analyzes the textbooks according to Aaker's (1997) five dimensions of brand personality: sincerity, excitement, competence, sophistication and ruggedness. The results suggest that these categories have a key role in the textbooks' content. Although all five dimensions do not usually appear simultaneously, the authors find several examples of features that fall under one or more of these dimensions. In one of the textbooks, for example, there is a story of a French entrepreneur who explains why he decided to stay in France in spite of the current economic crisis. According to Block and Gray (2018), from the entrepreneur's words, one can easily imagine that the values he would expect from his employees will be in line with some of the branding dimensions developed by Aacker. Furthermore, this story aligns with the dominant neoliberal ideology since it presents an economic crisis as an opportunity for entrepreneurs and does not mention the severe economic repercussions resulting from the crash of 2008.

Taken together, what all the critical studies from an economic perspective reviewed here show is a positive valorization of neoliberal values and practices in textbooks. We have also seen that textbooks from different languages are very similar in terms of cultural and social content, especially those produced in Western countries. On the other hand, little is known of the influence of textbooks in the process of teaching and learning a language since "there have been relatively few studies into the impact of coursebooks on learning" (Thornbury 2015: 101). In this vein, both Gray (2010a, 2010b) and Copley (2017) agree that future research should pay more attention to how the content of textbooks is perceived by the learners. Although the reception of textbooks might not be a field greatly studied, it is worth noting the following critical studies that have been conducted regarding the perception of textbooks for second language learning by the students or teachers who used them.

Reception of textbooks by teachers and learners

Some of the well-known studies from a critical perspective identify a certain resistance or rejection from students or teachers of the values and representations foreign language materials present. Suresh Canagarajah (1993), for example, examines the ways in which Tamil students in Sri Lanka rebel against the Western values that appear in their ELT textbooks produced in the United States. Through data such as annotations and drawings in the margins of the textbooks, this author shows that Tamil students supposedly demonstrate their discomfort with some of the representations which are very far from the reality of a rural Sri Lankan community. The representation in textbooks is closely related to consumerism, social mobility and mercantilism, values that are alien to them. Canagarajah concludes that the textbooks for second languages should include discourses relevant to the lives of the students and their social and political situation.

Another more recent study from Cosete Taylor-Mendes (2009) focuses on student and teacher perceptions of the images which appear in ELT textbooks used in Brazil. Through a series of interviews, the author discovered a critical position from students and teachers who detected racial prejudice in certain images and a tendency to promote a 'white elitism'. They observed that the United States was presented as a land of the white elite, in which white people represented power and wealth, and non-white characters were represented in relation to poverty. For example, one teacher commented on an image of a textbook, concluding that "the white man is in command. The Puerto Rican is working" (74). Another interesting result of the study was that white participants were the most critical about racial stereotypes: "neither Ronaldo, who is black, nor Casia, who is mulatto, nor Marta, who is of Japanese appearance and ethnicity, discussed colour or race as an issue in the images" (74). Furthermore, several participants also commented that the idealized reality that the pictures in textbooks present was far from their everyday lives and, in that way, they "reinforce a made-in-Hollywood version of culture that does not exist" (77).

Gray has also included the perceptions of teachers in several of his works about global ELT textbooks. In two studies, he collected and analyzed comments from English teachers from Barcelona about the cultural content of these materials. In the first study, Gray (2000) discovered how some teachers modified or censored parts of the content that they considered inappropriate for students, because they were not relevant or challenging enough or because they showed sexist attitudes and a stereotypical representation of Britain. In another study, which also included English teachers from Catalonia as informants, Gray (2010a) concluded that teachers tend to consider textbooks problematic for three reasons. First, language materials show certain stereotypes about ethnicity or gender. Second, parts of the content of textbooks are irrelevant to their educational context. Finally, teachers also detected in textbooks "the uncritical celebration of 'dominant culture' in which individualism, wealth and celebrity are central" (172). However, in a later study that I referred to before in which Gray (2012a) associated the large presence of celebrities with the promotion of neoliberalism, this author detects that the teachers' attitudes are not very critical and are

64 *Critical research on language textbooks*

mainly indifferent to this question. One of the teachers interviewed by Gray (2012a: 106) says that he is satisfied to use "anything legal" if it serves the purpose of motivating the students. Although further studies in this direction are needed, this apparent shift in teacher response to materials might mean that neoliberal ideology, and especially the cult of rich and famous people, is increasingly accepted among the community of educators. It may also mean that some teachers view the content of the textbooks as a vehicle solely for the teaching of grammar and that the ideological sub-text is trivial, even immaterial.

Beyond the perception of the textbook by researchers and practitioners as "a deeply problematic artifact" (Gray 2010a: 191), some authors have promoted an approach that challenges the hegemony of textbooks in foreign language courses. This approach was first proposed by Thornbury (2000) following a long tradition of rejection of textbooks and other forms of 'imported' materials in progressive education (Thornbury 2013). It is known as Dogme Language Teaching. This methodology gained its name from an analogy with the Dogme filmmaking movement initiated in 1995 by the Danish director Lars Von Trier, which rejects the use of digital special effects or other new technologies in cinema. Although Dogme Language Teaching is not explicitly critical in the sense that it does not seek social change as Thornbury (2009) has explained, it can be seen as an alternative approach to language education. Dogme Language Teaching is a communicative method of language learning which proposes the abandonment of pre-packaged materials (including published textbooks) and focuses instead on more spontaneous conversational interchanges between students and teachers through the learning opportunities that emerge in the classroom (Thornbury 2013). Dogme Language Teaching might also be understood as a kind of rejection of the proliferation of new technologies in formal or non-formal educational settings, especially of the digital devices and digital content (Selwyn 2015) that have accompanied neoliberalism.

Conclusion: a step forward

In the last four decades, critical researchers have made important contributions to the critical understanding of language textbooks. Their analyses have helped to uncover gender, racial and cultural bias and other kinds of exclusion and inequalities that appear in textbooks. Nonetheless, the emphasis on identity or recognition politics (gender issues, racial differences, culturalist approaches or the postmodern concepts of identity and ethnicity) may hide the most important injustice in our capitalist societies, located in the socioeconomic dimension. Most of these critical studies, influenced by postmodern theory, have shown a lack of interest in economic relations and therefore were not able to relate language textbooks to the larger capitalist organization of society.

Although antiracist and feminist struggles can contribute to constructing a more egalitarian world, they alone are not enough if they do not go together with the recognition of capitalism as the fundament of social and economic oppression. In fact, the celebration of gender, racial and ethnic differences is accepted and promoted by the ruling elites in the neoliberal age, because capitalism can survive when accommodating gender and racial demands, providing that economic redistribution remains intact. Indeed, as argued by Massimo De Angelis, "[c]apital does not have any problem in acknowledging difference and diversity, as long as it is diversity that finds the *common centre of* articulation within capitalist markets" (2007: 173; emphasis in the original). Due to the fragmentation of their approaches and the lack of interest in the redistribution paradigm, the postmodern critical perspectives of language textbooks do not currently represent a challenge to the capitalist order.

What I am suggesting then is that critical perspectives on language textbooks should now look at 'the very big picture' (Littlejohn 2012). As proposed by Block et al. (2012a) regarding research in general in applied linguistics, I also think it is necessary to view studies of language textbooks through the lens of economics, politics and history. This new approach, as Block (2014: 108) puts it, "would make it possible for sociolinguists to inform those who wish not only to effect change in the sphere of recognition, but also those who seek the transformation of capitalist society". The recent works of authors like Gray and Block which situate neoliberalism at the center of their interest in language textbook studies may represent a new way to contest current social relations within a global free-market paradigm and the neoliberal common sense that has flourished in all spheres of our contemporary lives, including the field of second language education. This book attempts to contribute to this new approach by analyzing language textbooks through their relations with dominant neoliberalism.

Notes

1 Queer theory refers to a set of ideas that problematizes essentialist understandings of gender and sexuality. It holds that gender and sexual identities are culturally and socially constructed rather than given by nature. One of the main interests of queer theorists is to examine "how discursive acts and cultural practices manage to make heterosexuality, and only heterosexuality, seem normal or natural" (Nelson 1999: 376).
2 I am using the acronym LGBT because it is used in the literature I have assessed. However, I am aware that by now some authors are including additional 'Q's for 'queer' or 'questioning' and producing the variants LGTBQ or LGTBQQ. Other authors refer to LGBTQQIA+ to include intersex, asexuality (or ally, i.e., straight people who support queer people) and the '+' symbol stands for other sexualities, sexes and genders that don't fall under another letter.
3 In *The Location of Culture*, Homi Bhabha (1994) also charts the irruption of a 'third culture' or a 'third space' in colonial contexts resulting from the collision between the imposed colonial culture and the indigenous or native culture. Bhabha's third culture refers to a hybrid culture influenced by the colonial power and preexisting traditions, and challenges any essentialist and fixed understanding of culture.

4 Analyzing textbooks from a political economy perspective

Introduction

In this chapter, I present a model for language textbook analysis which aims to contribute to an emergent approach investigating the links between language teaching materials and the global political economy (Chun 2009; Gray 2010b, 2012a; Gray and Block 2014; Copley 2017; Block and Gray 2018). However, I begin with the presentation of criteria for the selection of the corpus for analysis, followed by a brief description of that corpus. The books selected are addressed mostly to immigrants living in Catalonia, although some of them are also used in centers teaching Catalan abroad. This done, I explain the methodology developed to examine the relations between the texts from the corpus and neoliberal policies and practices dominant in the world today. This approach is especially important given the fact that one of the communicative method's general aims is to teach how language really happens in everyday life and that many authors of textbooks (at least of Catalan textbooks) state that they seek to include genuine situations in language materials. The methodology developed here will be applied later in this book to analyze the general socioeconomic portrayal of textbooks concerning social class and the topics of work and housing in the corpus. Although the impact of neoliberalism is visible in all spheres of our lives, from the organization of education and health care, to the way we travel, consume or engage in entertainment activities, I chose to focus on these two topics for several reasons. First, because texts and activities related to work and housing are widely found in language textbooks. Second, because in these two spheres of life the recent transformations of capitalism are very evident from a political economic perspective. The analysis of the world of work also allows me to compare the results of Catalan textbooks with similar results concerning global English textbooks (Gray 2010b). Finally, the study of housing-related content upon which I focus is especially relevant to the Catalan case, if we keep in mind the Spanish boom and the sizeable crisis in this sector in recent years, the consequences of which seriously affected the lives of immigrants (Human Rights Watch 2014), among the most important groups of Catalan language learners.

A *political economy perspective* 67

This study will take into account that the liberalization of the labor market has led to the creation of the self-interested and independent entrepreneur as the ideal worker, and the economization of all social spheres under the neoliberal regime has brought the marketization of housing, as we shall see below. In order to carry out my analysis, I have developed a mixed methodology which consists of a quantitative analysis followed by a qualitative one, similar to the one proposed by Gray (2010b) in his study of the representations of the world of work in global English textbooks. First, I analyzed the content quantitatively to determine the frequency of different topics in the corpus. Afterwards, I analyzed the corpus using a qualitative analysis from a political economic perspective.

Corpus selection

I decided to center my study on the so-called textbook (also known as 'student book' or 'course book') because it is the most frequently used didactic material in courses for Catalan to foreigners. Therefore, I excluded other complementary material from the corpus such as conversation guides, workbooks, vocabulary workbooks, bilingual dictionaries, audio-visual materials, etc. I also excluded from the corpus materials which usually go together with the student's book like the teacher's books or exercise books because they do not play as central a role in the process of second language teaching. However, during the qualitative part of the analysis, I consulted the teacher's books because on occasions they gave important information about the author's intentions.

In addition, I have included in my analysis the website *Parla.cat* because it is used as an online 'textbook' in various settings. *Parla.cat* is used in several Catalan language courses (for example in different centers belonging to the Consortium for Linguistic Normalization in Catalonia) and it is the most popular tool for the autonomous learning of Catalan. I have also included it because there are many students learning Catalan through this website and it is an example of a new kind of language learning material that will probably gain more momentum in future years. The corpus used in this analysis was selected according to the following criteria:

1   Materials for beginner, elementary and intermediate levels (A1, A2 and B1 from the CEFR). There are various reasons why I have chosen these materials. First, these are the levels in which students are introduced to the Catalan language and on many occasions it is the first time that the students become acquainted with Catalan culture. Second, these levels have the largest majority of students in Catalan language courses (especially A1 and A2). Third, these are the language materials that I know the best due to my 10 years of experience as a lecturer of Catalan language at the University of Belgrade, especially with beginner through intermediate levels. Finally, I chose materials from beginner, elementary

68 *A political economy perspective*

and intermediate levels because the majority of teachers with the least experience, those who in general most frequently use these commercial textbooks, teach these levels. I think that this last reason is worth mentioning because textbooks for these levels would presumably be the most used in Catalan language classrooms, although my study does not focus on the perception of textbooks by teachers and learners.

2   Materials for adults. This study is centered on textbooks for general Catalan with a diversity of texts about different topics. I have excluded from the corpus materials for special purposes (like commerce or tourism) and also for learners coming from a specific culture (for example, Catalan for Chinese speakers). Materials for children or adolescents have also been excluded from the corpus materials. Although it would be interesting to also study language materials for children, I did not include them in the corpus because the two main topics that I will analyze in this study (work and housing) are closer and more relevant to the adult population than to minors.

3   Materials published in Catalonia. The corpus is limited to materials published in the region of Catalonia because most of the Catalan language publishers are from this Catalan-speaking area, especially from Barcelona, although there are also some other materials published for example in Valencia, the Balearic Islands or abroad.

4   Materials published between 2005 and 2015 and currently in use.[1] The corpus is made up of the current textbooks that are most commonly used in classrooms as I have shown in my doctoral dissertation (Bori 2015).

Description of the corpus

The corpus consists of six series of textbooks (a total of 19 volumes) which correspond to A1 and A2 levels (12 textbooks) and B1 level (seven textbooks), and the six first courses (corresponding from A1 to B1 levels) of the *Parla.cat* online platform. All the textbooks' series are published by private publishing houses in Barcelona, except *Curs de català bàsic*, which was published by a public institution, the *Centre de Normalització Lingüística de Barcelona* (the Barcelona Center for Linguistic Normalization; hereafter CNLB), one of the main centers for teaching Catalan to foreigners.

The corpus includes the following books: *Veus 1, 2, 3* (Mas and Vilagrassa 2005, 2007, 2008); *Curs de català bàsic B1, B2, B3* (CNLB 2008a, 2008b, 2011); *Nou Nivell Bàsic 1, 2, 3* (Guerrero et al. 2010a, 2010b, 2010c) and *Nou Nivell Elemental 1, 2, 3* (Anguera et al. 2010a, 2010b, 2010c); *Passos 1* (Roig et al. 2011) and *Passos 2* (Roig and Daranas 2011); *Català Inicial* (Esteban 2012a), *Català Bàsic* (Esteban 2012b) and *Català Elemental* (Campoy et al. 2011); *Fil per randa Bàsic* (Vilà and Homs 2013a), and *Fil per randa Elemental* (Vilà and Homs 2013b). Moreover, the corpus also contains the six first courses (*Bàsic 1, 2, 3*, and *Elemental 1, 2, 3*) of the website *Parla.cat* (DGPL 2008). Table 4.1 presents the number of volumes, units and pages of each series of the corpus.[2]

A political economy perspective 69

Table 4.1 Textbook data

Title	Publishing house	Year of publication	CEFR level	Number of volumes	Number of units	Number of pages
Veus	PAMSA	2005/2008	From A1 to B1	3	18	376
Nou Nivell Bàsic/ Elemental	Castellnou	2010	From A1 to B1	6	42	684
Passos	Ocaedro	2011	From A1 to B1	2	48	520
Català Inicial, Bàsic, Elemental	Teide	2011–2012	From A1 to B1	3	55	528
Fil per randa	Barcanova	2013	From A1 to B1	2	36	512
Curs de català bàsic	CNLB	2008/2011	From A1 to A2	3	30	602
Parla.cat[3]	DGPL	2008	From A1 to B1	6	42	1,777
Total				25	271	4,999

One of the common aspects of all materials is that they follow the levels and the contents of the CEFR of the Council of Europe and Catalan language programs from the Catalan government. The mention of the CEFR level they correspond to usually appears on the cover of the books. The other thing these materials share in common is that they propose a task-based communicative approach[4] through situations that learners supposedly encounter in their everyday lives. Texts and activities tend to be bland and to have a very anodyne appearance. Their content is limited to the everyday situations and ordinary life of predominantly Western, middle-class individuals. The materials are filled with holidays and journeys, housing topics such as mortgage payments, work as part of a happy, problem-free daily routine, the lives of celebrities mixed together with expert advice on how to cope with anxiety and stress with a touch of good food, followed by a mandatory diet and the inevitable fitness exercises. It is not surprising then to say that Catalan language textbooks look somewhat like lifestyle magazines designed for women, minus all the clothing and makeup products. As is the case with global English (Gray 2010a) or French textbooks (Block and Gray 2018), Catalan materials also adopt a socially liberal approach dominated by gender equality, with characters from different origins and races, and several examples of same-sex couples.

Research paradigm

The research paradigm for this study is based on the reasoning of the Frankfurt School of critical theory, critical pedagogy and the most recent

70 *A political economy perspective*

currents in applied linguistics which call for a turn to the political economy in language-related issues, as was explained in Chapter 1. What these approaches have in common is that they place cultural, educational and language phenomena within their social, political and economic contexts. Another characteristic of this research is the political and moral commitment of the investigator in the research area. The aim of this research is to contribute to the transformation of the area of textbook studies, which, in its indifference to social and political issues, perpetuates a non-transformative, even unjust, status quo. This attitude of the critical investigators is in contrast to the terms 'instrumental', 'descriptive' or 'practical' which are usual in second language research from the positivist perspective.

If it is true that critical studies have preferred qualitative analysis to quantitative (Talmy 2010), there are more and more mixed methodologies developed every day, especially in critical studies on language textbooks and above all those that have inspired the approach of this book (Shardakova and Pavlenko 2004; Taki 2008; Gray 2010a, 2010b; Gray and Block 2014). Following the proposal from the book *Neoliberalism and applied linguistics* (Block et al. 2012a) to integrate political economy into applied linguistic studies, this book is interested in identifying not only which socio-economic reality is presented in the materials, but also the relation between the content and the current phase of capitalism: neoliberalism. To achieve this, I develop a method of work similar to that used by Gray (2010b) in his study of ELT textbooks and work on new capitalism. It consists of two phases. First, I will identify with what frequency the different topics in the corpus appear in order to quantitatively measure the appearances of the topics related to work and housing. The second phase is a more qualitative one in order to examine the content related to work and housing from an economic and political perspective.

Quantitative analysis

In order to find the most important topics that appear in textbooks and measure the importance of the content related to work and housing, I have conducted a quantitative analysis of the textbook passages which include written, listening and video activities and tasks. In this way, and in a clear and detailed manner, I am able to identify which spheres of life the materials present and emphasize to students through their content.

Quantitative analysis is centered on large texts. Similarly to Littlejohn (1992: 43), I consider a large text as one with more than 50 words. Texts with fewer words were disregarded because the information was not sufficient for analysis. Often these shorter texts are instructions telling students how to proceed, which are devoid of significant content. Among the texts longer than 50 words incorporated into activities, I included those associated with fill-in-the-blanks exercises, scrambled sentences, unfinished texts with enough information to be considered as texts, and lists of sentences

A political economy perspective 71

related to one topic (but not simple vocabulary lists) that give enough information about the socioeconomic reality that appears in the texts. The types of texts selected for the quantitative analysis are narratives in prose, dialogues, surveys, tests, news, poems or songs, announcements, CVs, letters of complaint, timetables and menus.

Once I had established the criteria for the text selection, I set about to describe briefly, but in detail, the predominant theme of each text in one or two sentences. For example: 'Different members of a family explain to the interviewer their daily habits, timetables and so on'. Next, I followed an inductive method to create a list of categories by topic, that is to say, after reading the texts I placed them into thematic groups according to their content descriptions. In that way, I obtained the first list of thematic categories that were refined and revised upon a second reading. It should be noted that the topic of the texts and the general topic of the unit usually coincided (work, shopping, housing, travel, etc.) and that the topic is often mentioned in the title of the unit. When creating the thematic categories, I reviewed the lists presented in the official guidelines that textbooks follow. The CEFR provides a list of 14 topics (Council of Europe 2001), which is the same as that proposed earlier by the *Threshold Level 1990* (van Ek and Trim 1991) from the Council of Europe. I also referred to a list of 13 topics for the beginner's level authored by the Catalan government (Generalitat de Catalunya 2001) and a list of eight topics for the elementary and intermediate levels authored by the same institution (Generalitat de Catalunya 2003a, 2003b). I made some small changes to these lists so that the final list would be operational for quantitative analysis. On occasions, I renamed some of the topics proposed in order to widen or reduce aspects that the category proposed. For instance, in the *Threshold Level 1990* there is a theme called 'house and home, environment' while I listed two different categories for these topics – 'housing' and 'environment'. And the topic 'environment' in my list also covers issues related to the *Threshold Level 1990*'s theme 'weather', that is not listed among my categories. In total, I established 14 categories to classify content according to these topics:

1 *Cultural information*: Information about Catalan and other languages (number of speakers, linguistic family, history), about demography, geography, rural and urban landscapes, rituals and traditions; the so-called 'culture with a big C' (literature, history, art, quotes from intellectuals) and also biographies of writers, scientists or artists; popular music (from traditional and children songs to pop music), texts about fairs, festivals, jokes, riddles and popular sayings. This category also includes texts about the political structure and territorial organization, information about emblematic places and institutions such as Antoni Gaudi's La Pedrera or the Catalan Parliament.

2 *Daily life and free time*: The everyday life of a person, habits, daily activities, timetables, frequency with which the things are done, personal

72 *A political economy perspective*

schedules; texts talking about the organization of free time activities like birthdays, weddings or stag parties; invitations and dialogues where interlocutors meet or decide to meet to do something together (or messages on the answering machines where someone asks a friend to respond to their call), comments on how to spend free time.

3 *Education*: Texts about studies, educational centers (language schools, for example), exams, enrollment for exams, motivation to study languages, ways of learning Catalan, information about teachers and professors.

4 *Entertainment and news*: Texts about TV and cinema, communication media (news, debates about news), books and magazines about entertainment, quizzes, social networks, self-help, sports, games, comics, horoscope, astrology, superstitions, the life of celebrities, surveys about entertainment. This category also contains information, opinions and reviews of spectacles (cinema, theater, the circus, expositions and concerts). Here I also included a series of texts about crime (murder, robbery and interrogations by the police) or urban legends because they all clearly serve the purpose of entertaining students and, in many cases, they are presented in the same form as the news published in the newspapers.

5 *Environment*: Climate, conservation and protection of the environment and related aspects (water, recycling, renewable energy, disasters caused by environmental negligence and so on).

6 *Food and drink*: Preferences and eating habits, recipes, menus, restaurants, ways of making and conserving food, cooks, utensils and so on.

7 *Health and well-being*: Illnesses, medical services, visits to hospitals, diets, healthy foods, recommendations for healthy living, alternative therapies.

8 *Housing*: Information about where people live, description of houses, home maintenance, house renovation and decoration, manuals about household appliances, warranties, housework, texts about buying and selling houses, renting and moving.

9 *Neighborhood*: Texts about neighbors, the neighborhood, the city, incidents on the street, questions about transit (car accidents, tickets for parking, how to change a tire, how to get a driving license), public transport, how to get to work or school. This category also includes texts about giving directions, municipal orders and norms, texts associated with the citizens' assistance office, post office and libraries.

10 *Personal information*: Personal data about someone (nationality, phone number, address, languages spoken), family, family trees, physical appearance, clothes, character, moods. I also included here problems related to people's love life, relations with friends, anecdotes or interesting events about somebody (weddings, childbirth, meeting a loved one), things somebody explained in the form of diary or a memory of how life was during someone's childhood.

A political economy perspective   73

11 *Shopping and consuming*: How a product or service is bought, when, in what way and why; complaints about buying a product or a service; announcements to sell a product or service, explanations of swindles related to buying a product or a service, texts about consuming (announcements posted in supermarkets, product labels, advertisements from companies and so on).

12 *Travel*: About travel, excursions and tourism, transport, places to stay, anecdotes related to travel (often in the form of emails and postcards that explain a journey with a friend or a family member), travel plans and so on. This category also includes texts that explain a place such as a tourist brochure; texts about what to bring, what to buy if you go on a journey, medical care, vaccines, clothes, visas and so on.

13 *Work*: Where people work, professions, working conditions, professional training, job perspectives. This category also includes job interviews, job announcements, curriculum vitae, and dialogues about work.

14 Other: Texts about content different than in the categories above. For example, the description of a nightmare (CNLB 2008b: 48), a dialogue about a woman who cannot find her keys (Roig et al. 2011: 71) or legal information about matrimony (Anguera et al. 2010b: 29).

When a text covered more than one topic from the list, I chose the topic which was most salient. In some cases, however, it was impossible to determine the predominant topic in the text. For these cases I created another category, number 15, which was called 'more than one topic'. For example, in a text taken from an internet forum where the people talk about "Who do you look like?" (Vilà and Homs 2013b: 96), there are certain comments about physical appearance and the character of the authors or some of their family, which could lead us to classify the text under the category 'personal information'. At the same time, there are comments about celebrities (like Marilyn Monroe or the Catalan model Judit Mascó) that could belong to the category 'entertainment and news'. As the results presented in Chapter 6 show, this 15th category always represents less than 10 percent of all the texts selected for the quantitative analysis.

Once all the texts were counted and placed in thematic categories, I could determine how much space different textbooks series dedicated to the content related to work and housing.

Qualitative analysis

For the qualitative or hermeneutic analysis of the content, I have adopted a multimodal critical approach (Kress 2010) which takes into consideration text and visual content. In other words, I have examined the textbooks' presentation, the titles of each unit and every subheading or subsection, the instructions for each task or exercise, all the written texts, the listening and audio-visuals incorporated into an exercise or a task and the artwork

74 *A political economy perspective*

(photographs, drawings, posters, videos and animations). On the other hand, I did not take into account the design of the materials analyzed (the composition of the pages, the arrangement of texts and images, colors, typography) because I did not find it relevant in obtaining information for the study. I did not analyze different symbols, icons or semiotic elements that are sometimes used to organize a unit because they carry little ideological content.

From a critical perspective, hermeneutics tends to build bridges between text and the external reality, the information and its wider context, and between the present and the historical circumstances. As stated by Luke (2002: 100), Critical Discourse Analysis is about putting into relation "the micropolitics of everyday texts and the macropolitical landscape of ideological and power relations, capital exchange, and material historical conditions". Critical pedagogues Joe Kincheloe and McLaren (2002: 98) use these words to sum up the critical hermeneutic methodology that I adopt in the qualitative analysis:

> Grounded by the hermeneutical bridge building, critical researchers in a hermeneutical circle (a process of analysis in which interpreters seek the historical and social dynamics that shape textual interpretation) engage in the back-and-forth of studying parts in relations to the whole and the whole in relation to parts. [. . .] A critical hermeneutics brings the concrete, the parts, the particular into focus, but in a manner that grounds them contextually in a larger understanding of the social forces, the whole, the abstract (the general).

Following the critical theoretical approach of this book, the interpretation of the content of the corpus tends to identify the ways in which different determined hegemonic discourses construct particular versions of reality (Apple and Christian-Smith 1991; Fairclough 1995) in the textbooks analyzed.

In order to relate the corpus with the economic and material basis of this phase of contemporary capitalism, so-called neoliberalism, I followed three steps. First, I established an overall portrayal of the socioeconomic reality that is presented in the textbooks through key dimensions of social class. Also, all the textual genres (job ads, rental contracts, surveys, etc.) and activities about work and housing proposed by textbooks. Second, neoliberal practices and values are identified in the content related to these two topics. These neoliberal characteristics, which will be described later in this chapter, were explained by other critical authors. To identify these aspects, I did an exhaustive reading, page by page, of all the content related to the topics which were the object of study. And finally, comments (with citations from the texts) were made about the examples of neoliberal practices and values, and how these were related to the wider political, economic and social aspects. To examine concrete examples, I adopted a critical perspective, taking into consideration the voices of the authors, the comments the

A political economy perspective 75

characters make, the experiences and results they talk about, the proposals for a task or activity given by the textbook or the visual material that accompanies the texts or a listening activity.

Social class

To describe the socioeconomic reality that appears in textbooks, I used the key dimensions of social class described by Block in Table 4.2, following his various works (Block 2012a, 2014). Block defines this concept, drawing on the ideas of Marx and Friedrich Engels, but also from other authors like Max Weber or Bourdieu, among others.

Even though we can look at the dimensions in Table 4.2 separately, they are clearly connected, as Block himself explains: "wealth might be associated with particular types of employment which require years of formal education leading to specific qualifications and with more manual professions requiring few or no educational qualifications" (Gray and Block 2014: 55). However, in the particular case of this study, I opted for a special emphasis on the most relevant dimensions in the corpus I analyzed such as occupation, place of residence, mobility and consumption patterns.

Table 4.2 Key dimensions of social class (Block 2015a: 3)

Dimension	Gloss
Property	Material possessions, such as land, housing, electronic devices, clothing, books, art, etc.
Wealth	Disposable income and patrimony (e.g., what owned property is worth in financial terms).
Occupation	The kind of work done: information-based or manual, specialized or unskilled, etc.
Place of residence	The type of neighborhood one lives in (poor, working-class, middle-class, gated community, an area in the process of gentrification) or the type of dwelling (individual house, flat, caravan).
Education	The level of schooling attained and the acquired cultural capital one has at any point in time.
Social networking	Middle-class people tend to socialize with middle-class people, working-class people with working-class people, etc.
Consumption patterns	Shopping at a supermarket that is "cost-cutting" or one that sells "healthy" organic products. Buying particular goods and brands.
Symbolic behavior	Including body movement, clothes worn, how one speaks, how one eats, pastimes engaged in, etc.
Spatial relations	The conditions in which one lives: dwelling size, bedroom size, proximity to others across day-to-day activities, etc.
Mobility	The means, disposition, time, and knowledge necessary for travel.
Life chances	Quality of life in terms of personal comfort, access to preventive medicine, life expectancy, etc.

76 *A political economy perspective*

Finally, to complete the general portrait the materials present about the topics of work and housing, I identify the type of text (discursive genre) and activities or tasks which are proposed because this data also permits me to consider the type of situations in which students are likely to be using the target language, and the types of roles they are expected to assume.

Neoliberal features in the areas of work and housing

In order to carry out the critical analysis of the two themes this study focuses on, it is necessary to briefly describe the main neoliberal practices and values that have emerged in recent decades in capitalist societies in the worlds of work and housing. The information presented below is extracted from other studies that have engaged critically in these two spheres of life, particularly from those interested in neoliberalism. The features described in this section will be used in Chapters 7 and 8 to discuss the relationship between neoliberalism and the content of language textbooks.

Work in the era of neoliberalism

Apart from it being one of the most common topics in textbooks for learning languages, the world of work is also the context in which the transformations of the capitalist economy are the most visible (Gray 2010b). In a post-industrial, globally deregulated and competitive economy, companies have opted for the subcontracting and externalization of production and services. At the same time, the global market has gradually changed into an oligopoly with large corporations stretching their involvement far beyond national frontiers (Boltanski and Chiapello 2007). Little by little, the majority of governments has abandoned the objective of full employment and have transferred the responsibility to get a job onto individuals (Garsten and Jacobsson 2004). This new organization of work has resulted in major labor precariousness with the rise of unemployment, subcontracting and part-time contracts (Boltanski and Chiapello 2007). The ideal workers in neoliberal times are the entrepreneurial selves, individuals who conceive themselves as personal enterprises engaged in a constant process of competition. In the same way that in the neoliberal era states are administrated through new public management, that is, with the logic of competition and methods of government in private enterprises, individuals should also act as managers of themselves, becoming "a sort of permanent and multiple enterprise" (Foucault 2008: 241). In the particular case of the world of work, among practices and values identified by critical authors as characteristics of neoliberalism are the following:

1 *Flexibility* (Sennet 1998; Lambert 2008): This refers to the ability of an individual to adapt to the necessities of the market. It can signify working long hours, as well as working part-time, or having a job unrelated to the educational field a person studied.

A political economy perspective   77

2 *Mobility*: This is another kind of labor flexibility and refers to the disposition of a worker to move according to the demands of the market.

3 *Zero drag* (Bauman 2007: 9): Closely related to flexibility and mobility, this refers to the capacity of an individual to adapt to the transformations of the labor market without any obstacles. It can also explain the versatility of individuals in fast changing circumstances to take risks in changing jobs or engaging in new projects.

4 *Lifelong learning* (Mitchell 2006; Olssen 2008): Also known as 'self-programmable labor' (Castells 2000), this refers to the disposition of an individual to constantly re-train him/herself, to acquire transversal skills especially those that would allow greater adaptability and mobility between businesses and countries. It promotes the flexibility of individuals. At the same time, it permits states and businesses to leave the responsibility for acquiring the necessary training and skills to the worker. In the last decade lifelong learning has been transformed into one of the pillars of educational policies in Europe and across the globe and is seen as 'a magical solution' for unemployment and the crises of schooling (Nóvoa 2002). Self-responsible individuals are to be prepared for a life of constant "skilling and re-skilling, training and retraining" (Rose 1999: 161) in order to find a proper position in the job market and at the same time help the rise of their countries' overall competitiveness (Nóvoa 2002).

5 *Self-branding* (Hearn 2008; Gray 2010b; Block and Gray 2018): To be successful in a highly competitive neoliberal environment, it is necessary to configure oneself as a brand in order to distinguish oneself from the other workers. Some of the most prominent features of personal branding are the importance to make visible the differences and particularities of oneself in comparison to other colleagues or competitors, the passion and commitment for work, the cultivation of self-image, the willingness to innovate and to change personal affiliations. According to one of the most popular gurus of management, Tom Peters, it is even necessary "to act selfishly – to grow yourself, to promote yourself, to get the market to reward yourself" (1997: section 5, para. 4).

6 *Entrepreneurship:* This refers to taking the initiative and not vacillating in the face of complicated decisions in the world of work and especially the willingness to take the risk of starting one's own business.

7 *Self-responsibility:* The responsibility to find a job (and keep it) in neoliberal times falls exclusively on individuals (Garsten and Jacobsson 2004), who must be able to construct a personality appropriate for a flexible, ever-changing and insecure labor market. As stated by Laura Servage (2009: 30), in the neoliberal era "the virtuous are individualists who care for themselves and their own and ask for little or nothing from the society in which they live" not only concerning employment but in all spheres of life.

8 *Risk management*: Due to the declining role of government and business in social welfare under the neoliberal regime, workers are increasingly

78 *A political economy perspective*

held responsible for risk management related to their health and safety (G.C. Gray 2009). By virtue of the self-responsibilization promoted by market forces, subjects must be able to access adequate information, make rational choices and, consequently, be responsible for the risks they run, especially concerning employment but also other vital spheres of life like education or retirement (Peters 2001).

9 *Expert knowledge*: In the configuration of an individual into a person capable of working, job experts such as consultants and career coaches play an important role. For example, they give detailed instructions on how to write a curriculum vitae or how to prepare and behave during job interviews, always according to neoliberal logic (Fogde 2007).

10 *Techniques to find a job*: In order to become competent job seekers, individuals must put into practice and demonstrate planning, self-reflexivity, entrepreneurial spirit, flexibility, self-responsibility and the ability to sell oneself during practices such as a job interview or writing a CV (Fogde 2007).

Housing in the era of neoliberalism

The world of housing and in particular the real estate sector plays a large role in Catalan language textbooks. These are some of the characteristics of the neoliberal housing concept:

1 *The commodification of housing*: Since the late 1970s there has been a significant transformation in the politics of housing which has been beneficial to the powerful capitalists with property and against the interests of the most vulnerable classes in society (Glynn 2009). As explained by Raquel Rolnik (2013), the new economic paradigm under the neoliberal regime promotes no direct intervention from the government in the housing sector through "the dismantling of housing welfare systems" (1060) and "the implementation of policies designed to create stronger and larger market-based housing finance models" (1058). As a result, having a place to live is seen through the lens of real estate value or "as an investment asset" integrated into the global financial market system (Rolnik 2013: 1059) rather than as a home, a social good, a basic human necessity or a fundamental right of every human being.

2 *The Celebration of Home Ownership*: This is one of the main values promoted by the neoliberal policy in the housing sector (Glynn 2009; Rolnik 2013). In most countries, as Richard Ronald (2008: 2) explains in his book *The Ideology of Home Ownership*, "the status of the home-owner has become a social ideal", the owners are considered "as a better type of citizen" while "renters and renting have become heavily stigmatized". Similarly, in the case of the United States, Peter Marcuse (2008) argues that private home ownership has become the embodiment of the American dream.

A political economy perspective 79

3   *Taking out a mortgage*: Becoming a homeowner in the capitalist economy for members of the middle and working classes especially, has been related to the practice of taking out a mortgage, a loan or credit from a bank. During the housing price bubble in the late 1990s and at the beginning of this century, in many Western countries the private sector was giving credits with low introductory rates and minimal initial costs to low and middle income citizens to finance their houses. The problems began when between 2006 and 2007 the prices of houses dropped rapidly and in the United States the so-called subprime mortgage crisis began (Marcuse 2008), which provoked a global economic crisis. One of the results of this was that millions of families lost their homes almost overnight, unable to meet their mortgage payments.

4   *The banking sector as the main actor*: In the market-based paradigm the financial sector plays a key role in housing since it gives credits not only for buying a house, but also to construct whole buildings. After the 2008 financial meltdown, many people were unable to pay their debt as their low-introductory-rate mortgages reverted to higher rates. Therefore, in many countries such as Spain the banks had to manage thousands of unsold homes and got more and more involved in the business of selling and renting houses (Cuesta and Velloso 2015).

5   *The rise of consumerism*: One of the main characteristics of neoliberalism is the vision of the world as a vast supermarket (Apple 1993), in the sense that individuals have to become compulsive buyers and that consumer spending should be the main driving force of the economy. The society of consumption is characterized by a great dependency on advertising which creates new necessities and desires to consume and by getting into debt in order to buy new products and services. What's more, as explained by Zygmunt Bauman (2007: 47), the key of the functioning of the contemporary consumer society is "to denigrate and devalue consumer products shortly after they have been hyped into the universe of the consumers' desires". In this way, a perpetual unhappiness is created among consumers who constantly seek new desires and needs. The rise of consumerism in the neoliberal era is a part of the so-called culture-ideology of consumerism, which assumes that happiness can be best achieved through consumption and possessions (Sklair 1998). In the sector of real estate, this ideological project is not only related to buying a house but also home remodeling, decorating and so on.

Example of critical content analysis

Any single text can generate different interpretations, depending on the interests, world views, and the social and cultural background of the investigators. My intention in this analysis is to situate the political economy at the center of the research and to challenge neoliberalism as the common sense of our times. One prerequisite for fitting into the new work order in

80 *A political economy perspective*

neoliberal times that I found in textbooks is self-branding. One of the paradigmatic examples of this practice can be found in the text below, under the title 'How to find the job of your life'. It is a text that has been extracted and adapted from a website of the Catalan career coach Carme Pla. It appears as the final reading of a work-related unit in the third book of *Nou Nivell Bàsic* which is addressed to students that want to achieve an A2 level of Catalan.

> *T'has marcat com a objectiu aconseguir una nova feina? [. . .] Molta gent pren la decisió basant-se en el sou, els càrrecs i les responsabilitats. És un error. En canvi, t'hauries de preguntar si t'inspirarà, et donarà energia i et permetrà fer un bon treball. [. . .] Aquí tens els passos que hauries de seguir per assegurar-te que la teva propera feina sigui perfecta:*
>
> 1 *Pren la decisió de canviar de feina sense vacil·lar.*
> 2 *Dóna't temps per trobar-ne una de nova.*
> 3 *Centra't en allò que t'agrada, no en allò que detestes.*
> 4 *Ignora el sou.*
> 5 *Ignora els detalls irrellevants.*
> 6 *Demana el que vols.*
> 7 *Fes que el treball sigui fenomenal.*
> 8 *Recorda que ets lliure de plegar quan vulguis.*
>
> *Si tens en compte tot això a l'hora de buscar i escollir una feina nova, segur que t'ho passaràs millor i tindràs més èxit.*
>
> [Is your goal finding a new job? [. . .] Many people form their decision based on salary, duties and responsibilities. This is a mistake. On the contrary, you have to ask yourself what is inspiring for you, what will give you energy and allow you to do a better job. [. . .] Here are the steps you should follow to ensure that your next job will be perfect:
>
> 1 Make a decision to change your job without hesitation.
> 2 Dedicate time to finding a new one.
> 3 Concentrate on what you like, not on what you hate.
> 4 Ignore your salary.
> 5 Ignore other irrelevant details.
> 6 Ask whatever you want.
> 7 Make your work phenomenal.
> 8 Remember that you're free to quit your job whenever you like.
>
> If you take into account these things when you are looking for a job, you will enjoy it more, and you will be more successful.][5]
>
> (Guerrero et al. 2010c: 79)

In the example above, I identified several neoliberal values and practices to transform oneself into a brand as explained by the marketing guru Tom

A *political economy perspective* 81

Peters (2008: x; cited in Gray 2010b: 718–19) in his recommendations on how to be successful in the working world. On the one hand, we see the evaluation of work especially through the possibility of personal fulfillment: "you have to ask yourself what is inspiring for you, what will give you energy and allow you to do a better job". Furthermore, the fourth piece of advice states that you do not have to think about the money you earn. On the other hand, I have already identified the promotion of flexibility, individualism and the freedom of choice in the world of work with the phrases found in the first and eighth pieces of advice. The passion for work also appears ("Make your work phenomenal") and is related to professional success ("you will be more successful"). The text is also an example of the increasing importance that the so-called experts in subjectivity (Rose 1990; Fogde 2007), such as job consultants and career coaches, have in today's working environments. Above all, the previous example argues that the worker should not be a mere conformist, a passive bystander in his job or life, but rather take pleasure in his performance, becoming "the subject of total self-involvement" (Dardot and Laval 2013: 288).

However, there are no economic, personal or social limitations in finding a job. The text presents a highly idealized reality and is addressed only to people without economic problems, belonging to a middle or upper social class. There is no mention of the problematic aspects of the neoliberal work setting such as unemployment and labor exploitation. Therefore, the values and practices of neoliberalism appear through a positive lens, full of personal and economic promise, reinforced with a photograph in color of 10 banknotes of 100 euros, although the text above stated that salary shouldn't be a driver. Moreover, the textbook presents this text uncritically, without any kind of question or activity related to it. The learners are only supposed to read it. Hence, it will probably depend on the teacher if any discussion about this neoliberal content should be opened among students in the classroom.

I am aware that the qualitative approach of this study may be taken to task for many reasons. Some of the critique may be quite similar to that which Critical Discourse Analysis (CDA) has received in the last 25 years, such as being too politically oriented and deterministic, or citing only the most extreme examples that seem to fit particularly well with the underlying thesis of the researcher (see Breeze 2011 for a review of criticisms of CDA). Needless to say, every methodology has its limitations. However, in the face of potential suspicions of political bias in my qualitative approach, I would like to emphasize at this point various aspects that should be taken into account. First, we have to bear in mind that each researcher has her/his own preconceived notions and the methodology always reflects the kind of issues with which one wants to deal. In this respect, I have explicitly stated my critical commitment at the beginning of this volume so the reader is acquainted with the main concerns of this study and can freely take a critical stance towards the approach I adopt. Second, I don't want to demonstrate in this

82 *A political economy perspective*

study that each aspect of the content of language textbooks is aligned with neoliberal ideology, but I will attempt to show the general ideological trends in the content of language textbooks. And, I will do so, providing multiple examples from the textbooks (not only the most 'sensational' ones), after several years of exhaustive and careful study of the language materials belonging to the corpus of study. Finally, my qualitative analysis builds on a strong tradition of critical and emancipatory approaches that date back at least to the works of Marx and Engels. Moreover, in contrast to many other language textbooks studies, my approach may have the advantage of being holistic, in the sense that it examines a cultural product such as a textbook in the light of its own wider social, economic and political contexts.

Conclusion

As I suggested in Chapter 3, critical language textbook analysis has tended to focus its attention on identity dimensions such as gender or race, but has been conspicuous for its neglect of the economic and material bases of society. This is why in this chapter I have proposed a framework to analyze language textbooks from a political-economic perspective. It starts with a quantitative analysis that is followed by a qualitative study centered first on dimensions of social class and later on the neoliberal practices and values in the worlds of work and housing. The aim of this approach is to examine to what extent the socioeconomic conditions of contemporary capitalism shape the content of language textbooks. Chapters 6, 7, and 8 discuss the results of the application of this framework to a sample of Catalan language textbooks for adults. Before moving on to the results of the analysis, in the next chapter I will present the particular socioeconomic and historical context of Catalan language textbooks.

Notes

1 I thought that it was a good idea to look at 10 years of publications and in particular this period (2005–2015), which includes the end of a boom in publishing Catalan language textbooks that began in the early twenty-first century (see Chapter 5).
2 The English translation of the titles of the textbooks of the corpus are as follow: *Veus* – Voices; *Curs de català bàsic* – Basic Catalan Course; *Nou Nivell Bàsic* – New Basic Level; *Nou Nivell Elemental* – New Intermediate Level; *Passos* – Steps; *Català Inicial, Bàsic, Elemental* – Beginner, Elementary, Intermediate Catalan; *Fil per randa* – In Detail. The website *Parla.cat* in English would be Speak ('.cat' is the Catalan language Internet Top Level Domain).
3 In Table 4.1, the number of volumes and pages of the online platform *Parla.cat* refers to the number of courses and activities, respectively.
4 As with many current foreign language textbooks, Catalan materials are not strictly task-based, in the sense proposed by Michael Long (2014), but follow an approach that is more accurately 'task supported', meaning that the syllabus is a linguistic one but the practice activities include communicative tasks.
5 All translations from Catalan to English in this book are my own.

5 The Catalan context

Introduction

The purpose of this chapter is to explain the development of the history of Catalan textbooks for non-Catalan speakers and to link this history to broader political and socioeconomic issues. Unlike mainstream approaches which isolate the evolution of textbooks from the macro context in which they originated, this book considers that a discussion of the development of textbooks is incomplete if it does not take into account the socioeconomic reality that created them, as explained in Chapter 1. First of all, in this chapter I will briefly present the particular case of Catalan, a 'medium-sized' language,[1] which is in a complex sociolinguistic situation. Then, drawing on my recent study about the evolution of Catalan language teaching materials from a socioeconomic perspective (Bori 2017), I will highlight two key moments in the history of Catalan textbooks. The first historical moment is in the 1980s, a time of great transformation in Spain after Franco's death in 1975 and Spain's accession to NATO in 1982 and to what was then the European Economic Community in 1986. In this period, Catalan institutions made the first attempts to teach the Catalan language to Spanish speakers living in Catalonia, after four decades in which the institutional and public use of this language was explicitly repressed. The second key moment brings us to the turn of the twenty-first century when Spain experienced rapid economic growth, which led to the arrival of hundreds of thousands of immigrants to Catalonia and a significant rise in students of Catalan as a second language. In this period, there was a proliferation of Catalan language materials addressed mainly to the foreign-born living in Catalonia.

The case of Catalan

The Catalan language is a Romance language, with approximately nine million speakers. In Spain, it is spoken in Catalonia, Valencia, the Balearic Islands and on the border with the Aragon region.[2] There are also Catalan speakers in Andorra, in the southwest of France and in the city of Alghero on the island of Sardinia. The Catalan case is rather unique when compared to other European medium-sized languages such as Dutch, Finnish or

84 *The Catalan context*

Czech, not only because of its lack of a sovereign state (with the exception of the microstate of Andorra where Catalan is the only official language), but also because of the bilingualism that exists in the territories in which it is spoken (Boix-Fuster and Farràs 2012). Catalonia is the Catalan-speaking region that has worked continuously and most explicitly to maintain the Catalan language and increase knowledge and use of it within Catalan society. There has been less activity of this kind in Valencia and the Balearic Islands. As a result, Catalonia is also where most Catalan language materials have been published.

Catalan-Spanish bilingualism has generated a large number of sociolinguistic studies, as well as studies in language policy and planning, not only in Catalan and Spanish, but also in English language research (Woolard 1989, 2016; Webber and Strubell 1991; Strubell and Boix-Fuster 2011). Bilingualism in the Catalan-speaking regions in Spain is asymmetrical, in the sense that Catalan speakers are bilingual while many Spanish speakers and immigrants are not proficient in Catalan. For example, in Catalonia, according to a governmental Survey on Language Use (Generalitat de Catalunya 2013a), 99.7 percent of citizens who are 15 years old and over can speak Spanish, while 80.3 percent can speak Catalan but only 65.6 percent can speak it fluently or relatively proficiently, which means that more than one-third of the population in Catalonia has little or no knowledge of Catalan.

The bilingualism question has raised not only academic, but also public interest in Catalonia, as manifest in debates on television and radio, as well as between people in cafés and during family dinners. It is even said that every Catalan speaker is an amateur sociolinguist, with a firm opinion about the vitality and survival of the Catalan language. One of the repeated debates in the last decades has been about the state of the Catalan language, its future and whether it is in danger of being eclipsed by the much larger language, Spanish (Argente et al. 1979; Prats et al. 1990; Junyent 1999; Pujolar 2007a).

During the 1980s, the Catalan government [*Generalitat de Catalunya*] initiated many policies to expand the number of speakers and the use of the Catalan language, after almost four decades of repression against this language during the fascist regime (1939–1975). The Franco government prohibited the use of Catalan (and also the use of Basque and Galician) in official institutions and formal public contexts. It imposed Spanish as the only language in education, newspapers, cinema and radio, and forbade the publishing of books in Catalan (Vallverdú 1984). Spanish was the only language allowed for the official names of people and places, for signs, advertisements, and any kind of written documents. Although in the later years of the Franco era the persecution of the Catalan language was not as ruthless as it had been in the beginning, the official use of Catalan was not re-established until the end of the 1970s. The Catalan language has since seen something of a resurgence, especially in local and regional administration and also in education. The use of Catalan as the dominant vehicular language in education is traditionally considered a success story (Strubell 1996) because all who completed their obligatory education in Catalonia had the ability to express themselves in both Catalan and Spanish. However, it is also true that although many people have learned Catalan in school, they never use it in everyday life. In fact, the Spanish language is often the dominant language outside the classroom in schools, especially in urban settings:

> despite the legislation and the efforts made by educational professionals to establish Catalan as the vehicular language in schools, the reality is that in many centres at all levels of education, Spanish is often the lingua franca used with classmates and in non-academic contexts.
>
> (Corona et al. 2008: 127)

Elsewhere, Eva Codó and Adriana Patiño-Santos (2014) have shown how in high schools in Barcelona's metropolitan area students from immigrant backgrounds (especially those from Latin American backgrounds) never use Catalan outside school. Differing language ideologies, as well as pragmatic reasons explain their preference for Spanish over Catalan:

> [T]heir lack of confidence in the language, the low value of Catalan within the global linguistic market, the limited language resources at their disposal to do in Catalan what they can do in Spanish (rap, insult, tell jokes, etc.), and finally, the absence of real contexts in which to use the language.
>
> (Codó and Patiño-Santos 2014: 62)

In a similar fashion, Víctor Corona (2016: 98) notes how some adolescents from South American backgrounds in Barcelona reject Catalan as "an imposition of the school that does not allow them to follow the lessons with normality". Nevertheless, six years later, these same participants in his study seemed to change their perceptions towards languages and now see Catalan as an instrument to get a better job:

> When they were young adolescents, they showed a very strong resistance toward all the languages outside from their Latino style. Now, when they are confronted with the necessity of finding a job, they accept the importance of multilingual skills to be more competitive in the job market.
>
> (Corona 2016: 105)

One of the most interesting findings in recent research on the use of Catalan and Spanish in Catalonia is that many from immigrant and working-class backgrounds consider Catalan a middle-class language and Spanish as the language of the working class (Woolard 2003; Frekko 2013; Codó and

86 *The Catalan context*

Patiño-Santos 2014). In her recent ethnographic studies with adolescents in the Barcelona area, Kathryn Woolard (2009, 2016) shows that the Catalan language now has more prestige than Spanish (also known as 'Castilian') among young people in Catalonia: "A corresponding perception of Catalan as a language of elegance and refinement and of Castilian as a coarser language has become nearly absolute for many of these students" (Woolard 2009: 147). Although it may be that Catalan is more identified as a middle-class language and Spanish as the language of the working class, it is also true that there are many Catalan speakers who belong to the working class and that Spanish has generally been considered the language of a part of the upper class, both now and before. We should remember, for example, that as early as in the fifteenth century with the arrival of a Spanish-speaking dynasty to the throne of Catalonia-Aragon, the Catalan aristocracy began to prefer using Spanish instead of Catalan (Frekko 2013). More recently, during the Franco regime, a large proportion of the Catalan-speaking bourgeoisie abandoned their native language and used Spanish to speak to their children. Today, even though Catalan is a language that might help improve someone's social status, the knowledge of which can enhance one's chances of working in the public sector in Catalonia, Spanish is still the predominant language in the business and private sectors among the highest classes of Catalan society.

In the post-Franco period, Catalan has re-established its place in the media (there are TV and radio stations, newspapers and websites in Catalan) and in some cultural sectors such as theater and, to a lesser degree, in the sectors of commerce and industry. However, Spanish continues to be the dominant language in the public sphere, in the media, as well as in social settings and the private sphere, especially in urban areas. After over 30 years of process of linguistic recuperation in Catalonia, it can be said that Catalan has become the dominant language in institutional life, but not in non-institutional social settings. Block (2016b: 115) sums up the current situation as follows:

> [T]he vitality of Catalan in the twenty-first century may be examined both with optimism (great progress has no doubt been made since the early 1980s, particularly as regards institutional uses of Catalan) and pessimism (there is little doubt that there is less Catalan spoken in the streets of Barcelona in 2015 than there was in 1995).

Recently, with the rise of the Catalan independence movement, the language has once again become the center of public debate with the question of what status should be given to Catalan and Spanish in a future state. While some language professionals, writers and academics argue that Catalan must be the only official language of a future Catalan republic (Grup Koiné 2016), other opinion holders and the two biggest pro-independence political parties in Catalonia defend the idea that both Catalan and Spanish should have joint official status.

The Catalan context   87

Among the significant events that have had an impact on the sociolinguistic situation in Catalonia are the two large migratory waves that have
occurred in the last 70 years. The first wave occurred more or less between
1950 and 1975, when the population of Catalonia rose from 3.2 to 5.6 million, resulting in a 75 percent increase in 25 years (Cabré and Pujadas 1984).
These migrants were mostly Spanish speakers who came from rural areas
of the impoverished south of Spain and other areas such as Galicia. They
settled in metropolitan areas, especially in Barcelona, to find work. These
were the years of what is known as the Spanish economic miracle, which
began in 1959 with the national plan for economic stabilization. After two
decades of a policy of economic self-sufficiency during the first period of the
Francoist regime, Spain adopted policies of economic liberalization aiming
at the integration of the country into the international capitalist economy
under the directives of the International Monetary Fund (IMF) and other
major international economic organizations (Prados de la Escosura et al.
2011). During the 1960s, Spain registered the second highest growth rate
in the world, surpassed only by Japan. Among the factors that best explain
this economic boom were the arrival of foreign investment (especially from
the United States and Germany); the loans provided principally by the IMF
and the Organization for Economic cooperation and Development (OECD);
US-Spain military cooperation agreements; the spectacular rise in international tourism; and the money sent home by Spanish emigrants working
abroad (especially in France, Germany and Switzerland). This period was
also characterized by the mass development of new areas of the Barcelona
metropolitan area, which coincided with a large movement of people to the
city. The international oil crisis and its aftermath in the mid-1970s brought
this phase of economic growth to an end.

The wave of migration that arrived in Catalonia from other parts of
Spain was one of the main reasons for Catalonian economic growth, which
soon became one of the economic engines of the Spanish economy. It also
provided an improvement in economic conditions of the host population
because "as the newcomers filled the plentiful lower order positions that the
booming economy provided, the old-timers quickly moved up into better-
paying technical or administrative positions" (Fishman 1991: 298). At the
same time, this migratory movement radically changed the sociolinguistic
reality of the region. Catalan ceased to be the predominant everyday language in informal settings in its historical territory, especially in the province
of Barcelona, which in 1975 comprised 70 percent of the total population of
Catalonia (Branchadell 2005).

The second migratory wave consisted mainly of people coming from countries outside the European Union, a wave that occurred primarily between
the mid-1990s and end of the first decade of the twenty-first century, against
the backdrop of neoliberal globalization, a point to which I will return later
in this chapter. Catalonia alone received more than a million immigrants,
the majority of whom considered Spanish and not Catalan as the language

88 *The Catalan context*

most useful for their life in a new society (Gore 2002; Branchadell 2015). Indeed, Catalan is today still very much secondary to Spanish in terms of its use in social and economic spaces and, as a consequence, immigrants usually choose Spanish as the language of their daily lives, although they maintain their first languages as the language spoken at home and among family members.[3] In the world of work, for example, knowledge of Catalan is an advantage and even required by some employers in the job market, but not as essential as Spanish (Heidepriem 2011: 229). According to Antonio Di Paolo and Josep Lluís Raymond (2012: 93), learning Catalan for adult immigrants is "much more a choice than a requirement or a need". There are many factors that may influence the decision to learn Catalan, such as individual characteristics (linguistic and educational background, the ability and motivation to learn languages, etc.), the sociolinguistic situation in the host environment (whether the Catalan language is the predominant one or not), but also, in some cases, immigrants learn Catalan to gain better job opportunities and "the prospect of higher earnings" (Di Paolo and Raymond 2012: 93). Nonetheless, Di Paolo and Raymond (2012) showed that Catalan proficiency was only rewarded with better incomes for well-educated individuals, while those with lower levels of education did not benefit from their knowledge of Catalan in terms of earnings. The study by Di Paolo and Raymond (2012) relies on data from 2006, which of course does not take into consideration the collapse of the Spanish economy after the 2007–2008 crisis – which depressed earnings and wage rises.

Another factor that might explain the reduced use of Catalan among immigrants in social settings, whether they are of Spanish origin or not, is the so-called code switching of Catalan speakers who abandon Catalan for Spanish in conversations with people they perceive as non-native Catalan speakers. An ethnographic study by Joan Pujolar (2007b) reveals much about the languages used during a Catalan course for adult immigrant women organized by a Catholic NGO in a small Catalan city. Pujolar discovered that even teachers of Catalan or Catalan-speaking administrators from the NGO often choose to speak Spanish to immigrants even during Catalan language classes. According to Pujolar, the tendency for Catalan speakers to always address immigrants in Spanish might be interpreted as "an informal politics of segregation" (337) because Catalan speakers themselves erect barriers that deny the immigrants access to the Catalan language.

Although the Catalan language is studied in more than 100 universities around the world (Institut Ramon Llull 2016), the textbooks that I will present below are mainly written for immigrants who live in Catalonia. Strangely enough, not one of the textbooks analyzed in this study contains a single reference to Catalan-Spanish bilingualism or to the increasingly multilingual situation, nor to the tendency of Catalans to change to Spanish when they speak to people seen as outsiders or as 'foreign'. The majority of learners in the 1980s and 1990s were Spanish speakers from other parts of Spain, while in the twenty-first century they are mostly immigrants with a variety of native languages from all over the world. According to official data, most immigrants registered in Catalonia (Idescat 2015a) are from Africa (28 percent), in particular from Morocco, from the EU (27 percent), especially from Romania, from Latin America (24 percent) and Asia (14 percent).

Having brief presented the sociolinguistic situation in Catalonia, I now move to a more detailed explanation of the history of Catalan language teaching to non-Catalan adult speakers, with an emphasis on the evolution of Catalan language materials from the 1980s until the present. I will connect the history of Catalan textbooks with the evolution of capitalism during the last four decades in Spain. For this reason, a discussion of the socioeconomic conditions in which Catalan textbooks have been published will be included. In doing so, I aim to highlight the fundamental argument of my book, by examining textbooks against the backdrop of the material conditions of capitalism. Catalan language teaching for non-Catalan adult speakers started during the last two decades of Francoist Spain, with courses organized by non-governmental organizations (very often clandestinely) and by the public libraries in the province of Barcelona. However, it was not until the 1980s, after the death of Franco, that the teaching of Catalan as a second language was established officially, as we shall see in the next section.

Teaching Catalan as a second language in the 1980s

The 1980s was a period of great transformation in Spain, as well as in Catalonia. Spain struggled to recover from the economic crisis of the 1970s, caused by the failure of the capitalist development model of the Franco regime, the structural deficits of an economy strongly dependent on the sectors of tourism and construction and the repercussions of the international oil crisis of 1973. Between 1973 and 1985, Spain experienced a severe capitalist economic crisis, with the decrease of investment in the industrial sector, very low growth of its GPD and extremely high inflation rates. Unemployment rose suddenly and by 1985 more than 20 percent of the Spanish working-age population was unemployed.

In the second half of the 1980s, Spain experienced an economic recovery driven by a period of growth heavily reliant on real estate and financial speculation (Rodríguez and López 2011: 41), which coincided with the accession of Spain to what was then called the European Economic Community in 1986. Between 1986 and 1991, the Spanish economy was rapidly incorporated into the European common market and the arrival of foreign investments provoked an increase in domestic consumption but not a decrease in social inequalities. It was in this period that Spain saw the rise of a new capitalist model, based on neoliberal politics of support for private capital, the reduction of public sector spending, the promotion of the mechanisms of the market, the increasing importance of financial and speculative capital, and radical changes in the organization of the world of

90   *The Catalan context*

work (Etxezarreta 1991). As Paul McVeigh (2005: 91) explains, the European integration of Spain required a profound economic liberalization of the country. The Social Democratic (PSOE[4]) government, with the support of the unions and employers, sought the opening up of the economy to external markets, assuming that this would facilitate the modernization of the Spanish economy in what was still a young democracy. For the new Spanish political and economic forces, European integration was identified at the time as a synonym for democracy and the welfare state. This so-called Europeanness meant a passive acceptance of all the economic and political conditions that came from outside. As Miren Etxezarreta has argued (1991: 57), the international powers and market forces guided the integration of Spain into the Western capitalist bloc.

Against the backdrop of this economic and political context, the Catalan government promoted policies to recover the use of the Catalan language, after four decades of repression and censorship by the Franco regime. Among its objectives, the linguistic politics of the Catalan government also included the teaching of Catalan to non-Catalan adult speakers. The main addressees were Spanish origin immigrants (or their descendants) that had come to Catalonia during the Francoist period and had not had the opportunity to learn Catalan, because Spain excluded Catalan from the formal and informal education systems.

With this end in view, at the beginning of the 1980s, the Catalan government promoted Catalan classes for the Spanish-speaking population, especially those who lived in urban areas and, in general, belonged to the working-class.[5] In practice, however, the most important group of non-Catalan adult learners were workers in the public regional administration, the majority of which were Spanish native speakers with a middle socio-economic status and who, in many cases, sought a certificate of Catalan to consolidate or improve their labor market position.

Once the program offering Catalan classes for non-Catalan adult speakers began, the Catalan institutions decided to follow the proposals of the Council of Europe regarding Communicative language teaching (CLT). Teacher training courses began to focus on how to use CLT in the classroom and how to work with CLT materials. Furthermore, as had occurred with the major languages of the European Community, the Catalan government translated and adapted *The Threshold Level* (Van Ek 1975) of the Council of Europe, a document that proposed that the main aim of learning a language is communication related to everyday issues. Although the Catalan version of this document would not be published until 1992, the first draft of the document was ready at the beginning of 1983. However, what most helped the expansion of the ideas of the Council of Europe in Catalonia was the diffusion of the popular multimedia course of Catalan called *Digui, digui* (1984/1985), which followed and elaborated upon the approach of *The Threshold Level*.

The recommendations of the Council of Europe met with rapid acceptance by Catalan educators, in the same way that had occurred in the majority of countries belonging at that time to the European Community. There was little debate as to whether these proposals, developed initially for English, could be adapted to the Catalan context. The reasons for this rapid and friendly acceptance and the later expansion of the proposals of the Council of Europe for the education of Catalan to non-Catalan speakers may lie in the Catalan sociolinguistic context. Historically, it has been a minority language with little political and economic power, so that its users have tended to affiliate with wider political trends, in this case to that of the European Community. Besides, the integration of Spain, first into NATO, and later into the European Economic Community, led the Catalan government, in parallel with the Spanish central government, to follow the economic and educational policies of the Western European countries. Given the overwhelming pro-European positions of the Spanish political class, all proposals coming from Europe were accepted uncritically and without question (Etxezarreta 1991).

In this way, during the 1980s and the 1990s, the European technocracy (the Council of Europe) was able to impose its proposals for Catalan teaching for adults, at a time when very similar approaches to the teaching of all foreign languages were being applied in the educational systems of the European Community. As explained in Chapter 2, these approaches were consistent with those implemented in neoliberal school reforms in most European countries, including Spain (Rodriguez 2011). Behind these ideas, although they were often presented as if they were neutral or even liberating, there were certain well-defined interests: improvement of the national economies; tightening the links between education, employment, productivity and trade; measurement of the results of students in accordance with the skills and competitions required by the new world of work; and the exertion of greater control over the content of curriculum and evaluation (O'Neill 1995: 9).

Digui, digui

Of all the Catalan language textbooks from the 1980s and 1990s certainly the most popular was *Digui, digui* (roughly translatable as 'Hello, hello' as this is what someone would say when answering the telephone, although it is worth noting that *digui* is the formal imperative form of the verb *dir*, which means 'say'). It was a course promoted by the Catalan government inspired by the English multimedia course *Follow me* created by the BBC with the support of the British Council.[6] During the entire process of materials preparation, the Catalan team counted on the advice of a group of experts from the Council of Europe (Trim 1992). The Council of Europe, as explained by Isidor Marí (1986), included this material as a pilot experience in Project 12, Learning and Teaching Modern Languages for Communication.

The course book is divided into two levels (Mas et al. 1984, 1985). Each of these courses had a student's book, a workbook, a teacher's book, a

92 The Catalan context

self-study book, and a collection of cassettes and videos. The preparation of this material meant a substantial economic investment for the Catalan government of around 150 million pesetas (almost 1 million euros), according to information from the Spanish newspaper *El País* (Galceran 1984).

The course followed a notional-functional syllabus and, as the teacher's book for Level 1 explains, aimed to empower students by equipping them with a real and immediate communicative competence:

> *Per explicar-ho ben planament: aquí no interessa tant que l'aprenent domini la morfologia verbal del català o els seus mecanismes de pronominalització; ni tan sols que pugui accentuar correctament una paraula com per exemple 'albergínia', ni que sàpiga que aquesta paraula vol dir 'berenjena' o 'aubergine'; ens interessa que, si ha d'anar a comprar albergínies, pugui realitzar tots els actes de paraula necessaris per dur a terme en català aquest acte comercial: demanar a quin preu van, dir com les vol, quantes en vol, fer valoracions de preu o de qualitat.*
>
> [To explain it simply: the interest here is not that learners gain a command of Catalan morphology or the mechanisms of pronominalisation or the ability to properly pronounce a word like *albergínia* [eggplant] or to enable them to understand whether this word means 'eggplant' or 'aubergine'. What interests us is whether when the learner goes to buy eggplants, she/he can accomplish all the necessary steps to carry out this transaction in Catalan: to ask the price, to express the types and sizes she/he would like to buy, how many she/he wants, and evaluate the price and quality.]
>
> (Llobera et al. 1989: 4)

At the same time *Digui, digui* was adapted so that learners could study Catalan through the daily newspapers, two TV channels and different radio stations. It was shown every day on TV as a daily series, the newspapers published a weekly page with entertaining activities and contests related to the social and cultural Catalan context, and radio programs had a teacher presenter who introduced activities and answered questions related to the course posed by both students and teachers (Gimeno 2012: 5). Owing to its presence in the mass media, *Digui, digui* quickly became very popular in Catalan society. It also became the most common material in Catalan classes for non-Catalan adult speakers, due to its promotion by Catalan institutions that organized several courses to train teachers to use *Digui, digui* in their classrooms.

In later years *Digui, digui* was also used in Catalan courses by many English, German, Italian and French universities, although it had been created mainly for Spanish speakers living in Catalonia. In the mid-1990s the authors of *Digui, digui* presented a revised version of the course book, published again with support from the Catalan government. Furthermore, the Catalan government also funded the adaptation of this course for Catalan students who had French, English, German and Italian as their native language. For these reasons, *Digui, digui* was used for many years in Catalan classrooms, until the early years of the twenty-first century. The last reprint of one of the *Digui, digui* course books was in 2005.

The introduction of the linguistic policy of the Council of Europe in Catalonia and the creation of *Digui, digui* in the 1980s began a process that, over time, would lead to a greater centralization and standardization of materials for teaching Catalan to non-Catalan adult speakers. Since teachers had a course book with so many resources provided by *Digui, digui*, they no longer had the need to create their own material for the classroom, as they had in the 1970s or during the early 1980s. Moreover, with the publication of *Digui, digui* and later of other similar products, commercial materials had more and more influence on the process of learning: which language should be taught, how should it be learned, with what content and even what type of interaction should take place in the classroom.

The organization of the units, the content and the general spirit of *Digui, digui* focused on the communicative teaching of an instrumental language would remain very similar in future Catalan textbooks, despite some small modifications. There is no data on how many students learned Catalan using this course book or to which extent *Digui, digui* was successful. What is clear, however, is that this course book represented a turning point in the evolution of Catalan materials first by promoting language learning as instrumental and as a vehicle for daily communication and second by promoting a new type of education related to the entrepreneurial culture that would continue to gain more and more popularity in the years to come.

The neglect of literature

One of the features of *Digui, Digui*, in common with more recent textbooks, is the marginalization of literature. Following the communicative approach, textbooks focused on day to day activities, as texts were about going shopping, eating, going to work and so on. The daily news and various kinds of advertisements also featured, along with a comic that occupied one or two pages in every unit. On the other hand, literary excerpts were practically non-existent. And when they featured, they tended to be short and related to the main topic of the lesson. The new concept of language learning, promoted among other institutions by the Council of Europe, placed great emphasis on communication through the uses of instrumental language to resolve everyday situations and practical needs. Within this new concept there was little or no space for literature.

Historically, literature has played a central role in language learning (Maley 2001) but, with the advent of audiolingual and communicative methods, literature moved from a core to a marginal position in language teaching. Although in recent decades more and more language professionals have argued for the benefits of incorporating literature in language

94 *The Catalan context*

classrooms[7] and empirical research has shown the positive results of using literature in foreign language courses (see Paran 2008 for a review), literary texts are still marginal in mainstream language teaching materials (Tomlinson et al. 2001: 97; Masuhara et al. 2008: 310; Gümüşok 2013; Skela 2014; Takahashi 2015)

In the field of Catalan textbooks of the 1980s, it is relevant to highlight the place of literature in teaching materials. And this leads me to consider briefly another Catalan textbook from the 1980s, one which presented a different kind of approach to language teaching than the one in *Digui, digui*. The book was entitled *Retalls* (Albó et al. 1980), which can be translated as 'Fragments', and it was a product of the experience of the authors who had worked as teachers of Catalan at the University of Barcelona. It had a total of seven editions. The course book was created before Catalonia implemented the policy of the Council of Europe, and it was different from *Digui, digui* because it used literature as the principal vehicle to teach the language.

The aim of this textbook was to teach a language that went beyond the instrumental, and it went against the communicative language teaching approach that was gaining momentum in Europe in that period. The authors explained this very clearly in their presentation of the book:

> [V]oldríem donar quelcom més que una llengua vehicular [. . .], ens sap greu donar-ne només un extracte o una mostra funcional que serveixi per preguntar quant val això i allò, a quina hora surt l'avió, i si us agrada la sopa de peix. El nostre desig i propòsit és comunicar-la d'una manera més plena i viva, intentant donar unes pistes de comprensió de l'esperit del nostre poble.
>
> [we would want to offer something more than a language as a vehicle [. . .], we would object to the provision only of an extract or a functional sample that serves to ask how much this or that costs, at what time the airplane departs, and whether you like the fish soup or not. Our wish and purpose are to communicate the language in a fuller and livelier way, and try to give clues for understanding the spirit of our people.]
>
> (Albó et al. 1980: 129)

These words represent a diametrically opposed approach to the one we saw in the eggplant example from *Digui, digui* where the authors explained that one of the main aims of language teaching was to give learners the means to resolve everyday financial transactions. In the first edition of 1980, *Retalls* consisted of two lengthy parts, the first a selection of literary texts in different styles and genres, organized by subject, and the second a series of exercises based on the literary texts. *Retalls* showed that there were other possible approaches to teaching a language, far from the communicative method that had then begun to become predominant in Europe. The approach of *Retalls*, however, was not replicated in future Catalan textbooks. With the rise to dominance of the communicative method, other textbooks opted to teach a practical language, very often through trivial situations. As a consequence, literature, despite its potential as a source of engaging texts, was relegated to a very marginal position in the new didactic materials.

Teaching Catalan in the twenty-first century

The 1990s represented the beginning of great changes in the economic and social situation in Spain. The country was incorporating an increasingly neoliberal economic model through the privatization of public enterprises such as the oil company *Repsol*, the energy provider *Endesa* or the telecommunications firm *Telefónica*. The decade also brought other measures such as the implementation of the 1992 Maastricht Treaty, reductions in public spending, the Spanish Land Act (which meant a greater liberalization of the residential construction sector) and banking deregulation, which led to an increase in financial speculation. Spanish GDP experienced an increase based especially on two key sectors: tourism and construction. This economic rise led to the creation of new jobs, but also greater levels of consumer debt, a dependency on credit, greater precariousness in the job market and what amounted to an environmental disaster, caused by extensive urbanization and intensive agriculture. As a result of this economic growth that was particularly high between 2000 and 2007, there was a strong demand for cheap labor in the tourist industry, in services for the elderly, in large-scale agriculture and especially in the construction sector, as there was a significant housing bubble during this period.

Meanwhile there was a rise in the inequality between rich and developing countries, caused by the expansion of neoliberal politics at the global level and promoted largely by transnational corporations and international institutions such as the International Monetary Fund, the World Bank, and the World Trade Organization. The diminishing economic role of nation-state economic regulation, with the reductions of tariffs and other trade restrictions on foreign investments and imports, along with the privatization of state enterprises and public services, led to the impoverishment of the majority of the inhabitants of most of the developing countries (Harris and Seid 2000). According to Harvey, one of the characteristics of neoliberal globalization is 'accumulation by dispossession', which means the transfer of wealth from the world's working class and poor to the ruling class and it includes the following phenomena:

> [C]ommodification and privatization of land and the forceful expulsion of peasant populations [. . .]; conversion of various forms of property rights (common, collective, state, etc.) into exclusive private property rights [. . .]; commodification of labour power and the suppression of alternative (indigenous) forms of production and consumption; colonial, neocolonial, and imperial processes of appropriation of assets (including natural resources); monetization of exchange and taxation,

96 *The Catalan context*

particularly of land; the slave trade (which continues particularly in the sex industry); and usury, the national debt and, most devastating of all, the use of the credit system as a radical means of accumulation by dispossession.

(Harvey 2005: 159)

The conjunction of these two factors (the greater demand for cheap labor in Spain due to economic growth and the impoverishment of large parts of the world population) caused a great increase in non-EU immigration to Catalonia, especially in the first decade of the twenty-first century. In the year 2000 Catalonia had a little more than six million inhabitants: by 2010 the figure was about 7.5 million. Foreign nationals registered in Catalonia in 2000 represented just 2.9 percent of the total population: by 2010 they represented about 16 percent of the total registered population (Idescat 2015b). The current economic crisis – provoked by the bursting of the financial and real estate bubble in 2008, which highlighted the underlying weakness of Spanish economic growth at the beginning of the twenty-first century (Etxezarreta et al. 2012) – has especially affected the immigrant population, which suffers from poverty, labor precariousness and difficulties finding a place to live or work.

The growth of the immigrant population has also meant an increase of Catalan language students. Proof of this can be seen in the increase of registrations during the first decade of this century to the Consortium for Linguistic Normalization (CPNL), the main center for teaching Catalan to non-Catalan adult speakers. Since the 2000–2001 course, when CPNL registered a total of 43,032 students, enrollments have increased year after year, reaching a maximum of 127,807 registrations for the 2009–2010 course (CPNL 2012). In recent years, the number of students at the CPNL has dropped because of the economic crisis and the consequent decrease of migration to Catalonia and the departure of many immigrants to their homelands or other countries.

Coinciding with the arrival of immigrants and the progressive increase in adult students of Catalan as a second language, Catalan institutions, like others in almost every European country, adopted the *Common European Framework for Languages* (CEFR) of the Council of Europe (2001). The Catalan translation of this document was published in 2003 by the Catalan, Andorran and Balearic governments (MECR 2003). Some parts of the CEFR, especially the definition of the levels and its descriptors, were received very favorably in Catalonia. Indeed, the CEFR's reference levels continue to be used to set levels for Catalan courses in both public and private language institutions, to design official language exams and to inform Catalan language teaching materials. At the same time, CEFR guidelines were also adopted in foreign language education programs at all educational levels in Catalonia and in the rest of Spain, from primary school through university. CEFR guidelines, especially the ones related to the six different language levels (from A1 to C2), are now considered in Catalonia to be a natural, common-sense way to organize a second or foreign language course by the immense majority of stakeholders involved in this process: political institutions, language center managers, authors and publishers of textbooks and, often, also by teachers.

The boom of Catalan textbooks

With the increase of immigrant students of Catalan, a consequence of increased migration in a neoliberal economic context, there was a dramatic increase of Catalan language teaching materials. New series of textbooks were published together with courses to learn Catalan online, materials for specific purposes, and a great variety of supplementary resources, such as graded readers, new bilingual dictionaries, vocabulary and grammar books for non-Catalan speakers, bilingual conversation guides and an increasing quantity of online resources to learn Catalan.

The majority of current Catalan language textbook series have significant similarities between them, not only in their design but also in their content. They usually have various supplementary materials (audio materials, workbooks, teachers' books), many instructions (given in detail in the teachers' books) and students' books are usually organized with very similar sequences, task-based instructions and a communicative approach to learning a practical language. The content of the books, as we shall see in Chapters 6, 7 and 8, is centered in features and lifestyles of Western middle and upper classes, which present multiple neoliberal values and practices in a positive light, as natural phenomena. Another common denominator of all current textbooks is that they note that they follow the Catalan government programs for the Catalan language and, in particular, that they take into account the CEFR's levels.

The greater production of Catalan language materials aligns with the ever-increased consumption and hyper-production that the new capitalist system requires. In recent years, Catalan publishing houses have identified Catalan as a second language textbooks as a source of potential income. Publishing houses such as Teide, Castellnou, Barcanova, Àlber, Ocatedro or Publicacions de l'Abadia de Montserrat (PAMSA) have published many different collections of textbooks and additional learning and teaching material. Textbooks in general, and not just for Catalan as a second language, have become the main source of income for publishing houses that publish in the Catalan language. In 2015, out of 11,348 titles published in Catalan, 3,524 are textbooks (Montañés 2016). According to data from the Association of Publishers in Catalan (Editors.cat 2016), the sales of Catalan language textbooks represented 108 million euros in 2015, which signifies almost a half of all the income from the books published in Catalan.

In the neoliberal age, macroeconomic strategy is characterized by the concentration of capital in the hands of a few (the hands are continuously

98 *The Catalan context*

fewer) in all sectors of the economy. This has been happening in vital sectors such as banking, communication, the food industry, construction and also publishing. The Spanish (and Catalan) publishing world has undergone a process of concentration so that the major publishers have been purchased by a few large corporations. Among the publishers that publish textbooks for Catalan as a second language, Barcanova is a paradigmatic example of this process. It was created in 1980 for the purpose of publishing teaching materials in Catalan and already by the following year it had been incorporated into one the biggest companies in the Spanish publishing sector, Grupo Anaya. In 2004 Barcanova, together with Anaya, were absorbed by the multinational Hachette Livre, one of the largest trade and educational book publishers in the world. Hachette Livre is a subsidiary of Lagardère, a multinational media conglomerate headquartered in Paris, which operates in 40 different countries. Lagardère is involved in a range of activities in a range of sectors: books, magazines and newspapers; radio, television and advertising; broadcasting and production; retail stores in airports and railway stations; and investment in the aeronautical and military industry (Rebelo 2010: 63).

My discussion here of multinationals buying up publishing houses is relevant to understand the business behind many current language textbooks. Moreover, through the previous example of the Catalan Publishing house Barcanova, we can become more aware that multinational corporations play a key role not only in the global economy, but also in the teaching of a language that is not international, such as Catalan. This point reinforces the overall argument of this book which is to connect textbooks with neoliberalism. As we shall see in the next section, large corporations have also recently become involved in digital resources to learn Catalan.

Digital learning resources

One of the characteristic features of the new knowledge economy or the information society – concepts tightly linked to the neoliberal economic turn of the past few decades (Levidow 2007) – is the development of information and communications technology (ICT) in a range of social spheres, from the worlds of finance and global industry to the field of education. Jernej Prodnik (2014) argues that the transformations that brought the knowledge economy (for example, the increasing importance of ICT) are associated with much wider political, economic and social changes. Prodnik (2014: 147) contends that the development of new technologies did not usher in a "social revolution" as its apologists contend, but "a deepening, expansion, and acceleration of the capitalist accumulation and commodification on the one hand, and an intensification of control on the other". From a critical perspective, several researchers relate the development of ICT in education with the imperatives of the neoliberal economic agenda, such as the conception of students as consumers and entrepreneurial selves. Les Levidow (2007: 246) explains that online educational technologies not only "discipline, deskill, and/or displace teachers' labor" but also change "the role of students, who become consumers of instructional commodities". In a similar vein, Neil Selwyn (2015: 237) argues that digital education "demands increased levels of self-dependence and entrepreneurial thinking on the part of the individual, with educational success dependent primarily on the individual's ability to self-direct their ongoing engagement".

In the last few years, in the field of Catalan as a foreign language, multiple online language learning resources have appeared. The most famous of these is the website *Parla.cat* (DGPL 2008) which is the result of a project carried out by the Catalan Government in collaboration with the Ramon Llull Institute and the Consortium for Linguistic Normalization. It is a virtual learning space that offers a total of 12 courses organized and distributed in four learning levels according to CEFR criteria. It contains more than 4,000 exercises and information in four different languages. The courses are offered in two different modalities: autonomous learning or with the support of a tutor who guides and encourages the students.

The Catalan government invested more than four million euros and contracted two large multinationals from the new technologies sector to put into motion this online learning resource. The company *Informática El Corte Inglés* (pertaining to one of the biggest business groups in Spain) developed the technical part of the website, whereas another large corporation, Capgemini, was responsible for the e-learning methodology, the contents, the programs and the graphic design. Capgemini, one of the world's largest consulting, technology and outsourcing companies, not only benefited from the contract for this language learning website, but a couple of years later obtained a contract to develop ICT for the Catalan administration, with an annual income of close to four million euros (Generalitat de Catalunya 2013b).

Parla.cat was made available in 2008 just at the outbreak of the real estate and financial crisis in Spain. The number of students registered on this website is impressive and in 2016 there were more than 200,000 registrations (Generalitat de Catalunya 2016). However, this data does not reflect how many of those registered have actually followed any of the courses, nor to what degree they have improved their knowledge of Catalan with the use of this resource. In spite of the innovative spirit of *Parla.cat*, the organization and the content of the units are very similar to that of Catalan language textbooks published in the first years of the twenty-first century. The only noticeable difference is the use of videos and animations (in addition to written texts and audio material) and the ability to quickly access many other online resources. *Parla.cat* follows a communicative approach to teaching and learning the Catalan language, as well as the recommendations of the Council of Europe.

Conclusion

This chapter has shown how Catalan language teaching materials for non-Catalan adult speakers have followed the recommendations of the Council of Europe since the 1980s with the publication of the popular textbook *Digui, digui*. The proposals of the Council of Europe were accepted during a period of greater integration of Spain into the European capitalist economic system, characterized by what was in effect a Europeanist position among Spanish and Catalan political powers, who accepted all guidelines that came from Europe in an unquestioning and uncritical way (Etxezarreta 1991).

The adoption of the methodological recommendations of the Council of Europe continued through the early years of the twenty-first century, with the incorporation of the CEFR in the teaching of Catalan as a second language. Coinciding with the era of neoliberal globalization, there has been a rise in the number of immigrant Catalan language students and an increase of Catalan textbooks. The Catalan language teaching materials have appeared in different formats, with a greater presence of online resources, of which the online platform *Parla.cat* is a clear example. Large multinational companies have also gained power in the world of Catalan language materials publishing.

At the same time, there has been an increased process of standardization, centralization and homogenization of Catalan materials, in the sense that the approaches, content and design of the various materials are very alike. All of them are designed in accordance with CEFR descriptors. As we shall see in Chapters 7 and 8, they propose a communicative language learning of practical and useful language in the service of the interests of the new neoliberal economic order (see also Chapter 2 for a discussion about the relation between the CEFR and neoliberalism developed by Kubota 2013 and Boufoy-Bastick 2015). Although Catalan is a medium-sized language embedded in an extremely complex bilingual (and progressively multilingual) situation, textbooks have adopted the same approaches as textbooks for the large global languages such as English (Gray 2010a) without making an effort to introduce important parts of Catalan culture into language curriculums such as, for example, its literature, as explained above.

Following this introduction to Catalan language textbooks, in the next three chapters I will discuss the results of the application of the analytical model proposed in Chapter 4 to current Catalan language materials, starting with the quantitative results and the key dimensions of social class that appear in the corpus. Several of the economic and historical issues covered here will be addressed again in the following chapters to develop a critical analysis of the impact of neoliberalism on the content of Catalan textbooks. All of this with a view to making more broadly applicable statements about the interrelationship between political economy and language teaching materials, the focus of the ninth and final chapter of this book.

Notes

1 'Medium-sized' language is a term that challenges the dichotomy between 'majority' and 'minority' languages or between 'greater' and 'lesser' used languages (Vila 2012). It has been coined by Catalan sociolinguists to classify those languages that have neither many millions of speakers nor only a few thousand speakers (Vila and Bretxa 2012). Generally speaking, these languages have between one and 25 million speakers. It is estimated that there are more than 300 languages in the world that fall into this category (Vila and Bretxa 2012).

2 Since the approval of the Spanish Constitution in 1978, Spain has been divided into 17 Autonomous Communities. Among these 17 Autonomous Communities, Catalonia, the Basque Country and Galicia are widely regarded as 'historical nationalities'. Together with Spanish, Catalan is the official language of Catalonia and the Balearic Islands. Catalan is also the co-official language of Valencia, but in this Autonomous Community the Catalan language is called 'Valencian'.

3 In Catalonia, about 600,000 people out of a population of approximately 7.5 million inhabitants speak a language other than Catalan or Spanish as their first language (Generalitat de Catalunya 2013a). The Research Group on Endangered Languages (GELA, University of Barcelona) has recorded more than 300 languages spoken today in Catalonia. More information available online: www.gela. cat/doku.php?id=llengues (accessed 27 April 2017).

4 PSOE stands for *Partido Socialista Obrero Español* (Spanish Socialist Workers Party).

5 In addition to Catalan language courses for non-Catalan adult speakers, the Catalan government also organized courses for adult Catalan speakers who could not write in their native language because Franco had banned the Catalan language from the educational system.

6 The teacher trainer John McDowell, head of studies at the Barcelona British Council, was a key figure at this time in the introduction of new methodologies in Catalonia, both for ELT and for teaching Catalan as a second language. In 1983, he was appointed as the head of training for teachers of Catalan to adults by the Catalan government. He collaborated with the production of the course *Digui, digui* and contributed several articles to *COM ensenyar català als adults*, a specialized journal for teaching Catalan to adults published by the Catalan government between 1982 and 1997.

7 It is argued that literature exposes students to non-trivial texts that have meaningful topics, genuine contexts and interesting characters. Furthermore, literary texts, by their very nature, contain a strong ambiguity and imaginative power that allow multiple interpretations, thus encouraging critical and creative thinking among students (for a review of the benefits of incorporating literature in language classrooms, see Skela 2014: 116–18).

6 Social class in textbooks

Introduction

This chapter will present the first part of the results of the application of the political economic approach to Catalan language teaching materials analysis explained in Chapter 4. I begin by presenting the results of the quantitative analysis of the corpus: the number of large texts selected and their classification into categories according to the predominant topic. In this way, it will be possible to see what proportion of topics related to work and housing appear in the corpus. This will be followed by an interpretation of the content through the key dimensions that index social class. The objective is to gain a general understanding of the socioeconomic situation presented in textbooks through looking at the materials using the social class dimensions explained by Block (2015a). For this purpose, following the theoretical perspective adopted in this study, I will present several examples of social class from Catalan textbooks, and I will discuss them against the social and economic backdrop of Spain in the era of neoliberalism. At the end of the chapter, I will present an analysis of the main textual genres and activities which feature in the materials in order to see which roles are given to students. All direct citations from the textbooks presented in this chapter and the two following chapters have been translated from Catalan into English by the author.

Number of texts

The total number of large texts[1] (more than 50 words) selected for the quantitative analysis is 2,537, as can be seen in Table 6.1. The online platform *Parla. cat* is the source with most large texts, followed by the *Passos* series from the publisher Octaedro, whereas the *Català Inicial, Bàsic, Elemental* textbooks from the publisher Teide are those with the least number of large texts.

Parla.cat is different from all other series because more than a half of the texts counted are in the form of listening activities, which appear alone (17 texts) or accompanied by the transcript of the audio text (310 texts), or videos and animations (32 texts). In the rest of the items from the corpus,

Table 6.1 Number of large texts in the corpus

Textbooks Series	Publisher	Number of large texts
Veus	PAMSA	283
Nou Nivell Bàsic/ Elemental	Castellnou	351
Passos	Octaedro	414
Català Inicial, Bàsic, Elemental	Teide	242
Fil per randa	Barcanova	324
Curs de català bàsic	CNLB	283
Parla.cat	DGPL	640
Total		2,537

however, the presence of listening activities is less apparent. In *Veus* we find almost half of the texts in the form of listening activities (132 out of 283), but in other series the percentage of large texts as listening activities is always less than a third of all the texts. *Parla.cat* is also different from the other materials because it includes videos and animations. The physical appearance of this platform is similar to the scenes and TV programs for language learning from the 1980s like the Catalan *Digui, digui* or the British *Follow me*. In general, the videos in *Parla.cat* are short (between one and two minutes) with one or two fixed planes where the units' protagonists appear, repeating in a dialogue the structural patterns and vocabulary similar to the ones which appear in previous or later activities.

Main topics

After examining the content of large texts, I have grouped them into 15 thematic categories, as explained in Chapter 4. The absolute and relative results are presented in Table 6.2.

As can be seen from Table 6.2, the thematic categories 'Work' and 'Housing' are important and recurring issues in Catalan language teaching materials, but the percentage of large texts that address these topics varies considerably in each series. 'Work' is among the three most represented topics in four out of seven series analyzed, while in *Parla.cat* and *Veus* work occupies the fifth and sixth place, respectively. In only one series, *Passos*, is this topic covered less frequently. On the other hand, the 'Housing' category has a significant presence in *Fil per randa* and to a smaller degree in *Parla. cat*, *Curs de català bàsic* and *Veus*. The large texts which explicitly deal with this topic in *Nou Nivell Bàsic/Elemental*, *Passos* and *Català Bàsic, Inicial, Elemental* are much less common.

'Travel' is another of the most frequent thematic categories in Catalan textbooks. It is found among the three most represented topics in six out of the seven series analyzed, with the *Passos* series in fourth place. In Table 6.2 we can also see that texts belonging to the category 'Personal information'

Table 6.2 Number and percentage of large texts in each textbooks series according to their thematic category

Thematic category	Veus (PAMSA)		Nou Nivell Bàsic/ Elemenal (Castellnou)		Passos (Ocatedro)		Català Inicial, Bàsic, Elemental (Teide)		Fil per randa (Barcanova)		Curs de català bàsic (CNLB)		Parla.cat (DGPL)	
	Texts	%	Texts	%	Texts	%	Texts	%	Texts	%	Texts	%	Texts	%
Cultural information	19	6.7	76	21.6	49	11.8	40	16.5	15	4.6	20	7.1	30	4.7
Daily life and free time	19	6.7	27	7.7	30	7.3	19	7.8	18	5.6	17	6	80	12.5
Education	0	0	4	1.1	18	4.3	5	2.1	16	4.6	10	3.5	3	0.5
Entertainment and news	41	14.5	30	8.6	18	4.3	11	4.5	16	4.9	29	10.2	72	11.2
Environment	5	1.8	11	3.1	15	3.6	6	2.5	6	1.8	3	1.1	15	2.3
Food and drink	23	8.2	11	3.1	25	6	7	2.9	10	3.1	17	6	28	4.4
Health and well-being	16	5.7	11	3.1	20	4.8	5	2.1	32	9.9	17	6	14	2.2
Housing	24	8.5	21	6	26	6.3	9	3.7	39	12	24	8.5	58	9.1
Neighborhood	5	1.8	23	6.6	23	5.6	22	9.1	13	4.1	22	7.8	28	4.4
Personal information	43	15.2	18	5.1	75	18.1	16	6.6	15	4.6	22	7.8	67	10.5
Shopping and consuming	12	4.2	17	4.8	34	8.2	5	2.1	24	7.4	22	7.8	41	6.4
Travel	29	10.3	33	9.4	30	7.3	47	19.4	48	14.8	30	10.6	70	10.9
Work	22	7.5	40	11.4	20	4.8	29	12	48	14.8	25	8.8	65	10.1
Other	3	1.1	6	1.7	8	1.9	4	1.6	2	0.6	3	1.1	9	1.4
More than one topic	22	7.8	23	6.6	23	5.6	17	7	23	7.1	22	7.8	60	9.4
Total	283	100	351	99.9	414	99.9	242	99.9	324	99.9	283	100.1	640	100

have a major presence in *Passos, Veus* and *Parla.cat*, whereas the category 'Entertainment and news' is given significant coverage in *Veus, Parla.cat* and *Curs de català bàsic*. There are also three series (*Nou Nivell Bàsic/ Elemental, Català Inicial, Bàsic, Elemental* and *Passos*) that feature a significant number of large texts on the category classified as 'Cultural information', a category which gathers all texts related to so-called culture with a big C (literature, art, history) and popular culture (traditions, songs, riddles, popular sayings). In general, the texts in this category are linked to the predominant topic of the unit like personal information, work, travel, housing, food, shopping, free time and so on. The category 'Daily life and free time' also occupies an important place in all materials, especially in *Parla.cat*, where it represents around 12 percent of all texts.

The categories 'Shopping and consuming', 'Neighborhood' and 'Food and drink' are not the most common topics in any of the materials, but tend to fall in the middle range, as can be seen in Table 6.2. In general, the texts related to 'Environment' and 'Education' are the least frequent in all series. The texts related to 'Health and well-being' are also more rarely found in the materials, except for *Curs de català bàsic* and *Fil per randa*, where there are many texts dedicated to this topic. The category 'Other' has a small presence in all series, representing always less than 2 percent of all the large texts counted. Finally, the category 'Texts with more than one topic' represents between 5 and 10 percent of the total texts counted in each series. This category covers texts that mention more than one of the themes noted in the other categories.

Work and housing content relevance

As one can see in Table 6.3, the category 'Work' represents more than 10 percent of all large texts recorded in four out of the seven textbooks series, and in *Català Bàsic* and *Veus* the topic represents 8.8 percent and 7.5 percent, respectively. Only in *Passos* is the percentage of texts which address this topic less than 5 percent. According to the results of this quantitative analysis, the housing world is also a common category in almost all series. It represents between 8.5 and 12 percent of the total of longer

Table 6.3 Percentage of work and housing-related large texts in materials

Textbooks Series	Work (%)	Housing (%)	Total (%)
Veus	7.5	8.5	16
Nou Nivell Bàsic/Elemental	11.4	6	17.4
Passos	4.8	6.3	11.1
Català Inicial, Bàsic, Elemental	12	3.7	15.7
Fil per randa	14.8	12	26.8
Català bàsic	8.8	8.5	17.3
Parla.cat	10.1	9.1	19.2

106 *Social class in textbooks*

texts in focus in *Veus*, *Fil per randa*, *Curs de català bàsic* and *Parla.cat*. In two additional series (*Passos* and *Nou Nivell Bàsic/Elemental*), it represents around 6 percent of the total texts recorded. Only in one series (*Català Inicial, Bàsic, Elemental*) is the percentage of texts related to housing less than 5 percent.

To sum up, the topics of work and housing together represent between 15.7 and 26.8 percent of all the large texts recorded in the quantitative analysis, except in the *Passos* series where these two themes are less common (they represent 11.1 percent). In Chapters 7 and 8, I shall analyze qualitatively the topics of work and housing in Catalan textbooks in relation to neoliberal values and practices. In the next section, I will present a qualitative analysis of the general content of the materials of the investigation through an examination of the representation of social class.

Social class

Textbooks tend to present an upper-middle class reality according to the jobs that characters do, trips they take, the pastimes they engage in and the kind of houses in which they live. The life of the participants is not limited by any economic restriction and their choices depend only on their personal preference. The most frequent characters are middle and upper-middle class people between 20 and 40 years of age, usually well educated with university degrees, who socialize with people of the same economic status. The everyday life of Catalans is portrayed as relaxed and happy in which young people, without budgetary constraints, enjoy eating out, attending cinemas and theaters, and buying expensive tickets to watch Formula 1 races or football matches.

One important example of social class representation can be found in a text called "Catalonia, a land of encounters" (Mas and Vilagrassa 2005: 34–5), where Asha, an adopted daughter from India, presents her family. The activity related to this text consists of reading the text and completing a table by entering data about Asha's relatives (their age, nationality, place of residence, profession and the languages they speak). The text is accompanied by a very large image of an outdoor barbeque with all the members of her family present. We find that her grandparents are from Germany and the Czech Republic, her father and uncle have foreign names, and her aunt is French. They all live in Catalonia and speak Catalan. We see that they all belong to an upper Catalan class: her father is a lawyer, her uncle and aunt live in Sitges, an upmarket coastal town south of Barcelona, and they are pictured elegantly dressed, engaged in what seems to be a cheerful Sunday outdoor meal. In choosing to portray this kind of family under the title 'Catalonia, a land of encounters', the authors seem to advocate a privileged immigrant, one who is evidently rich. It could be hypothesized that this could have a prejudicial effect on students of Catalan as a second language, the majority of which do not belong to upper-middle class families. What is being hidden in this text is that Catalonia is also a country of poor, socially disadvantaged, struggling-to-survive immigrants. In this sense, it is relevant at this point to describe in some detail the economic, social and political situation of recent immigrants to Spain. In so doing, I aim to highlight the contrast between the ideological representation of reality in textbooks and the lived human experience in today's world.

Generally speaking, foreigners in Catalonia and in all of Spain are more socially disadvantaged than the indigenous population, above all the economic immigrants from the global south and east. They have difficulties earning an income that allows them a decent living or to access adequate housing. Most non-EU immigrants arrived in Spain at the end of the twentieth century and the beginning of the twenty-first century as 'gap fillers' in the workforce, which means that they did the jobs that the autochthonous population did not want to do (Gil-Alonso and Vidal-Coso 2015). They worked in sectors with precarious, temporary and uncertain jobs that very often afforded them no social rights and were badly paid, such as the construction, hotel and catering industries, intensive agriculture or domestic services. During that period, the autochthonous workforce raised its 'job acceptability' level for various reasons such as economic growth, the improvement of welfare standards (although the distribution of this improvement was not equal for all people), a better level of education and the rise in expectations of upward social mobility (Cachón 2009: 3–6). In this way, Spain developed a 'dual labor market structure' (Gil-Alonso and Vidal-Coso 2015: 101). On one hand, nationals did white-collar jobs in sectors with relatively high salaries, the possibility of promotion and greater labor regulation. On the other hand, immigrants did the poorly paid, unskilled jobs that have been characterized as the 3Ds: *dirty, dangerous, demanding* (Cachón 2009: 17).

Since the start of the economic crisis in 2007–2008, foreign workers are among those who have suffered most from the negative consequences of the economic recession in Spain (Colectivo IOÉ 2012), especially after 2011 when nationals slowly started to return to work in niches that had been left to foreigners during the previous economic boom period (Gil-Alonso and Vidal-Coso 2015). In fact, most immigrants face many of the problems experienced by persons with Spanish nationality such as poverty, unemployment, a shortage of adequate housing, homelessness or a lot of difficulties making ends meet. But immigrants (especially the non-EU economic immigrants) have to face further problems, such as racial discrimination, difficulties gaining work or residence permits and political exclusion since only a few of them have the right to vote (Cachón 2009).

Not all students who learn Catalan are socially disadvantaged foreigners, since many university exchange students and middle-class professionals learn Catalan, but many learners of Catalan in Catalonia belong to lower social groups, although textbooks tend to present a reality mainly associated with the upper social strata. In the next sections I will comment in more detail on the four key dimensions of social class as explained by Block (2015a) that are highlighted among Catalan language materials. Later, the social class erasure[2] that appears in textbooks will be commented on.

Occupation

In Catalan textbooks, there are more examples of white-collar jobs such as managers, doctors or professors than lower paid ones such as supermarket workers, hairdressers or mechanics. One typical example of the professions depicted in textbooks is that of a Catalan lawyer in *Parla.cat* who does a lot of work-related travel:

> *Treballo com assessora d'un grup d'hotels. Viatjar forma part de la meva feina: agafo l'avió almenys dos cops a la setmana, de vegades tres. El millor de la meva feina és que no és gens avorrida, perquè cada situació és diferent, és nova per a mi. El més dur és passar tants dies lluny de casa, perquè trobo a faltar la família i els amics.*
>
> [I work as an assistant manager in a hotel chain. Traveling forms part of my work: I take a plane at least two times a week, sometimes three. The best thing about my job is that it is not boring at all because each situation is different and new for me. The worst thing is spending so many days away from home because I miss my family and friends.]
>
> (DGPL 2008: Elemental 1, Unit 3, 2.17)

In some of the series we also find young people with university degrees and upper-middle class lifestyles doing low paid jobs. For example, James, one of the main characters of *Nou Nivell Bàsic*, is a publicist who works as a cashier in a supermarket, lives in a big flat and has no problem paying for an expensive hotel room when going out of town for a weekend. The characters usually demonstrate satisfaction with their jobs or are enthusiastic when talking about the possibility of finding a new one. Conflicts or problems related to work are not presented. The visual content also reinforces this idealization with the people smiling while working. For example, in one work-related exercise, there is a photo in which different workers (a waitress, a nurse or a cook) appear smiling and looking into the camera (Anguera et al. 2010a: 32). The unemployed, on the other hand, are rarely mentioned in the textbooks. When they appear, they are mentioned in simple phrases such as "I haven't had a job since April" (DGPL 2008: Bàsic 1, Unit 5, 2.7). Nowhere are the reasons for the lack of jobs mentioned. We do not know, for example, if this person lost the job because their firm moved to another country or because there has been restructuring of personnel due to the cuts imposed by the government or the company.

Mobility

The characters who travel in textbooks are usually young or middle-aged tourists with all of the trappings of the Catalan upper-middle class. In the series *Veus*, for example, a group of Catalans are traveling on a "luxury

Social class in textbooks 109

cruiser" (Mas and Vilagrassa 2008: 9) or others are staying in a "marvelous hotel" (Mas and Vilagrassa 2007: 37). In *Parla.cat* there are also young Catalans taking a "cruise ship to visit various Greek islands" (DGPL 2008: Elemental 3, Unit 4, 1.2) or a young woman from Barcelona is asked to go to New York on a shopping tour to "the most expensive shops on Fifth Avenue, where members of the upper class in the city live" (DGPL 2008: Bàsic 2, Unit 2, 1.8). In other textbooks we see a similar trend. In *Català Elemental*, a couple rent a "house with a garden" in a village in the Catalan Pyrenees (Campoy et al. 2011: 20). In textbooks from the Barcelona Center for Linguistic Normalization, two people go on a safari in Africa (CNLB 2011: 33). In *Nou Nivell Bàsic*, a young man does not think twice about making a reservation for a room in a hotel in a country where the rooms cost between 70 and 95€ per night (Guerrero et al. 2010b: 28). And finally, in *Fil per randa*, a client in a luxury hotel wants to rent a suite with a "hydro massage bath" (Vilà and Homs 2013b: 200). Only the *Passos* series includes a few examples of travel dedicated to the economically well off, while in the others well-to-do travel predominates.

Although there are some characters who take their holidays at camp sites or hostels, the tendency is for the materials to present an upper-middle class reality and in general people who do not have money problems. Characters in textbooks not only have the means and the time to go on a trip, but also have the knowledge necessary to travel, which can be seen in this excerpt from a dialogue between friends in *Fil per Randa Bàsic*:

[Persona 1]:   *Ja tinc els bitllets d'anada i tornada a Nova York . . .*
[Persona 2]:   *Encara es necessita visat per anar als Estats Units?*
[Persona 1]:   *Ara, amb el passaport electrònic, ja no se'n necessita si hi vas de vacances menys de noranta dies. I tampoc no t'has de posar cap vacuna, és clar, però jo em vaig haver de renovar el passaport perquè feia tres mesos que m'havia caducat!*
[Persona 2]:   *Sort que te'n vas adonar! Jo, com que vaig a Angola, necessito de tot. Sort que fa molt temps que preparo el viatge.*
[Persona 1]:   *És clar: passaport, visat i t'has de posar la vacuna de la febre groga . . .*
[Persona 2]:   *Sí, la de la febre groga és obligatòria. Però jo ja he demanat hora per posar-me'n dues més: la de l'hepatitis i la de la meningitis.*
[Persona 3]:   *Jo no tindria temps, ara, de fer tants tràmits . . . Em sembla que aniré a l'Alguer. És que m'ha caducat el passaport i no tinc temps de renovar-lo. I ara no tindria temps de posar-me vacunes, sol·licitar un visat . . . Per anar a Itàlia no necessito res. Només el DNI, és clar.*

[Person 1:   I already have my return tickets to New York . . .
Person 2:   Do we still need a visa to enter the USA?

110 *Social class in textbooks*

Person 3: With an electronic passport we don't need it anymore, if you go there on vacation for less than 90 days. You don't have to get any vaccinations either, of course, but I have to renew my passport because it expired three months ago!

Person 2: Lucky you've remembered. On the other hand, I go to Angola and need everything. Luckily, I have been preparing for the journey for a long time.

Person 1: Of course, you should have your passport, a visa and the vaccination against yellow fever.

Person 2: Yes, the yellow fever vaccination is obligatory, but I asked to be vaccinated against two more illnesses: hepatitis and meningitis.

Person 3: I think that I don't have time now to do all these things . . . I think I'll just go to Alghero. My passport expired and I don't have time to renew it. And I wouldn't have time for vaccination; visas . . . To go to Italy I don't need anything, except my ID, of course.]

(Vilà and Homs 2013a: 197)

This dialogue offers students linguistic resources and information about how to use Catalan to prepare for travel. The exercise related to this dialogue has a very pragmatic purpose since it consists in listening to the conversation and writing down things needed to travel to various destinations, such as vaccinations, passports, visas and foreign currency. However, the reality offered by this dialogue may be very far from the real experience of the majority of Catalan students, most of whom are economic immigrants that rarely travel abroad and, when they do travel, usually go to their country of origin. According to data from 2014 taken from the Consortium for Language Normalization (CPNL 2014: 50–1), the principal center for learning Catalan as a second language in Catalonia, the vast majority of foreign students in beginner courses in this institution come from non-Western and impoverished countries, especially from South and Central America (46 percent) but also from Africa (24.4 percent) and Asia (17 percent). Yet, the participants in this long dialogue belong, evidently, to the wealthier classes. None of the characters show any concern about travel, accommodation and catering costs to go to New York, Angola or Italy. Besides having time and money to travel, the characters demonstrate knowledge typical of the upper-middle class tourist regarding the documentation and vaccines they need to travel. In a similar vein, the next section will show that most of the characters in these textbooks belong to the most affluent social classes, according to their consumption patterns while traveling.

Consumption patterns

Catalan textbooks place a great emphasis on content related to travel, as the quantitative results presented here have shown. Looking more closely at their treatment of this topic, these language materials emphasize the culture-ideology of consumerism (Sklair 2002)[3] by means of the trappings of tourism (consuming accommodation, transport, medicines, tourist services) or travel experiences, which the learning materials explain. In their treatment of the tourist theme, we can also more clearly identify consumption patterns in Catalan textbooks that are typical of the middle and upper-middle classes. One example of the culture-ideology of consumerism and upper-middle class consumption patterns is in the dialogue and the emails in *Veus 3* between two Catalan friends in which one of them called Pere receives advice about traveling to India (Mas and Vilagrassa 2008: 16–17). The advice is mostly about products that Pere should consume, such as vaccines and medicines, means of transport, clothes or guidebooks. Through such advice we can see that both characters have a fair amount of disposable income: "If I were you I would take a couple of credit cards in case you lose one, along with money in cash. When you arrive there, it's worth your while to rent a car with a driver". About India, all that is said is that it is not a dangerous country and that it is very hot. And about its culture and people, we only learn that there is poverty, that cows are allowed in the streets and that "women don't show their legs!".

Another example of this consumerist perspective in content related to travel is a letter of complaint written by a character in *Català Elemental* to a tourist agency that had organized a journey to Costa Rica for her (Campoy et al. 2011: 138). The letter consists of a series of complaints about and disappointment with the services encountered. The traveler expected to stay in a five star hotel but unfortunately for her: "Upon reaching the hotel, we found that it did not have five stars as we had agreed upon, but three stars, and it was in deplorable condition". She had also expected better quality transportation: "Once we went outside the capital, they put us in a bus without air conditioning, although they had said that we would travel in off-road vehicles with eight people at most and with air conditioning". In the entire lengthy text about Costa Rica, there is no mention of the local culture or people. It is exclusively dedicated to making consumer complaints. What these two examples above reveal is a form of travel of people without economic problems where consumption takes priority together with a complete lack of interest in the reality of the places and their culture and people.

I also identify consumption patterns and travel only affordable to people belonging to the upper-middle classes in other Catalan textbooks. For example, a character in *Curs de català bàsic B3* explains her trip to New York mostly with the products she consumes, such as shows, meals and drinks in nightclubs (CNLB 2011: 23). The textbook series *Català Inicial, Català Bàsic* and *Català Elemental* stands out from the other textbooks by including a lot of activities related to alternative tourism, which as I shall explain below is also characteristic of middle-class people. It presents sojourns in rural houses, hiking, ecotourism or cultural tours through Catalonia. It seems that tourists in these textbooks are perhaps more sensitive, educated,

112 *Social class in textbooks*

helpful and more open than the ordinary summertime-resort type of travelers. There is even a text about a family who goes on an environment saving trip, shown in the following excerpt:

> *Nosaltres proposem una sortida força profitosa per el medi ambient. Es tracta de participar en la neteja de camins i fonts d'una zona del Montseny. Ho porta un grup de bombers voluntaris i tot està pensat per fer-ho amb famílies.*
>
> [We propose a trip which is quite beneficial for the environment. It consists of taking part in the cleaning of paths and springs in the Montseny's area. It is led by a group of voluntary fire fighters and is intended for families.]
>
> (Esteban 2012b: 90)

The volunteer tourist proposal of the previous example illustrates the increasing importance of individual responsibility in the era of neoliberalism, in particular the withdrawal of the states from community spheres of life (in this case, the conservation of a natural space). Jim Butcher and Peter Smith (2010) see in the recent boom in volunteer tourism an attempt to create "morally justifiable lifestyles" (30). Following the decline of alternatives to the current free-market capitalism, volunteer tourism may be understood as a means to "make a difference" in such a way that reflects how "aspects of our lives that were previously unproblematic (shopping or holidays for example) have become politicized (or moralized)" (Butcher and Smith 2010: 33).

One of the most frequently offered alternatives to mass tourism in these textbooks is trekking and especially mountain climbing, a practice with a long tradition in Catalonia, initially with a patriotic, scientific and erudite component (Martí Henneberg 2005) which Catalan textbooks do not mention. In *Català Bàsic* (Esteban 2012b), for example, there are two stories about climbing the Catalan mountains, a meeting of hikers at the top of a mountain, a father and a son who climb a mountain to reach a sanctuary, and advice about a route on foot through the Pyrenees. Similarly, another textbook presents a survey with the following question: "Do you consider yourself an athlete?" (CNLB 2008b: 49). After that, there are various sports-related photos (bungee jumping, white water rafting, horse-racing, etc.) with an activity with questions like: "In your view, what is the worst and the best adventure sport?".

As Nigel Harwood (personal communication) points out, these examples are in contrast with the travelers discussed earlier in this section who do not seem to be the least interested in the countries to which they are going (India and Costa Rica). I am naturally in agreement that eco-friendly travelers and mountaineers usually do take interest in the places to which they are going. However, my point here is to highlight alternative tourism as an indicator of social class, and above all to link the content of textbooks with neoliberalism, the issue to which my study is devoted. Thus, according to

Robert Fletcher (2008), adventure sports and alternative tourism in general are the typical practices of professionals belonging to the middle-classes in contemporary capitalist societies. They are people without financial limitations, yet with the desire to differentiate themselves from those who enjoy mass tourism. For Fletcher (2008: 323), the practice of these sports implies a contradiction for the people who engage in them: "although athletes' discourse often suggests that they engage in risk sports to resist or escape mainstream social values, their actual practice embodies many of the very values that they claim to reject". In other words, many of the values associated with adventure sports – individualism, risk management, self-dependency, personal progress thanks to new challenges, good physical condition and resilience – are congruent with the societal ideas that neoliberalism promotes. In this sense, it is relevant to mention the increasing frequency of courses of adventure sports organized by companies for their workers, with the aim to teach them to manage risk and the labor uncertainty in the world of work in neoliberal capitalism. In the next section, I will continue the general portrayal of the socioeconomic situation presented in textbooks by reviewing and analyzing the kind of dwellings depicted and the neighborhoods where characters live.

Place of residency

Most characters in these textbooks are depicted as current or prospective property owners. In a form similar to the one in ELT textbooks analyzed by Auerbach and Burgess (1985: 481) and the French textbooks studied by Kinginger (2004: 225), Catalan textbooks tend to present a type of housing accessible only to the wealthy social classes. Characters usually live in big apartments in the city or in individual houses with gardens in residential neighborhoods. The apartment that Pere in *Parla.cat* bought is a typical example of the kinds of houses we find in textbooks:

Pere: *Et truco per dir-te que al final ens hem comprat un pis a Moià.*
Paul: *Ah, sí? I com és el pis? És gaire gran?*
Pere: *Sí, és molt gran, fa 150 metres quadrats.*
Paul: *Què, quant fa?*
Pere: *Fa 150 metres quadrats. Hi ha quatre habitacions, totes són bastant grans. Té dos banys, però un és força petit, només hi ha un vàter i un lavabo.*
Paul: *I la cuina?*
Pere: *La cuina . . ., home la cuina és massa gran. Ja saps que no cuinem gaire, i a més no hi mengem.*
Paul: *Ha, ha, ha, sobretot tu.*
Pere: *Hum! Però escolta: el que m'agrada més d'aquest pis és que té . . . dues terrasses!!! Bé, eh?*
Paul: *Genial!*

114   *Social class in textbooks*

[*Pere:* I'm calling you to say that I finally bought an apartment in Moià.
Paul: Oh, really? And how is it? Is it big?
Pere: Yes, really big, it's 150 m2.
Paul: What? How big?
Pere: 150m2. There are four pretty big rooms. There are two bathrooms, but one is really small, there is just a sink and a toilet.
Paul: And how about the kitchen?
Pere: The kitchen . . . man, the kitchen is too big. You know that we don't cook much and we also don't eat at home.
Paul: Ha, ha, ha, especially you.
Pere: Hm! But listen: what I like best about this apartment is that it has . . . two balconies!!! Pretty good, huh?
Paul: Great!]

(DGPL 2008: Bàsic 2, Unity 1, 1.10)

Dwellings more typical of working-class families (such as small cheap apartments without central heating or trailer homes) appear very rarely. On the other hand, expensive houses and apartments appear regularly, for example in real estate announcements for an apartment for 563,000 euros or a house for 482,000 euros (Anguera et al. 2010a: 38), in a description of an apartment of 105 m2 for two people (Campoy et al. 2011: 30) or in a text about a family looking for a house with six bedrooms, a swimming pool and a garden (Vilà and Homs 2013a: 180). On occasion, the visual material reinforces this upper-middle class reality with pictures and drawings of luxury houses, such as two photographs of a kitchen and a living room in *Veus* (Mas and Vilagrassa 2008: 60) that are very similar to the ones found in home decoration magazines. As demonstrated by the analysis so far, Catalan textbooks tend to present very little socioeconomic diversity, a theme that I will develop in more detail below.

Class erasure

In all materials, Catalonia is presented as a prosperous country, without poverty, without class differences, that offers great job opportunities, possibilities to travel around the world and live in comfortable houses and apartments. Similarly to the contemporary global ELT textbooks studied by Gray and Block (2014), Catalan textbooks are mostly inhabited by middle and upper-middle class members. The working class, when it appears, is almost always related to immigrants such as Emil from Romania who works in a restaurant (Mas and Vilagrassa 2005: 89), Vilma from Ecuador who is a hairdresser (Mas and Vilagrassa 2005: 96) or Mammadou from Senegal who makes home deliveries for a supermarket in *Nou Nivell Bàsic*. There are very few situations in which economic problems or difficult living conditions are represented and when they are, it is by non-Western immigrant characters. For example, in the following excerpt taken from *Nou Nivell*

Bàsic 2, Mammadou, the aforementioned immigrant from Senegal, explains his arrival in Catalonia:

> *Em va costar molt trobar feina . . . Vaig viure uns quants anys a Barcelona amb uns amics senegalesos. Va ser una època bastant dura, perquè no tenia feina i no teníem prou diners per pagar el lloguer i comprar el menjar.*
>
> [It was very hard to find a job. . . . For a couple of years, I lived with my friends from Senegal in Barcelona. It was quite a difficult period because I didn't have a job and we didn't have enough money to pay the rent and buy food.]
>
> (Guerrero et al. 2010b: 58)

As a result, it seems that the few people who appear to be from a lower class in Catalan textbooks all come from non-Western countries, which might contribute to a sense of inferiority for non-Western newcomers in Catalan society and make these roles seem inevitable. The only exception to this approach is *Passos*, which includes working-class characters who are not only immigrants, but also Catalans. In this series Catalans have jobs as hairdressers, mechanics or shop assistants. One Catalan man, for example, explains the professions of his family members (Roig et al. 2011: 48, 50): His wife is a geriatric nurse, the older son is a mechanic, the next son studies and works in a bar and his youngest daughter does not have a job. In the same textbook, there is a text about Rosa, a disabled woman who sells lottery tickets (100).

Another series, *Fil per randa*, includes the only mention of a workers' strike I recorded in all the materials. On the first page of the unit entitled "I have problems" there is a drawing of a supermarket whose workers are on strike (Vilà and Homs 2013b: 140).

The shop remains open, but only a skeleton staff is working and there is a long queue of customers. In the speech clouds of the drawing, a customer shares her worry about the strike because she will be late to pick up her son from school. Another customer exclaims: "I will demand a complaint form. Many products are past their sell-by date". And another customer says to one of the employees who decided to work: "Don't worry dear. It's not your fault". The motives for the strike are not mentioned and it seems that the characters are not really interested in them. Instead, in the introductory activity that accompanies the drawing are: "How would you react when in a situation similar to that of the picture? Are you calm or do you get irritable if you have to wait in a line? Or do you think this depends on the day? What would be the reason for your reaction?". In order to comment on a labor strike, this textbook opts to present the point of view of the customer and not of the worker. Throughout the unit, there is no mention of workers' rights. On the contrary, the unit is based solely on the customers' rights with various activities in which the students learn how to fill in complaint forms.

116 *Social class in textbooks*

To sum up, the only appearance of a labor strike in the world of work in these textbooks seems to have the objective of teaching students the rights of consumers during or after the purchase of a product or a service. Students learn the ability to use their power as consumers to get what they want. As described by Wolfgang Fellner and Clive Spash (2014: 9) regarding contemporary capitalist societies, in my sample of Catalan textbooks any reference to class conflicts or to the economic structure of the society are suppressed.

In a similar fashion, more than two decades after the critical pedagogue Michael Apple (1993) pointed out that neoliberalism had transformed societies into vast supermarkets, the authors of *Nou Nivell Bàsic* decided to place the entire narrative action of their books in a supermarket, a symbol of the hyper-productivity and consumerism espoused by neoliberal capitalism. Furthermore, this series implicitly denies the inequality that exists in the real world. For example, in a dialogue between the workers and the directors of the chain of supermarkets accompanied by a drawing, we see the characters' interacting as equals, in a casual, cheerful atmosphere, with the majority of characters smiling (Guerrero et al. 2010a: 20). In a similar way, in the following dialogue between a cashier (James) and the supervisor (Santiago), we see a highly cordial conversation, much like one between close friends. This, despite the fact that the cashier has arrived late for work:

[Santiago:]	*Què t'ha passat?*
[James:]	*He resllicat quan sortia de la dutxa i m'he donat un cop al genoll.*
[Santiago:]	*Vaja, i et fa mal?*
[James:]	*No gaire, però m'hi ha sortit un blau.*
[Santiago:]	*Doncs jo ahir em vaig cremar amb la planxa, perquè va sonar el telèfon i no la vaig desendollar . . . M'ha sortit una butllofa. . . .*

[Santiago:	What happened to you?
James:	I slipped when I was getting out of the shower and I hurt my knee.
Santiago:	Oh, and does it hurt?
James:	Not much, but I have a bruise.
Santiago:	Well, just yesterday I burned myself with an iron because the phone rang and I didn't turn it off . . . I have a blister . . .]

(Guerrero et al. 2010b: 46)

The previous dialogue presents a conversation between a cashier and a supervisor as if the two parties were friends engaged in a conversation about everyday matters. The supervisor is acting not as a person in a position of power but as an equal – a situation highly unlikely to happen in a hierarchical occupational structure such as that of chain stores. It would be fair to say that these conversations might take place (during lunch breaks), but this is not the issue. The issue is that the textbooks only emphasize the positive aspects not just of working conditions but every other sphere of life, making their content completely unrealistic and yet always reminding us (the teachers and the students) that we are in a process of learning linguistic repertoires associated with the 'real life'.

As explained by Gray and Block (2014: 68), this erasure of social inequalities and the under-representation of working-class issues and characters in language textbooks must be understood "as part of a more general and profoundly ideological attempt at reconfiguring reality in such a way that the concept of class is seen as being redundant" in the era of neoliberalism. Philip Mirowski (2013: 117) summarizes the neoliberal doctrine regarding social classes as follows:

> The rich and the poor have become so evanescent as mental categories that they are rarely ever accorded the right to occupy space in the real world. The rich are continually quoted as not feeling "really" rich, while the poor are cued to deny that they are poor, to avoid opprobrium. If they confess to poverty, they are examined for personal failings, rather than class membership.

Avoiding working-class topics and assuming the neoliberal mantra that 'there is no such thing as social class', textbooks do not help students consider or understand the ways that wealth is unequally distributed, or why some people are poor and others are embarrassingly rich. To sum up, the textbooks not only hide the social class structure, but also block the development of a class conscience among students of Catalan. To complete the introduction of the portrait of the content of Catalan textbooks that I shall further discuss in Chapters 7 and 8 in relation to the topics of work and housing, in the next section I will identify the principal types of texts and activities the textbooks use when dealing with the subjects of the world of work and housing.

Textual genres and activities about the world of work and housing

The world of work topic mainly utilizes the following types of texts: CVs, job interviews, job ads, business letters, letters of complaint, surveys about labor conditions, journalistic articles about work, advice from experts about how to start a business or how to prepare for a job interview, and finally dialogues about work between friends or colleagues. On the other hand, in the content related to housing, the most common texts are adverts for buying, selling or renting a house, dialogues between real estate agents and clients, descriptions of dwellings, rent contracts and leases, texts with expert opinions about buying, selling or renting a house or obtaining a loan

118   *Social class in textbooks*

or a mortgage, journalistic articles similar to those in magazines dedicated to home decor and opinions about housing issues.

Following the task-based communicative approach, the activities proposed by the materials have an explicitly instrumental purpose. Work-related content presents activities that consist of preparing for a job interview, writing CV's, elaborating and presenting business initiatives, setting up business projects, reading, commenting on, responding to or writing job ads and organizing the delivery of company goods. The activities related to the world of housing also have an instrumental purpose with a heavy emphasis on consuming, for example reading or writing ads to buy or rent a house or an apartment, simulating dialogues between real estate agents and clients, debating whether it is better to obtain a mortgage from the bank or rent, giving advice to future buyers or renters, calculating loan interest rates, creating ads for real estate agencies or writing texts for a home decor magazine.

Activities like writing a CV, a business project or an ad to rent or buy a property have been in fashion in language learning textbook content in recent decades, as these practical tasks have become a tool of survival in the world of late capitalism. Moreover, textbooks also include recommendations about how to adapt to the new work order or what to do in order to buy or rent a house. With these types of activities and texts the textbooks might contribute to building the roles of consumers and workers in students. On the other hand, these are not activities and texts in which the students are invited to critically reflect upon the socioeconomic context. Nor do they provide students with tools to combat the injustices and discrimination that exist in the neoliberal era.

Conclusion

All textbooks that were analyzed follow the task-based communicative approach to language learning and teaching. So, instead of making grammatical structures the center of their content, these textbooks claim, as stated in one of the textbooks, "to give students basic competences to get by in Catalan with a minimal level of autonomy in everyday contexts and situations and also to facilitate the learners' integration into the country" (CNLB 2011: 5). Inside this everyday and useful content that these textbooks transmit, the worlds of work and housing occupy an important space as the results of the quantitative analysis have shown.

In the content of these textbooks, almost everything is represented as a neoliberal fairytale in which economic growth, attractive cosmopolitan careers and expensive journeys appear together with new houses and apartments and cars. This is, of course, a reality out of reach for a large portion of the world's population, to say nothing of the majority of Catalan language students, especially those who are poor and working-class immigrants. The textbooks emphasize the good, rich life of Catalan citizens and their capacity to consume. They also emphasize all the possible lifestyles of upper-middle class men and women, creating an idealized picture of Catalonia as a country where everybody lives a happy life. It seems that poverty, if it exists, is reserved for the so-called third world, and that inside Catalonia there are no economic divisions and unequal wealth distribution. The people of Catalonia live in a society where everybody is taken care of. And if by any chance, someone is sacked from his/her job, it is his/her fault. However, those who lose their jobs need not worry; they will find a new and better one.

The students using these textbooks will learn how to write CVs and simulate job interviews as well as how to conduct negotiations with their bank, which will provide them with a loan or a mortgage. They will also learn how to prepare business projects and different kinds of ads. With this clear instrumental purpose to language education, in which the tasks of the neoliberal economic and social order are taught and practiced, these textbooks provide no space for students to question any of these practices. In addition, no reasons are provided as to why language learners have to learn them the way that they do. The only explanation given by the authors is that they 'represent real life' and that their content is 'meaningful'. By choosing to present only the practical side of human endeavor and making invisible other important parts of human expression, such as literature, art or philosophy, these pedagogical tools become nothing more than manuals on how to become a good capitalist citizen. To form a more in-depth critique of the neoliberal ideology that appears in textbooks, the next two chapters will provide a further analysis of the content related to work and housing from a political-economic perspective.

Notes

1 Texts here refer to written or spoken words within textbooks, not to images or pictures. However, in the qualitative analysis of this study I will take into account not only the verbal texts but also the visual ones when they are relevant for the purpose of the research.
2 In this study, social class erasure refers to a tendency in textbooks not to present characters and issues of different social classes. This fact is in line with the neoliberal ideology which aims to get people to believe that social class is not relevant anymore and that there isn't any existing conflict based on different class interests.
3 The culture-ideology of consumerism is a concept developed by Leslie Sklair which refers to the spread of consumerism in all spheres of life in the era of capitalist globalization. Its aim is "to persuade people to consume above their 'biological needs' in order to perpetuate the accumulation of capital for private profit" (Sklair 1998: 3). According to Sklair (2002: 166), consumerism consists mainly of creating what he calls "induced wants". Tourism is one paradigmatic example of these 'induced wants', in which "the advertising profession and tourism industry continually tells us we need" (Higgins-Desbiolles 2010: 122).

7 The world of work
Constructing an entrepreneurial identity

Introduction

This chapter presents the results of the qualitative analysis of the textbook content related to work. In the framework proposed by the communicative approach to language education in which the emphasis is on practical goals and everyday life, the world of work has become one of the key topics in textbooks for learning languages. Indeed, in the first efforts by the Council of Europe to develop a communicative method for language learning in the 1970s, one of the main objectives was to help immigrant and guest workers incorporate themselves into the new labor market of the European countries they were coming to, as explained in Chapter 2. Four decades later, language education continues to be oriented towards the training of workers in order to develop more competitive economies. In current language textbooks, the world of work tends to have a central place (Gray 2010a).

The application of the neoliberal capitalist labor model in Western countries since the 1980s has led to major insecurity and precariousness in the world of work. In Spain, for example, the seven labor reforms that have been implemented over the last few decades (1984, 1994, 1997, 2001, 2006, 2010 and 2012) represented the renunciation of the earlier objectives of full employment and permanent contracts.[1] They all debilitated the working class and gave more and more power to the employers (Ruiz 2006; Otxoa 2007). These reforms have promoted temporary and part-time jobs, internship contracts and offers by private agencies of temporary work. They also broadened the grounds for dismissals and reduced the duration and amount of unemployment aid. Neoliberal labor reforms have been approved by Social Democratic and Conservative governments with the (eventual) support of the two main Spanish trade unions. The latter organized massive strikes against labor reforms in the 1980s and the early 1990s. However, in recent years, they have accepted neoliberal labor policies, giving their support to the 1997 and 2006 labor reforms (Otxoa 2007). In other words, the two biggest Spanish unions have accepted measures that prioritize and promote a flexible job market.

The world of work 121

The latest labor reform was passed by the conservative government in 2012 without any negotiation with the unions. It was approved at a time when the economic downturn initiated in 2007–2008 reached its peak. The law was adopted under the pressure from international institutions and organizations such as the European Central Bank, the European Commission and the International Monetary Fund, the so-called Troika. The reform made dismissals easier and cheaper, weakened sector-wide collective agreements and gave companies more flexibility to reduce salaries or increase working hours if their competitiveness and productivity depended upon it. The spirit of the latest labor reforms in Spain is based on the concept of 'flexicurity' promoted by neoliberal theorists and political leaders to deal with the greater precariousness in the job market. This new paradigm is explained by Francesco Di Bernardo (2016: 12) in the following words:

> Flexicurity is based on the idea of providing workers a moderate degree of social security, particularly in assisting workers moving from one job to another and supporting them financially in this phase, while preserving the 'flexibility' of the job market.

Although it is presented as helping workers in response to declining job security, flexicurity represents the promotion of employers' interests, the elimination of state employment protection and the legitimation of casual labor contracts (Di Bernardo 2016).

Neoliberal labor reforms in Western countries have led to the creation of 'a reserve army' of labor (Marx 1976 [1867]: 781–94) consisting of millions of unemployed and millions of people working under different kinds of precarious conditions, especially young people and immigrants. After the start of the 2007–2008 crisis, Spanish unemployment grew rapidly surpassing 26 percent in 2013 according to governmental data (INE 2016a), which meant that more than 5 million people were officially without a job. In recent years, Spanish unemployment has reduced slightly, but temporary work has also increased. In 2016, for example, only one of every 20 new contracts was for a full-time job (Garrido 2016).

A recent report by the Catholic charity Caritas (Fundación Foessa 2016) states that 15 percent of Spanish workers live in conditions of poverty, which means that one out of six workers in Spain is poor. The situation is even worse among the unemployed: the poverty rate of those without a job stands at 44.8 percent (Fundación Foessa 2016). These high rates of poverty mean that a lot of people in Spain don't have sufficient income for making a living, either because they don't work or they have a poorly paid job. The precariousness of the Spanish labor market is the result of a neoliberal political economy that during recent decades has done very little to fight unemployment and to create better working and living conditions for the working classes. With this in mind, this chapter will now go on to identify

122 *The world of work*

and comment on the representation in Catalan textbooks of neoliberal values and practices in the world of work.

Flexibility

The theme of labor flexibility, one of the main characteristics of the neoliberal world of work, was recorded in all collections of textbooks. Robert Sennet (1998: 57–8) suggested that flexibility in the workplace was fueled in the mid-twentieth century by the rise of "more middle-class women" into the workforce, who joined poor and working-class women "who were already employed in lower-level service and manufacturing jobs". These working women needed more flexible timetables to combine part-time work and full-time parental obligations (Sennet 1998: 58). However, with the advent of the neoliberal economy, 'flexible labor' quickly spread throughout the entire world of work and in recent decades flexibility has become a characteristic associated with both female and male employment.

In one of the most frequent textual genres related to work in Catalan textbooks – the job interview – flexibility usually appears as a precondition for getting a job, whether it is timetable flexibility (Vilà and Homs 2013b: 14) or the willingness to work extra hours (Vilà and Homs 2013b: 18). As we see in the following example from one of the books of the Barcelona Center for Linguistic Normalization, the interviewer demands work-time flexibility as a non-negotiable condition from the candidate in order to get a job:

- *Bona tarda, he llegit el seu anunci i m'agradaria treballar aquí.*
- *Ha treballat alguna vegada en una botiga?*
- *Sí, com a dependenta a la botiga de comestibles de la meva família, a Roses.*
- *I en algun bar o restaurant?*
- *També, els estius faig de cambrera.*
- *Busquem una persona que tingui flexibilitat horària, perquè nos sempre hi ha feina. A vegades hi ha molta gent i, a vegades, gens.*
- *A mi ja em va bé. Puc treballar en règim de torns, a temps parcial o només el cap de setmana, com prefereixin.*
- *I quan pot començar?*
- *Puc venir demà mateix.*

[– Good afternoon, I have read your announcement and I would like to work here.
- Have you ever worked in a store?
- Yes, as a shop assistant in my family's food store in Roses.
- And how about bars or restaurants?
- Yes, I also work as a waitress during the summer season.
- We are looking for someone to be flexible with working hours because there isn't work all the time. Sometimes there are more people, sometimes less.

The world of work 123

–   I'm fine with that. I can work in shifts, part-time or even only on week-
    ends, whichever you prefer.
–   And when can you start?
–   Tomorrow.]

(CNLB 2008a: 157)

In the example above, work-time flexibility is presented as a positive thing
not only for the interviewer but for the job applicant as well, who demonstrates the willingness to work at times convenient to the employer without
showing any concern. I have also identified the ability/willingness to be flexible as a habitual practice in dialogues between friends. For example, Joan,
one of the characters in *Fil per randa*, explains to a friend that he works
long hours and weekends (Vilà and Homs 2013a: 48). He himself admits
that this practice is tiresome but he is not complaining about it because of
the money he earns: 2,500 euros net per month. Therefore, the ability to be
flexible confers advantages on the employee.

One of the few negative representations of labor flexibility was identified
in the dialogue between two friends in *Fil per randa*:

–   *Ei, Pau, què fem?*
–   *Bé, però estic fart de les pràctiques! Treballo el dissabte i el diumenge
    de vuit a dues i de tres a vuit i em paguen una misèria!*
–   *Uf . . ., són moltes hores en dos dies. A més, treballar el cap de set-
    mana . . . Tan poc et paguen?*
–   *Quatre-cents euros al mes! I durant la setmana vaig de cul amb la uni!
    Ja no tinc vida social!*

[–   Hey, Pau, how are you doing?
–   Fine, but I am fed up with this internship! I work on Saturday and on
    Sunday, from eight to two and from three to eight, and they pay me a
    tiny wage!
–   That's awful . . ., that's a lot of hours in two days. And what's more,
    you work on weekends. . . . They really pay you so little?
–   Four hundred euros a month! And during the week I'm up to my eye-
    balls in work at the university! I don't have a social life anymore!]

(Vilà and Homs 2013a: 48)

Pau, the student from the above dialogue, in contrast to the characters from
previous examples, is complaining about his work, his timetable and his low
salary. So, in this dialogue flexibility as a neoliberal practice does not appear
in a positive light. Indeed, it is worth mentioning this example because it
presents flexibility from a negative perspective, a fact that is highly unusual
in the textbooks analyzed since they almost always follow the storyline of
neoliberal rhetoric that associates flexibility with ever-greater personal freedom, self-fulfillment and better social and economic expectations. Despite

124 *The world of work*

all its promises, the emphasis on flexibility in the new work order, together with short-term contracts and labor instability has, in reality, created a growing disorientation and anxiety among many workers (Sennet 1998).

Labor flexibility and adaptability also appear when various characters from textbooks explain how they adapted themselves to work in a line of business unrelated to their university qualifications. Thus, we meet a journalist who works as a secretary (Mas and Vilagrassa 2005: 25), a psychologist who works as a supermarket stocker (Guerrero et al. 2010a: 58), another psychologist who works as a saleswoman, a musician who works as a truck driver (Roig et al. 2011: 91) and an architect who works as a shop assistant, first in a clothing store and then selling furniture (DGPL 2008: Bàsic 2, Unit 3, 1.10). Highly educated men and women take low paying jobs in which they cannot use their university qualifications. These so-called skills mismatches are also one of the consequences of the neoliberal work order. However, not one of these 'mismatched' workers in the textbooks expresses any concerns about this situation. For example, the visual images of the 'overqualified' workers from the supermarket in *Nou Nivell Bàsic* often portray them as smiling and happy. When an individual doing an MA in journalism is asked if he still works as a cashier at the supermarket, he responds: "Yes, I still work there, and to tell you the truth I really like it" (Guerrero et al. 2010a: 81).

Not being able to find work related to one's university degree or other qualifications is not seen as an anomaly in the world of work. It is presented as a natural phenomenon, to which the textbook characters do not express surprise or outrage. In this sense, these materials at least acknowledge this reality in contemporary capitalist societies. However, they do not make any reference to the consequences that the practice of job mismatching has on workers such as stress, constant job switching or disaffection (Kalleberg 2007). There are no references to be found about the economic system which has provoked and is using this practice in order to build up and sustain its own competitiveness.

Indeed, one of the few times we see workers complaining is when they talk about their low salaries. For example, one shop assistant complains of earning 500 euro per month (DGPL 2008: Bàsic 2, Unit 3, 1.17). However, the characters never explain how they came to be in these situations or comment on the political and economic circumstances that caused them. Some teachers may argue that it might be difficult to discuss political or economic issues with students who are at beginner levels. However, we should also take into account that, although their language knowledge is limited, students have the capacity to think deeply, and even with little language knowledge they may be able to express their opinions and feelings about this issue. Surely, they have their points of view about working conditions, enriched by their background and lived experiences. In short, I am of the view that the limited language proficiency of learners should not be an excuse to avoid 'problematic' issues in language classrooms and to underestimate students' intellectual capacities.

Mobility

Another type of flexibility that appears in textbooks as an indispensable prerequisite for a job is mobility, meaning among other things location flexibility, which presumes the willingness to relocate for a job, as illustrated in the following job interview from *Fil per randa*:

- Té experiència com a banquer en empreses estrangeres?
- Sí, fa molts anys que m'hi dedico i he treballat a Londres, a Zuric i a Nova York. Els detalls apareixen al currículum que els he deixat.
- Ho dic perquè a la plaça a la qual vol accedir és molt important ser flexible i estar disposat a canviar de ciutat sovint.
- Miri, de fet, és precisament per la falta de mobilitat en altres bancs que he decidit buscar feina a la seva entitat. Com deu haver vist, tinc molt bones referències ja que sempre estava ben considerat quan he deixat una feina per assolir un nou repte professional.

[- Do you have experience working as a banker in foreign companies?
- Yes, I have been working as a banker for many years and I worked in London, Zurich and New York. The details appear in my CV, which I've given you.
- I ask you this because in the job position for which you applied it is very important to be flexible and well-disposed to moving from one city to another often.
- You see, it's precisely because of the lack of mobility in other banks that I've decided to look for a job in your firm. As you can see I have very good references and have always been considered a good employee when leaving job positions to cope with new professional challenges.]

(Vilà and Homs 2013b: 18)

In this example, mobility is presented as a desirable labor practice, not only on the part of the company, but also on the part of the future employee who demonstrates his desire to frequently move to other countries. Furthermore, it is also interesting to note that this worker positions himself as an ideal neoliberal worker, which includes his willingness to constantly change jobs and 'to cope with new professional challenges'. With the emergence of the 'risk society' (Beck 1992), workers are increasingly encouraged by employers to be risk-takers who eschew stability and long-term commitment but pursue self-investment and innovation.

Another example of mobility is found in the words of a Catalan scientist from *Veus 3* who worked in a medical laboratory in her home country, but now has to go to work in Switzerland because the funding for scientific research in Catalonia is insufficient (Mas and Vilagrassa 2008: 125). She is an example of the many workers with advanced degrees in the era of neoliberalism who are forced to relocate because there are no job prospects

126   *The world of work*

where they live. Although the character expresses sorrow for having to leave her home country, the job change seems a natural process to her. There is no mention of the reasons why Catalonia cannot support scientists and give them a chance to work in their own country, unlike in other countries such as Switzerland (or the UK or the United States).

Parla.cat dedicates an entire unit to workplace mobility, with the objective of teaching students how to prepare for a business trip. The main character in the unit is Ralko, a salesman from Holland who travels to Majorca on business. Apart from Ralko, we also get to know other characters (a singer and a university professor) who also travel for work. In a dialogue where these three meet, Ralko sums up his job using these words: "I think that the best things about my job are the journeys and contacts with the clients. The hardest part is working the whole day, from breakfast to dinner" (DGPL 2008: Elemental 1, Unit 2, 2.10). The entire unit is full of examples of the importance of mobility, together with a work ethic that sees long working hours as unproblematic. For example, in a test under the title "Are you a professional traveler?" there are options such as "I take a plane three or four times a week", or "I almost never watch the movies on the plane. I prefer working on my laptop" (DGPL 2008: Elemental 1, Unit 2, 2.12).

The only negative perspective about labor mobility is identified in the commentary of a man who has been working for five years and has lived in 10 different places. He compares his situation with those of his parents and grandparents who always lived and worked in the same place and defines his labor mobility as "chaos!" (Mas and Vilagrassa 2008: 125). This character, unlike the others in these textbooks, does not consider location flexibility as something desirable and natural.

Zero drag

In the neoliberal era, employers are increasingly looking for employees with zero drag, meaning workers who are infinitely flexible, adaptable and disposable. This type of worker appears, for example, in a listening exercise where different characters are responding to job advertisements (Anguera et al. 2010a: 25). In one of the dialogues, a woman who wants a job as a teacher does not feel that relocating or working late at night is an inconvenience. In another dialogue, the candidate looking for a job as a truck driver is more than happy to spend a couple of nights away from home, and travel to Paris or London. Moreover, for the job of truck driver, the employer also demands a good command of foreign languages, another characteristic of work in neoliberal times. Because of the high levels of unemployment, companies can ask for better training and university degrees from people applying for manual jobs.

Characters in textbooks also do not find any inconvenience when it comes to changing jobs, as can be seen in a personal account from a character that has changed jobs, extracted from one of the textbooks from the Barcelona Center for Linguistic Normalization:

He fet d'infermera durant dos anys. El que més m'agrada era el tracte amb els pacients i el que menys, els canvis de torn. Ara faig de tècnica de laboratori i estic molt contenta amb l'horari. A més, guanyo el doble.

[I worked as a nurse for two years. What I liked best was working with patients and what I liked least was working different shifts. I now work as a technician in a lab, and I'm very happy with my schedule. What's more, I earn double.]

(CNLB 2008b: 66)

In the previous extract, we can identify two neoliberal practices: timetable flexibility and flexibility in changing jobs. The first is presented as negative: "what I liked least was working different shifts". And the second practice is seen as positive, reinforced with a photo of the main character smiling. In a listening exercise in the same textbook series, we again see job mobility and flexibility as a usual practice (CNLB 2011: 71). The first character is a Catalan woman working for a Japanese multinational corporation who decides to go and spend three years in the company's center in Tokyo. The second character is an operator in a factory who has been forced to take early retirement. The third is a self-employed woman who works in advertising and wants to take a year off. In all three cases, they are very positive about their situation. For example, although he was taken aback initially, the worker forced to retire early explains that "the truth is that I needed some free time and I am happy not to go to work and get my retirement paycheck at the end of the month". This positive representation of the change in someone's job situation and the risk involved is addressed in the following exercise in which different celebrities explain how the change was good for their lives and how it helped them become even more successful (CNLB 2011: 71). For example, we learn that the Catalan scientist Eduard Punset studied law at Harvard University, worked as an economist at the IMF and as an advisor to the Catalan Ministry of Finances. The change that is highlighted is that he left politics for scientific research, and later it is said that in 2011 he won the *Creu de Sant Jordi* (the Cross of Saint George), a prestigious award for life achievements, sponsored by the Catalan government. This disposition for change and the risk that it brings is a characteristic encouraged by neoliberalism and also appears in English textbooks (Gray 2010b), especially if the change serves to find a job which brings personal fulfillment.

In the collection *Fil per randa*, which proportionally has more work-related content than the other books in my dataset, job loss is repeatedly seen as an opportunity and not as a problem, as is illustrated in the following dialogue, in which one of the interlocutors is happy to be out of work:

– *Hola, com estàs?*
– *Bé, força bé. Vinc d'una entrevista de feina i m'ha anat molt bé.*
– *Però, tu no treballaves en una companyia telefònica?*
– *Sí, de moment sí, però d'aquí a poc se m'acaba el contracte.*

128   *The world of work*

–   *Ostres, quina mala sort.*
–   *No! I ara! Prefereixo canviar de feina, la veritat.*

[–   Hi, how are you?
–   Well, very well. I've just come from a job interview and it went really well.
–   But I thought you were working for a telephone company . . .
–   Yes, for the moment, but my contract will expire soon.
–   Bummer, that's bad luck.
–   Oh, no! On the contrary! I would like to find a different job, really.]
(Vilà and Homs 2013b: 15)

The reaction to losing a job in the example above is in line with the neoliberal economic utopia where job insecurity and uncertainty are "celebrated as 'liberating' transformations" (Zimmerman 2008: 233). In a similar fashion, in the following dialogue in this same textbook, losing a job is not seen as a real problem, but more as a fortunate event. When one of the people in the dialogue discovers that one of his old colleagues has lost his job he says: "I'm sure you'll find a new one quickly. It might even be a better one!" (Vilà and Homs 2013b: 15). There is yet another similar dialogue following this one. A worker accepts his layoff as something natural and which was foreseen, without expressing any kind of worry, anger or doubt. His words in the text are: "Don't worry, I've been expecting it" (Vilà and Homs 2013b: 18). The only negative representation of losing a job I found is a drawing of a man who has just lost his job with his head down and his hands on his head (Vilà and Homs 2013b: 16). If we bear in mind the massive layoffs and the difficulties that people were having finding a job in Catalonia at the time this collection was published, it seems that *Fil per randa*, like other textbooks, opted not to present a realistic portrait of Catalan society. Obviously, unemployment and precarious working conditions are nothing new in capitalist countries, but the labor situation has further worsened since the 2007–2008 crisis, also impacting wider sectors of the middle class:

> In large parts of the labor market, employment has become less secure and the low-wage sector has expanded in many countries. Together with high levels of unemployment, this has resulted in an increase in precarious living conditions. While precarity has always existed on the margins of society, it is now more widespread, expanding the zones of vulnerability and insecurity.
> (Flecker et al. 2017: 8)

One of the best-known neoliberal practices to combat unemployment is to demand that workers constantly re-train themselves in order to adapt to market necessities. This practice is known as lifelong learning or 'self-programmable labor' (Castells 2000). Lifelong learning has been in vogue in all important EU official documents concerning education since the late 1990s (Mitchell 2006). The goal behind this practice is to prepare individuals for the changing labor market. In textbooks, this practice is also frequently presented, as we shall see in the next section.

Lifelong learning

In Catalan textbooks, lifelong learning is usually presented as a solution for the unemployed. For example, Koldo, one of the characters of *Curs de català bàsic B2* from the Barcelona Center for Linguistic Normalization, explains to his friend Joana that when he lost his job he immediately started a course in occupational training (CNLB 2008b: 69). Even though Koldo still does not work, this situation is not presented as problematic because Joana assures him that he will surely find a job. Meanwhile, Joana recounts to Koldo her labor experience in recent months. She decided to leave her old job in a supermarket six months earlier and is now working for an advertising agency. In Joana's story, we can see an individual willing to risk changing jobs in order to find one that will be personally fulfilling, something that neoliberal ethics encourages. The result, in this case, is positive because Joana has found a better job in an advertising agency. Furthermore, the experience of Joana gives us the impression that to change a job is a very easy choice: she left the old one because she was tired of it and found a new position relatively quickly, which is a very idealized vision of job switching if we bear in mind that the long-term unemployment rate in Spain has affected more than 10 percent of the working-age population since 2012 (INE 2016b).

Similarly, in the following dialogue between two friends from another textbook of the Barcelona Center for Linguistic Normalization retraining is explained as an opportunity for the unemployed to open their own business:

Mirta: *Ah, doncs, jo ara que sóc a l'atur vull aprofitar per estudiar i posar-me al dia.*

Nora: *Molt bé! Jo, quan vaig estar aturada, vaig fer un curs de dones emprenedores de 300 hores i em va anar genial. Mira, sis mesos després vaig obrir l'empresa que tinc ara.*

[Mirta: Oh, well, since I am unemployed now I want to use the time to study and get myself up to date.

Nora: Great! When I was unemployed I took a course for women entrepreneurs that lasted 300 hours and it was great. Look, six months later I opened my own firm.]

(CNLB 2011: 105)

The perspective towards lifelong learning in the example above is clearly positive. We notice it from the cheerful tone of the conversation coming

130 *The world of work*

from both interlocutors (although Mirta is unemployed) and from Nora's professional success. It is also interesting that we get no information about the process and the steps between point (a) taking a course, and point (b) opening one's own firm. Again, textbooks tend to present job switching as a very easy process.

In a unit in *Passos* dedicated to lifelong learning (Roig et al. 2011: 187–93), learners are given a menu of vocational courses which they can take in order to find a better job. In a conversation between Raquel and Gloria, we hear that Raquel, who worked as a part-time babysitter, is now taking an occupational course to become a geriatric assistant. The course is offered by a civic center, and she says it will give her the opportunity to have a job which includes pension and sickness benefits. In the examples of this textbook, lifelong learning refers to permanent adult education and the courses presented are conducted with the help of the state or non-governmental organizations. This textbook appears to promote the view that lifelong learning should be backed by the state through voluntarily accessible education for adults, as was the case formerly when free educational courses were regularly offered by the state (Tuschling and Engemann 2006). Today's concept of lifelong learning in which the individual learner creates spaces for learning aligns to some extent with older iterations of education. Both concepts stress the need for a self-reflective, self-responsible individual who accesses education as a vehicle for liberation. What has changed, however, is the role of the state, which once had the obligation to provide funding for learning which was seen as a personal right, while now it forces its citizens to learn in order for their countries to keep up with the global economy (Biesta 2006).

Lifelong learning is not only presented as a solution for the unemployed. It is also seen as an opportunity for students to gain specialized training and is often offered by their companies. One of the textbooks explains that universities offer their students training in companies, which is seen by the students as a very positive practice because they can demonstrate their "value to the company" or because it gives "added value" to their curriculum (CNLB 2011: 70).

Self-branding

Apart from constant training and flexibility, another prerequisite for fitting into the new work order in neoliberal times that I found in textbooks is self-branding. For example, in *Català Elemental* there are four short fragments from answers to job interview questions from which students are to construct appropriate questions. In the responses offered, we can identify the candidates' spirit of self-branding in sentences such as the following: "I am a resolute, decisive person with initiative, things that I find important when it comes to being an accountant. And I have an MBA from the University of Manchester" (Campoy et al. 2011: 188). Lifelong learning and personal commitment to the future company also appear in these answers. One of the candidates says: "I would like to take an MA in Business Management; in that way my education would be more complete, and I could be more engaged in the management tasks of the firm" (188).

The journalist in the following excerpt from *Veus 3* is also an example of a self-branded worker, as she shows passion for work, flexibility and the willingness to innovate:

> *Sóc periodista i he treballat a diversos diaris i revistes. Cada un tenia avantatges que l'altre no tenia. Però a tots havia de fer un horari molt estricte i força absurd. Al final, m'he decidit! M'he fet autònom. Treballo des de casa i envio els articles per internet. És fantàstic!*
>
> [I'm a journalist and I have worked for various magazines and daily newspapers. Each of them offered advantages that others didn't have. But at all of them I had a strict and really absurd schedule. Finally, I decided! I became self-employed. I work from home and upload my articles on the internet. It's great!]
>
> (Mas and Vilagrassa 2008: 125)

This text promotes the idea of labor flexibility as the journalist criticizes her "strict and really absurd" timetable. This example also shows self-branding values in the willingness to change personal affiliations and adopt an entrepreneurial spirit, as the character decides to leave a job and become self-employed. In an enthusiastic tone and with the final exclamation ("It's great!") this text demonstrates a celebration of these neoliberal practices and values. The extract above is also an example of labor mobility through distance working, a practice growing in popularity due to the recent accelerated developments of information technology and the outsourcing and decentralization of production in the global economy. In the neoliberal era, both public and private enterprises are generally interested in having an increasing number of remote workers because this offers them more advantages than drawbacks:

> Such arrangements save money on offices, give a company access to a broader pool of talent (and retain women after childbearing), allow it to operate extended days, reduce office politics and colleague interruptions, and are more environmentally friendly. Drawbacks include lack of informal information sharing and less *esprit de corps*.
>
> (Standing 2011: 38)

Of course, 'telework' can also have many benefits for the workers, since it may offer a more comfortable way of working, particularly for those with family commitments or who live very far from their workplace. However, it should also be noted that working at a distance implies the complete individualization of the workers since, as Guy Standing (2011: 53) noted in *The Precariat*, this isolates employees and limits "their space and opportunity

132 *The world of work*

for collective action". Furthermore, remote jobs have also blurred former boundaries "between work and private life" (Flecker et al. 2017: 2) because the traditional physical spaces of the world of work such as the factory or the office no longer exist. Although these workers can organize their time as they see fit, working at a distance often implies that employees work longer and longer hours to earn better incomes and to show commitment to the company. All this may prepare "the ground for devotion and the self-exploitation of workers" and, ultimately, for the construction of the entrepreneurial identity required by the employers (Flecker et al. 2017: 15).

So far, we have seen that Catalan materials present very similar kinds of characters as those who appear in textbooks for learning English (Gray 2010b; Copley 2017) and French (Block and Gray 2018) (see Chapter 3). The typical character in contemporary language textbooks greatly resembles one who Michel Foucault (2008) would consider the ideal neoliberal subject and also called by Block (2018a) the 'neoliberal citizen'. In the work-related content in textbooks, this is the kind of individual who does not maintain long-term commitments, who is willing to take risks and engage in constant training, and who demonstrates entrepreneurship, self-branding and self-responsibility, as I will discuss with further examples in the next section.

Entrepreneurship and self-responsibility

In *Nou Nivell Bàsic*, a supermarket stocker plans to become a small business owner by opening her own jewelry shop (Guerrero et al. 2010c: 34), whereas a man who works as a courier at the same supermarket looks for a job in the IT sector (Guerrero et al. 2010c: 70) after having completed a course in IT. They both seem happy with their low paid jobs in the supermarket, but at the same time they aspire to better ones. The textbook appears to celebrate and encourage this attitude as witnessed by the general support that the two individuals receive from all their colleagues who encourage them to take the risk, leave their current job and look for a new one. Inside of this idealized work setting, it seems that finding another job or opening a business is the easiest task in the world. For example, when the supermarket supervisor discovers that his courier wants to quit his job and find a new one, he says: "Oh, very good! I'm sure you'll find another one immediately!" (Guerrero et al. 2010c: 70).

Català Elemental dedicates a whole unit to developing the entrepreneurial spirit among learners using the unit title "Help us! Let's start a business" (Campoy et al. 2011: 207–16). The first question this unit poses is: "Are you entrepreneurial?" (208). The question is followed by a questionnaire in which students see whether they have an entrepreneurial spirit or not. This is revealed after they comment on a series of 12 statements such as the following: "An entrepreneur [. . .] cannot stand to waste her/his time with unimportant things" (208). Later, there is a listening activity about a business center created to help young entrepreneurs with their ideas in order to promote private initiative (209). The unit continues by making students imagine starting their own business. Once they have chosen an idea, they should explain "the viability of the idea and the resources needed to start the business" (210). After deciding on the business idea they want to develop, the next step in this unit is to elaborate a business plan following an example of a business plan given by the textbook. Later, learners are asked to explain their ideas in front of the class with other students suggesting ways to improve their business projects (211). Finally, there is a model of a business proposal from which students can improve their business plans and ideas (213).

Entrepreneurship and market competitiveness are as important to the neoliberal order as is individual responsibility. Dardot and Laval (2013: 290) explain this as follows:

> [N]eoliberal rationality produces a subject it requires by developing the means of governing him so that he really does conduct himself as an entity in a competition, who must maximize his results by exposing himself to risks and taking full responsibility for possible failures.

Textbooks also highlight the relevance of workers' individual responsibility in the new economic order, as for example in a dialogue between a head of a company and his employee who has recently been late for work because he has three little children and his mother-in-law in the hospital. Although his personal situation is complicated, his superior focuses on his lack of punctuality, and the employee completely agrees that it is definitely his own fault: "You are right. This has happened because of my lack of planning. The situation with my mother-in-law has taken us by surprise. I am asking you to forgive me" (Vilà and Homs 2013b: 153). The answer of this character is a model of the ideal attitude that a submissive employee should have towards the neoliberal work order: he recognizes his individual responsibility and apologizes for something that obviously is not his fault. Another example of self-responsibility featured in textbooks is related to the issue of workplace safety, as we shall see in the next section.

Risk management

The notion of risk has changed in the current neoliberal phase of capitalism because the state is increasingly tightly linked to the market, which directs the behavior of the state, society and individuals. In the workplace, as Garry Gray (2009: 326) explains, states (and firms) are less and less responsible for workplace safety, and they have transferred this responsibility onto individuals:

> Workplace safety is undergoing a process of 'responsibilization'. While employers have traditionally been the target of health and safety law,

134 *The world of work*

workers are increasingly assigned greater responsibility for their own safety at work and are held accountable, judged, and sanctioned through this lens.

Related to risk management lies another important practice and that is self-regulation, which includes "strict abstention from dangerous practices, constant self-control, and a regulation of one's own behaviour that blends asceticism and flexibility" (Dardot and Laval 2013: 186). The evolution of responsibility and risk management in the workplace goes hand in hand with the neoliberal attributes of "autonomous, self-determined, and self-sustaining subjects" (Shamir 2008: 380) who should be responsible for all spheres of their lives, from education and work to their retirement. In the words of Michael Peters (2001:61): "The duty to the self – its simultaneous responsibilisation as a moral agent and its construction as a calculative rational choice actor – becomes the basis for a series of investment decisions concerning one's health, education, security, employability, and retirement".

Treatment of risk management is evident in several textbooks. *Passos* dedicates an entire unit to occupational risks (Roig and Daranas 2011: 58–67). It starts with a text from the Spanish Construction Association about occupational risks and hazards in which students are given the definitions of occupational risks, accidents and illnesses and what is to be done to prevent them. The text states that "prevention means acting responsibly by the company and the worker respectively in order to avoid accidents. Prevention means being informed" (60). This definition situates workers and employers with shared responsibility towards work safety. However, as pointed out by Garry Gray (2009: 326) despite the apparent equality in what he calls "the neo-liberal discourse of 'equal partnership'" between workers and employers, the responsibility falls more heavily on the workers because of their "direct exposure" to the unsafe working conditions. Later, the unit gives advice on how to promote individual responsibility in order to minimize labor-related risks. There are recommendations on how to lift a heavy object safely in nine steps with pictures (62), and what to do in order to avoid accidents at a construction site, accompanied by a picture of a bricklayer (63).

Much like an imitation safety-at-work manual, the textbook continues with instructions for waiters and cooks on how to prevent work-related risks. There is an exercise with a table called "risks in the kitchen" that students are to fill in, with columns related to explaining and defining the risk, naming the type of injury and finally how to prevent it (65). Later, there is a text taken from a daily newspaper which explains an accident that happened to workers in a medical center in Tarragona. The case involved a nurse named Carmentxu Atin and 22 of her colleagues, who had to give up their jobs due to severe health problems arising from having been poisoned by the inhalation of chemicals following a "fumigation conducted by the company" (66). The text explains the state Carmentxu is in and what kind

The world of work   135

of life she has lead since the accident. However, the nurses' employer was not to blame, according to the text. In the activity which follows, students complete a table in which once again they themselves have to explain the risks described in the text and the possible prevention. In the final task of the unit, students are asked to think of all the means of prevention for various types of occupations and write them down (67).

Nou Nivell Elemental also dedicates space to occupational risks with examples of professions and the risks they entail, followed by a newspaper article on farmers not being responsible enough when it comes to preventing risks and two short personal accounts about accidents that have happened or can happen (Anguera et al. 2010a: 27–9). In all texts dedicated to risk, there is an emphasis above all on personal responsibility and company-worker collaboration when it comes to finding solutions. The state, local government and unions are mentioned only as intermediaries between workers and employers, whose job is to draw up regulations to ensure that individual responsibility is exercised.

The examples cited here suggest that these textbooks are in line with the neoliberal policies of the individualization of responsibility and promote the self-regulation practices related to safety at work. The European Agency for Safety and Health at Work Report (2013) features a slogan that seems to fit perfectly with the textbooks' treatment of this topic: "Safety and health at work is everyone's concern. It's good for you. It's good for business." (EU-OSHA 2013: 1). Responsibility for one's personal safety without a doubt has its benefits. However, the apparent equality which is stressed here between the worker and the employer in the matter of safety at work can also mean that the state no longer has any responsibility for the well-being of the workers. It is now a matter of 'self-responsibilisation', whereby the state gives way to the corporate-backed economy, such that individuals are no longer protected by the state. In the case of these units, safety and avoiding danger are notions that have more to do with the individual workers than with the state and the social system establishing mechanisms for their protection.

Other textbooks do not treat the topic of occupational risks this extensively. However, they all have units related to health and well-being, which are mostly dedicated to personal 'responsibilization' for being healthy and accident free. Furthermore, as I have already explained in this chapter, these textbooks also emphasize lifelong learning and entrepreneurship as practices in which self-responsibility is a key to managing the uncertainty and risks related to the new work order.

An important role in the process of configuring a neoliberal identity for the working world is played by managerial discourse and texts such as those in self-help guides for success, written by the so-called experts in subjectivity (Fogde 2007). The 'expertise in subjectivity' is a concept developed by Nikolas Rose (1990) who argues that these new professionals base their social authority upon "their capacity to understand the psychological aspects of

136 *The world of work*

the person and to act upon them, or to advise others what to do" (3). In the work order, the experts in subjectivity include career counselors, job consultants, occupational psychologists and personnel managers. As we shall see in the next section, the experts in subjectivity are also featured in the work-related content in textbooks.

Expert knowledge

In neoliberal times, states (and companies) have shifted the responsibility of finding a job to individuals, who are now responsible for becoming entrepreneurial, flexible and self-branded workers in order to retain their job or get a new one. Textbooks include several texts by experts, such as job consultants and career coaches, with advice on achieving success in increasingly competitive, changing and insecure work settings. In *Nou Nivell Bàsic 3*, there is a text from a website addressed to workers, employers and future professionals where learners can read expert advice related to work, such as for example how to ask for an increase in salary or how to create their own business (Guerrero et al. 2010c: 74). This text is accompanied by a picture with three elegantly dressed business men and women smiling in front of a laptop, which presents the idealization of the new work order.

In a similar vein, in *Fil per randa*, a psychologist gives advice to the unemployed suggesting how to manage future job opportunities:

> *Tu, com tothom, al llarg de la vida has conegut moltes persones. Fes això: apunta'n unes quantes, les més importants, en llistes per temes, llocs. . . . Quines són les persones que es repeteixen més? Identifica'n deu o dotze. Ara no tens feina, fa temps que en busques, però aquestes persones es poden convertir en els teus contactes. Ho pots comprovar avui mateix.*
>
> [Like the rest of us, you have met a lot of different people during your life. Try to do this: make a list of some of them, the most important ones, by topics, places. . . . Which people appear most? Identify ten or twelve of them. You don't have a job now, you have been looking for one for a long time, but these people can become your contacts. You can try that out today.]
>
> (Vilà and Homs 2013b: 88)

Once again, in the previous example, the textbook highlights the simplicity of the process of finding a job. It seems that if one follows this exercise, she/he will become employed as if by magic! Moreover, this text suggests that the responsibility to look for a job depends solely on individuals and should be considered part of the self-managing entrepreneurial process. It is also interesting to note that sometimes the textbooks' authors take on the role of experts in the new work order. For example, they give advice to learners on how to get ready for a job interview, such as to prepare a script beforehand with all the possible questions and to make sure to answer all of the questions (Campoy et al. 2011: 189), not to swear (Vilà and Homs 2013b: 89), to look the interviewer in the eye (DGPL 2008: Bàsic 3, Unit 6, 2.7), or "to be on time, wear proper clothes and explain with certainty what you want" (CNLB 2008b: 68). Similarly, in a final task of writing a job announcement for the student's imagined company, textbooks authors also give advice to students on how to make their advertising campaign more successful: "The advertisements serve to convince. So, you have to present the company as important, one that can help both workers and other companies!" (Vilà and Homs 2013b: 19).

Contemporary techniques to find a job

The neoliberal work order also encourages the manufacturing of a self-employable worker through training techniques such as how to write a CV or how to prepare for a job interview (Fogde 2007). These practices are found in all textbooks and are usually preceded by activities such as reading and commenting on job ads, writing letters of application or reading and listening to recommendations from advisers on how to get a proper job. Like the managerial texts, these kinds of activities seek to enhance to students' employability in neoliberal times.

A typical unit introducing these practices can be found in *Català Elemental* under the title "Interview for a new job" (Campoy et al. 2011: 179–92). The unit starts with a one-page photo of an unemployment office and a line of people (179). In one of the first activities there are a number of job ads (for an administrative worker, hairdresser, salesman, secretary, cashier and air hostess) that students are invited to analyze according to certain criteria and skills, such as knowing languages or having a drivers' license or owning a vehicle, and whether these are important for obtaining the jobs published in the ads (182). The job ads give brief descriptions of the person who would fit the position advertised. After this activity, learners are asked to prepare a job ad. Later, there is a model of a CV listing personal information, education and work experience (183). Students are then asked to write their own CV (184). The unit continues with a model and instructions to write a letter of application (185), also one of the typical steps in the process of finding a job in contemporary working life. Next, students are asked to comment on their experience of job interviews and how they should prepare themselves for an interview (186). This exercise continues with an activity in which students fill in their suggestions on how to perform well at a job interview. After that, they compare their own suggestions with those given by an expert that they listen to in another activity. The text below presents the expert's advice on what needs to be done to be successful in a job interview:

> *En la salutació i la presentació, cal donar la mà d'una manera decidida i cordial. Convé mostrar amabilitat i somriure. Procura evitar ser el primer de parlar. Convé esperar que l'entrevistador prengui la iniciativa.*

138 *The world of work*

[When introducing and presenting yourself you need to shake hands in a decisive and cordial manner. It is advisable to show friendliness and to smile. Try to avoid being the first one to talk. It is best to wait for the interviewer to take the initiative.]

(Campoy et al. 2011: 186)

Finally, after reading answers to job interview questions and a list of instructions about how to get ready for a job interview, students do a simulation of a real job interview with one group of learners posing as interviewers and another as job applicants (190).

The textbooks from the Barcelona Center for Linguistic Normalization include two work-related units with similar approaches. In one of them, there are four job ads, two pages of preparation for a job interview and an activity in which one student acts as an interviewer and the other as a job candidate (CNLB 2008a: 157–8). The other unit is dedicated to showing learners how to write a CV, a job application and what to do in a job interview (CNLB 2008b: 65–77). In *Fil per randa* there are also two units in which students use a similar set of exercises, from reading and writing CV's, motivational letters and job ads to a simulation of a job interview. The first unit is called "On work" (Vilà and Homs 2013a: 44–55) and the other one is "I have a job interview" (Vilà and Homs 2013b: 8–19).

As a whole, these units not only aim to teach the language and to show students how the new work order functions, but also seek to instruct students about how to become self-responsible individuals suitable to work in very flexible and competitive work settings. Language lessons, in this way, serve as one more link in the chain of neoliberal working practices, encouraging language students to conform to the pragmatics of job seeking in neoliberal times.

In that regard, the techniques for finding a job taught in Catalan textbooks resemble those proposed in job-guidance centers for immigrants, as in a center in Italy studied by Del Percio (2017). Professional counselors in this center teach newly arrived immigrants ways to become self-entrepreneurs to fit into a neoliberal work order characterized by labor flexibility and employment insecurity. The Italian center places an emphasis on teaching linguistic abilities to immigrants, such as how to read job announcements, how to write a CV or how to behave and communicate in a job interview. Del Percio (2017) suggests that these counseling practices do not help immigrants find a job, and actually contribute to maintaining the neoliberal rationality which dominates the current economic system.

Conclusion

The findings presented in this chapter suggest that Catalan textbooks tend to promote the neoliberal revival of *Homo economicus* (Peters 2001, 2016), constructing an entrepreneurial identity among learners. In the world of work, practices related to the entrepreneurial self (the ideal neoliberal citizen) usually appear in a positive, desirable and normalized way. The typical worker in Catalan language materials, similarly to their equivalent in global ELT textbooks (Gray 2010b), is one who has no commitments or attachments, is easily adaptable and adjustable to any kind of job condition, for whom insecurity is a form of a personal and professional challenge, while stability and lifelong security are outdated. The characters tend to show satisfaction with their work or are excited at the prospect of finding a new job. Labor conflicts or problems very rarely feature. Visual content reinforces the idealization of the neoliberal work order with several images of people smiling while working. In addition, the tasks in the textbooks require students to exercise their entrepreneurial spirit by having them imagine starting their own business or learning and developing techniques to find or maintain a job in a highly competitive, flexible and insecure labor market. The precarious working conditions and the high unemployment that affect many people in Catalonia, including immigrants (the main actual and potential group of learners), are very scarcely addressed in textbooks.

In concluding this chapter, it is worthwhile to highlight that the promotion of an entrepreneurial identity in textbooks is in line with the dominant discourse in Western societies in the era of neoliberalism. To demonstrate this point, I will focus on a report published by the European Commission (2012), called *Rethinking education: investing in skills for better socioeconomic outcomes*. It gives advice to European Union Members on what should be done to improve education in future years. According to this communication, entrepreneurship in education is crucial to increase productivity and assure future prosperity. Therefore, the European Commission calls for the incorporation of entrepreneurial skills into the curriculum at all levels:

> Member States should foster entrepreneurial skills through new and creative ways of teaching and learning from primary school onwards, alongside a focus from secondary to higher education on the opportunity of business creation as a career destination. Real world experience, through problem-based learning and enterprise links, should be embedded across all disciplines and tailored to all levels of education.
>
> (European Commission 2012: 4)

The proposal presents this educational reform as the solution to the major problem of unemployment in Europe. It states that all young people should have "at least one practical entrepreneurial experience before leaving compulsory education" (European Commission 2012: 4) and cites as an example of good educational practice the participation of entrepreneurs from private businesses in classrooms (European Commission 2012: 11). Together with entrepreneurship, the European Commission (2012) calls for the mobility of students, the adjustment of educational outcomes to the new requirements of the economy and to increase the partnerships between private and public institutions in education, which is in line with the neoliberal reorientation of schooling in recent decades (see Chapter 2). The promotion of entrepreneurship illustrated in this communication of the European Commission also appears in other documents of the same institution or of several EU member states, as Block (2018a) shows in the cases of the call for research projects of the *Horizon 2020* program by the European Commission and the 2013 Spanish law on support for entrepreneurs. It is worth noting that this law, passed by the conservative government, states that the educational system should develop an entrepreneurial culture to teach students the abilities needed to become entrepreneurs (Block 2018a), which is fully in accordance with the educational proposals stated above from the European Commission (2012) for its state members. Furthermore, Block (2018a) illustrates the dominance of the entrepreneurial and self-branding discourse in the neoliberal era using the figure of Josef Ajram, a paradigmatic example of a self-branded personality. Ajram is a Spanish businessman, broker and athlete who has become a celebrity with his books, conferences and interventions in traditional and new media about how to become economically successful in times of economic crisis. Block (2018a: 131) points out two factors that contribute to his enormous popularity:

> First, there is his physical appearance: he has an athletic body covered in tattoos and at times adorned with piercings. He usually dresses very informally, jeans, a tee-shirt and trainers being a typical combination, and on the whole, he projects an image that we might call 'youth cool'. The second factor which has contributed to his success is his exceptional stage presence, and indeed, charisma as a speaker.

As the previous examples and the ones belonging to the Catalan textbooks have shown, it seems that becoming a successful entrepreneur can be a reality for everyone, which of course is not the case, particularly for those belonging to the lower classes of society (Block 2018a: 130). Indeed, the effects of the 2007–2008 crisis have clearly shown that the neoliberal fantasy that everybody should be transformed "into little one-person corporations" (Fleming 2015: 39) has resulted in a deterioration of the living conditions of many working-class people who believed that by becoming self-employed they could succeed economically and climb up the social ladder. However, Catalan textbooks seem not to take this state of affairs into account. Seemingly a part of the capitalist utopia that the textbooks represent is a reality that rewards people who demonstrate entrepreneurship and self-branding. In the final chapter of this book, I will return to the dominant neoliberal discourse in our capitalist societies to address the question of why textbooks are presented as they are.

In the next chapter, the critical analysis of Catalan language textbooks will continue examining how neoliberal practices and values find expression in the content of textbooks and how they are presented as a matter of common sense. The focus will be on housing, another important social concern, which in recent years has become a matter for national debate in Catalonia and across Spain, because of the forced evictions of working-class people who could no longer pay the mortgage on their homes, and also because of the protests against evictions by the *Plataforma d'Afectats per la Hipoteca* (Platform for those Affected by Mortgage).

Note

1 The Francoist dictatorship encouraged full and permanent employment. The fascist regime intended to compensate for the lack of trade unions and political freedom with employment stability. The Spanish government stated that the situation in the labor market was very near to full employment, but this did not mean quality and well-paid jobs (Vilar 2012). The apparently low unemployment rate during the Franco era, especially from the time of the Spanish economic boom in the 1960s, can be explained by the fact that most women in that period were excluded from the regular job market and by the emigration abroad of around two million Spanish workers (Vilar 2012).

8 The world of housing
Creating a neoliberal fairytale

Introduction

The impossibility of providing decent housing for everyone in a capitalist society is an issue that has been repeatedly discussed since Friedrich Engels published *The Housing Question* in 1872. In this essay, Engels entered into the controversy over the shortage of affordable housing for workers in European urban centers during that period. He dismissed the alternative housing models within the capitalist system to solve the housing crisis, such as workers purchasing their own dwellings, which would require workers to take on heavy mortgage debt, or the possibility that factory owners provide their workers with housing. For Engels (1970 [1872]: 17), the housing crisis was just "one of the innumerable smaller, secondary evils which result from the [. . .] capitalist mode of production". He proclaimed prophetically that capitalism never addresses this problem, or rather that it does so "in such a way that the solution continually poses the question anew" (Engels 1970 [1872]: 69). According to him, the only real solution to the housing question was the elimination of the exploitation of workers by capitalists through the proletarian revolution and the abolition of private property.[1]

Almost a century and a half after the work of Engels, the 2007–2008 financial crisis again "elevated housing issues to the level of national and international debate and protest" (Pattillo 2013: 509). While capitalist economies have promoted the transformation of land (and housing) into a commodity, many people have protested against the lack of affordable housing for low-income groups and also against the evictions of millions of families across capitalist societies. Protesters claim housing as a universal right and a basic human need.

Spain is a paradigmatic example of the transformation of housing in recent decades because it suffered one of the highest boom and bust cycles in the housing and credit market in the capitalist world (Akin et al. 2014: 224). During the first years of this century, the construction of new dwellings in Spain was higher than the total number of new-builds in France, Germany and Italy together (Akin et al. 2014: 228), and real estate and construction constituted around 20 percent of the nation's GDP. The economic recession, which started in 2007–2008, meant that thousands of families were not able to pay their mortgage debts due to mass unemployment and were evicted from their homes.[2] It is also in Spain that one of the strongest social movements against neoliberal housing policy has emerged in recent years: the *Plataforma d'Afectats per la Hipoteca* (Platform for those Affected by Mortgage; hereafter PAH). It started in Barcelona in 2009 and expanded rapidly throughout Spain. The PAH concentrates its energies on giving practical and moral assistance to mortgage victims, fighting and stopping evictions, attempting to change legislation concerning evictions and, last but not least, raising public awareness of the social injustice of the current housing situation in Spain (De Weerdt and Garcia 2016). According to public opinion surveys from 2013, PAH had an 81 percent positive approval rating among members of the public and only 10 percent of the people stated they believed in the government system (De Weerdt and Garcia 2016: 479). Another indication of the popularity of the PAH is the victory in Barcelona's municipal elections of the leader of the movement, Ada Colau, who became the mayor of the capital of Catalonia in 2015.

The story of the neoliberal economic policy that led to the Spanish construction boom and to the bursting of the Spanish housing bubble in 2008 goes as follows. From the year 2000, the construction sector grew spectacularly, fueled by the 1998 Land Act, also known as 'the build anywhere law', which facilitated the acquisition of building permits and made a huge amount of land available for construction (López and Rodríguez 2011). At the same time, financial institutions began to relax credit requirements for construction companies and property developers, but also for families to buy property (Naredo 2009). In fact, in this period, Spanish banks "offered the lowest mortgage rates" in the Eurozone (Akin et al. 2014: 228). During the real estate bubble in Spain, housing prices continually rose with an increase of 50 percent between 2001 and 2006 (Gentier 2012: 346), which led many people to decide to buy a house with a 30, 40 or 50-year mortgage. There was the general belief that buying a house on a mortgage was a secure investment since the price of the property would never go down and there would always be the possibility to sell it, if necessary. However, this 'house of cards' suddenly collapsed in 2007–2008, with the outbreak of the mortgage subprime crisis in the United States, which expanded rapidly all over much of the planet (Etxezarreta et al. 2012). In Spain, immigrants with low incomes and large debt were among the first groups severely affected by the housing crisis and, in many cases, were evicted from their homes (Human Rights Watch 2014). As the crisis and unemployment have continued, more and more people, including those belonging to the middle classes, have also faced foreclosures (Human Rights Watch 2014). Indeed, at the time of writing this chapter in the summer of 2017, the Spanish crisis continues to hinder the access to an affordable home for many people.

This chapter will present and comment on examples of the commodification of housing, the celebration of private property, the practice of taking on

144   *The world of housing*

a mortgage and the central role of the banks and consumerism that appear in Catalan textbooks. I do not aim here to compare the content that appears in textbooks and the reality of learners in the field of housing since there is no data available about how Catalan language students feel about the issue of housing. My purpose is to identify neoliberal practices and values in language textbooks and to determine the extent to which they are presented as natural and desirable in our societies.

The commodification of housing

The commodification of housing (Rolnik 2013), which characterizes the neoliberal economy (see Chapter 4), appears in all of textbooks that I analyzed. *Veus 1* explains the problems that today's Catalan youngsters face when looking for a home under the title "Finding an apartment for the young population: a problem with solutions".

> *Hi ha diversos factors que provoquen aquesta situació, però el més important és la dificultat de trobar un habitatge adequat a les necessitats dels joves i les seves possibilitats econòmiques. Els pisos de lloguer tenen uns preus impossibles i pràcticament no n'hi ha. Per comprar (aquí tothom vol comprar per allò de "vas pagant però al final és teu") normalment necessites hipoteques de 30 a 40 anys. I ja se sap, per obtenir una hipoteca s'ha de tenir una feina estable o l'ajuda dels pares. . . . Tot això és normal, ja que la gent, en general a Catalunya, dedica 66.9% dels seus ingressos a les despeses l'habitatge i a la zona de Barcelona, un 82,4%!!!*
>
> [There are several factors that cause this situation, but the most important one is the difficulty young people have in finding a house to suit their needs and their budgets. Rental apartments have impossibly high prices, and they are scarce. To buy an apartment (here everybody wants to buy because of the thing about "you pay but in the end it's yours") one usually needs a mortgage of up to 30 or 40 years. And, as everyone knows, to obtain a mortgage one must have a stable job or the help of parents. . . . This is all typical, since people in Catalonia generally devote 66.9 per cent of their income to housing expenses and, in the area of Barcelona, 82.4 per cent!!!]
>
> (Mas and Vilagrassa 2005: 72)

According to this textbook, it is "typical" for a young person from Barcelona to spend almost all her/his revenue on housing expenses. The textbook authors express surprise over this situation using exclamation marks at the end of this excerpt, but they consider it natural to apply for credit from a bank and pay for it over three or four decades. Moreover, the text above contends that to own a flat is a commonplace practice in Catalonia: "here everybody wants to buy". In this regard, we should recall that the lack of rental apartments that this text mentions did not occur on its own, but it was the result of a specific economic policy that fiscally rewards private property ownership and does not favor the renting of a home. In addition, the construction bubble stimulated the further accumulation of debt and speculation in real estate, since many investors bought properties in order to sell them shortly afterward for a higher price. In that way, Spain faced a paradox regarding housing: "[I]n spite of an over production in the housing market, there is always a crisis in the lack of [affordable] accommodation" (Gentier 2012: 344). The exercise that follows the reading of this text asks the learner to supply definitions for a series of terms such as mortgage, revenue, expenses, rent or savings (Mas and Vilagrassa 2005: 73), terms related to the world of modern housing and integral to capitalism.

In the content related to housing, I also identified the frequent appearance of consumers' organizations and, above all, the real estate agencies. In *Nou Nivell Elemental*, for example, there is a text adapted from a document belonging to the Organization Catalan Consumers with detailed information on the purchase of a house (Anguera et al. 2010a: 46). It explains different kinds of real estate purchase agreements and includes an extensive list of expenses related to selling or buying a property. Meanwhile, *Fil per randa* dedicates a whole unit to real estate agencies (Vilà and Homs 2013a: 176–87). On the opening page of this unit there is a drawing of a real estate agency in which six people are working as telephone operators giving information about the property they sell or rent. Almost all the dialogues in this unit are between people who want to buy or rent a place and a real estate agent. One of the activities involves checking a real estate agency's website, commenting on its content, and answering questions such as "Is it better to buy or to rent a house?" (183). In the final task, students are asked to create a radio advertisement for a real estate agency (187).

Textbooks from the Barcelona Center for Linguistic Normalization also pay a great deal of attention to real estate agencies in housing-related content. I found dialogues between customers and real estate agents in all three books in this series (CNLB 2008a: 54; CNLB 2008b: 39; CNLB 2011: 38). There are also advertisements of real estate agencies (CNL Barcelona 2008a: 54) and a story about a young woman who calls a real estate agency three times a day to find an apartment (CNLB 2008b: 39). This series also includes an activity which asks students to assume the role of a real estate agent to write an advertisement to rent or sell their houses (CNLB 2008a: 54), and a role play in which the students have to simulate phone calls between people who rent apartments and those who are looking for one (CNLB 2008b: 40). Furthermore, one of the textbooks asks learners to read a part of an apartment rental agreement and to answer questions related to the duration of the agreement, the names of the contracting parties and whether the flat is furnished or not. Students are also to read the whole contract at the end of the book which includes sentences such as these:

> *Les despeses generals pel manteniment adequat de l'immoble, els seus serveis, tributs, càrregues i responsabilitats que no siguin susceptibles*

146 The world of housing

d'individualització, i, en general, les que corresponguin al pis arrendat d'acord amb la seva quota de participació en règim de propietat horitzontal, són a càrrec de l'arrendatari.

[All general expenses for the appropriate maintenance of the dwelling, its services, taxes, fees and other costs that are not incurred by the individual rental unit, and, in general, those that correspond to the flat leased according to the participation fees under the terms of the 'horizontal property' law, are to be charged to the tenant.]

(CNLB 2008a: 189)

In this text, the textbook authors clearly opted to present to beginner students of Catalan a very specialized language related to the market aspects of housing. Likewise, *Català Elemental* also dedicates a whole unit to housing in which students are treated as potential experts in the real estate business (Campoy et al. 2011: 25–40). The unit begins with a series of questions posed to students such as:

Què consideres més convenient per a una parella jove: que s'hipotequin amb un habitatge ampli per no haver de pensar-hi més, o que comencin amb una compra més modesta i confïin que en el futur ja podran finançiar un habitatge més gran i més car. [. . .] A l'hora de pagar la quota mensual d'una hipoteca, fins a quin percentatge dels ingressos d'una família creus que s'hi pot destinar? El 30%? El 50%? Més?

[What do you consider best for a young couple: to take out a mortgage and buy a large house and not think about the matter further or to begin with a more modest purchase in the belief that in the future they will be able to finance a larger and more expensive house? [. . .] What percentage of a family's income do you think should be dedicated to monthly mortgage payments? Thirty per cent? Fifty per cent? More?]

(Campoy et al. 2011: 26)

Later, students are asked whether they are aware of the most important questions related to finding an apartment and if they are already familiar with the vocabulary from the real estate sector (28). One of the main activities in this unit requires students to formulate a series of questions after they are divided into three groups (32–3). The first group should debate about which questions are important to prepare before contacting a real estate company. The second is asked to write about the most relevant details to take into account when visiting a house. And the third group is to discuss the questions one should ask before buying or renting a property. The textbook authors help students to elaborate on the points that are considered important, such as the value of the apartment: "[I]f the real value of the house is less than the asking price, the buyer loses and the bank, if it is involved, will not grant a mortgage for the asking price, but only for the actual value of the house" (Campoy et al. 2011: 33). With such activities, textbook authors focus on teaching students how to behave in a neoliberal environment, probably on the assumption that being knowledgeable of the field of real estate and its vocabulary should be beneficial for learners. These practices undoubtedly pertain to late capitalist societies in which real estate investments, the market and everything else involved have become a daily 'normality' for people who live in societies governed by this economic model.

Català Elemental continues with the listening of a dialogue between a woman who wants to sell her flat and a real estate agent who is helping her with her decision. The real estate agent says: "The best advice that we can give you is to have confidence in us. Our agency has been working in this neighborhood for more than 30 years" (34). Although real estate agencies may help people buy or sell properties, it is worth noting here that during the housing boom real estate agencies have played an important role in capturing clients for banks, going regularly to the workplaces of low-income immigrants to promise a good deal with the banks for a mortgage, and often providing dubious loans for home buyers (Human Rights Watch 2014: 3–4). After listening to a conversation between a real estate agent and a client, students are asked to write down all the expressions that might influence the decision of the buyer, as though the class is studying to become experts or sellers in the real estate business, or maybe owners of homes. Finally, students are to continue by reading texts in which, once again, recommendations about buying a property are presented and learners are expected to use expert knowledge and specialized vocabulary related to the real estate business.

The quantity of texts and activities dedicated to the commodification of housing confirms the importance the authors give to this topic. I am aware that many teachers and learners would welcome any textbook that provides some help both with the local practices related to finding housing and with the vocabulary involved, although some of them probably realize that today it is difficult to find decent housing. However, what I want to show here is how neoliberal common sense has penetrated language education to the extent that many people in education believe that it is not possible to approach language teaching without following the market ideology that runs the world of housing in capitalist societies. In contrast, I am suggesting that it would be possible to teach a language that is not simply a utilitarian tool to find an accommodation or to buy a property. Indeed, it would be perfectly conceivable that students would manage to deal with the home finding process without the necessity of teaching them in language classrooms such dense and specific vocabulary related to neoliberal economic transactions. What's more, if the textbooks want to offer a view of the 'real world', they should at least be open to questioning this state of affairs, and offer activities and texts that contrast mainstream views. For example, it is worth recalling that everything related to the housing industry, including real estate, has in recent decades evolved into a huge multimillion-euro

148 *The world of housing*

business that makes some people very rich but which serves to sustain socio-economic inequalities. People who are able to buy more property are the ones who rent to the less fortunate. But these are also the buyers who, if they are able to raise an easy low-interest mortgage, are the most likely to have difficulties in paying it and eventually may be evicted from their homes.

Related to the commodification of housing, I also identified in textbooks the concept of housing as an investment. For example, there is a text about a huge project which involves the reconstruction of an old textile colony and the construction of 229 apartments at a cost of 12 million euros (Anguera et al. 2010a: 43). In another activity, there is an article about the increase in housing auctions where, among other things, it is said: "Many construction developers have huge buildings to sell and those who have bought a new house are now forced to sell their old one" (Campoy et al. 2011: 28). Both examples are illustrative of how big the businesses of the real estate and construction sectors in Spain were at the beginning of the twenty-first century when property speculation flourished. During this period, Spain opted for a model of unbalanced growth in which the construction business had a central place, thanks to very flexible legislation regarding construction requirements, a fiscal policy favorable to the acquisition of housing property and cheap mortgages for companies and families. However, none of the textbooks include any reference to the bursting of the housing bubble in 2008, or to its negative consequences, such as rising unemployment in the construction sector and thousands of evictions.

The celebration of home ownership

Another value that I identified in housing-related content is the celebration of home ownership (Ronald 2008). In *Nou Nivell Elemental*, for example, there are three dialogues about the buying of a house in an exercise to practice Catalan pronouns (Anguera et al. 2010a: 42). In the first dialogue, a young woman explains to her friend that she has just bought an apartment with a mortgage. Despite the implications of this decision, the young woman says that she did so "without giving it a lot of thought". The friend congratulates her and suggests throwing a party to celebrate the decision. In the second dialogue, a character recommends that a friend buys a house as quickly as possible because there is always the possibility that somebody else will buy it first. In the third dialogue, two friends discuss buying a house in a similar way. When talking about buying a house, one friend says: "It must have cost you a lot of money!". And the other one answers: "Yes, indeed it has, but we don't regret it at all. We couldn't wait to buy it". In these three dialogues, we can identify a minimization of the problems of buying a house (such as spending a lot of money or taking out a mortgage) and above all the celebration of home ownership. Nevertheless, my point here is not to discuss whether this kind of approach resembles the reality on the ground, nor whether it is considered appropriate by some teachers or

The world of housing   149

learners. What I simply want to show is that the celebration of home ownership plays a prominent role in the content of Catalan language materials,
and in that way the textbooks may contribute to making home ownership a
commonly held value in our societies.

I also identified a great emphasis on private property in the series published by the Barcelona Center for Linguistic Normalization, such as in the
following excerpt:

> *A l'estat espanyol, per tradició són poques les famílies que decideixen
> viure de lloguer tota la vida. La idea que el patrimoni familiar pot cré-
> ixer gràcies a l'adquisició d'un habitatge sempre ha estat molt atractiva
> per a molta gent que opina que el lloguer a la llarga és més car. El
> cert és, però, que en general llogar és una opció millor perquè permet
> canviar fàcilment quan hi ha trasllats per feina, canvis familiars, etc.*

> [Traditionally, in Spain there are very few families that decide to live
> in rented houses their whole life. The idea that a family's estate can
> grow thanks to the acquisition of a house has always been very attrac-
> tive for a lot of people who believe that renting is, in the long run, more
> expensive. The truth is, however, that in general, renting may be a bet-
> ter option because it makes moving easier when there are job transfers,
> changes in family size, or other similar changes.]

(CNLB 2011: 41)

The example above refers to a supposed Spanish cultural tradition of owning
houses, which would be congruent with neoliberal values. Although today
the majority of families in Spain supposedly own a house, many do so by
means of a mortgage, which means that the family could lose the property
if it doesn't repay the debt to the bank. Actually, this cultural tradition is
inaccurate because until the mid-twentieth century there were more Spanish
families who rented their homes than owned them (Pereda 2013). As noted
earlier, home ownership is a practice promoted by recent economic policies
that reward the buying of a property and penalize the renting of a home.
This policy also boosted the private construction sector to the detriment of
public housing (Pereda 2013). The origins of this policy can be found in the
last two decades of the Franco dictatorship in Spain, which aimed to promote private property above class solidarity (Sola 2014). Franco's Housing
Minister, José Luis Arrese, synthesized the spirit of this policy in 1957 with
a sentence that over time would become famous: "*Queremos un país de
propietarios, no de proletarios*" [We want a country of [home] owners, not
proletarians] (Sola 2014: 107). After Franco's death, the idea of creating a
society of homeowners continued with the housing policies of the various
Spanish governments. The so-called Boyer act, passed in 1985 with a Social
Democratic party in power, made home renting an expensive and precarious
option (Delgado 2010). Later, neoliberal policies such as the 1998 Land Act,
passed by a Conservative party government, speeded up the construction of

150 The world of housing

private houses and apartments. In addition, the incorporation of Spain into the globalized economy made it easier for families to take out a mortgage as a route to home ownership.

The same textbook also presents dwellings as commodities (in the sense that they are investment assets), rather than as homes, as can be seen in the following example:

> *Ser propietari d'un habitatge és una de les aspiracions més communes, per la satisfacció personal i els beneficis financers [. . .]. Si es ven al cap d'un temps se solen obtenir guanys i pot suposar un estalvi a l'hora de pagar impostos.*
>
> [Being a homeowner is one of the most common aspirations for personal satisfaction and financial profit [. . .]. If the home is sold after some time, it has usually gained value and can bring a saving when paying taxes].

(CNLB 2011: 41)

This idea of a home as an investment became very popular in Spain during the period of the real estate bubble. In those years, some wealthy individuals "were able to take advantage of the bubble and improve their financial investments in the process" (Daly and Zarco 2015: 40). During this period, control over the housing sector switched from public to private hands, and taking out a mortgage became a very common practice for many Spanish people. However, in 2011, the year of publication of this particular textbook, the bubble had already burst with devastating effects for the most disadvantaged classes of society. Nevertheless, this is not mentioned in this textbook or in any of the others in my corpus.

Taking out a mortgage

The most frequent practice that I identified in housing-related content is acquiring a mortgage. Characters in textbooks decide to take out a mortgage in order to buy a house, as can be read in the following conversation between two friends taken from *Curs de català bàsic B3*:

- *Pedro! Com va tot? Fa molt temps que no ens vèiem! Encara vius en aquell pis del Carmel?*
- *Ui noi! L'any passat em vaig comprar un pis.*
- *Caram, quin canvi? I això?*
- *Doncs perquè al pis de lloguer on vivia no em renovaven el contracte i havia de marxar. Com que tenia diners estalviats i m'acabaven de fer indefinit a l'empresa, vaig fer un cop de cap.*
- *Ben fet!*
- *Sí, sí, ara estic molt content. [. . .]*
- *I vas trigar gaire a anar-hi a viure?*

>   – Va ser *rapidíssim. Vaig poder negociar bones condicions per a la hipoteca amb el banc i vaig signar l'escriptura de seguida. Al cap de deus setmanes ja hi vivia.*
>   – *Enhorabona, de debò! Jo segueixo al meu pis de lloguer. Així, no em sento tan lligada i si me'n canso o em surt alguna feina fora, el puc deixar i estrenar-ne un de nou!*
>
>   [– Pedro! How's everything? Long time no see! Do you still live in that flat in Carmel?
>   – No, man, last year I bought a flat.
>   – Wow, what a change! Why?
>   – Because they didn't renew my lease for the rented flat I was living in and I had to leave. Since I had savings and I've just got a long-term contract at my company, I made the decision.
>   – Well done!
>   – Yes, yes, now I am very happy. [. . .]
>   – And did it take a long time before you were actually living there?
>   – It was very fast. I negotiated a good mortgage rate with the bank and I signed the title deed immediately. And after two weeks I was living there.
>   – Congratulations, indeed! I continue to rent my apartment. That way, I don't feel so tied down, and if I get bored or another job appears somewhere else, I can leave this apartment and move to a new one!]
>   (CNLB 2011: 40)

The dialogue above presents taking on a mortgage as a natural and necessary step in order to buy a house in Catalan society, which is a general trend in all these textbooks. Taking out a mortgage is seen in a positive light, taking into account that Pedro highlights the good deal he achieved with the bank and that his friend congratulates him enthusiastically for having bought a flat on a mortgage, although she says that this choice is not suitable for her because she does not want to feel "so tied down" and to be able to move more easily.

Moreover, the materials also present detailed information about mortgages, as in the dialogue below from *Nou Nivell Elemental 1* between an employee of the Housing Office and a person that wants to buy a house with a mortgage:

>   – *Miri, el primer que ha de fer és mesurar les seves possibilitats econòmiques. Segurament deu voler demanar un hipoteca . . .*
>   – *Sí, és clar . . .*
>   – *És recomanable que la quota mensual de la hipoteca no superi una tercera part dels ingressos de cada mes. D'altra banda, si opta per una hipoteca d'interès variable, pensi que estarà subjecta a fluctuacions al llarg dels anys.*

152   *The world of housing*

–   *Què vol dir, d'interès variable?*
–   *Les hipoteques poden ser de tipus fix, en què el tipus d'interès es manté
    constant fins al final; de tipus mixt, que vol dir que el tipus d'interès es
    manté constant durant els primers anys, però es converteix en variable
    un cop passat el període inicial, i de tipus variable. En aquest últim cas,
    el tipus d'interès es determina sumant a l'índex de referència el diferen-
    cial que s'hagi pactat amb l'entitat financera. Les revisions s'acostumen
    a fer cada sis o dotze mesos, i per tant la quota mensual pot pujar o
    baixar.*
–   *Així, quan vagi al banc hauré de decidir quin tipus d'hipoteca em convé
    més?*
–   *Sí. També és important que compari entre diferents entitats financeres i
    negocïi al màxim la rebaixa de les comissions.*

[– Look, the first thing you must do is to evaluate your financial situation.
    You would probably want to take out a mortgage . . .
–   Yes, of course . . .
–   It is recommended that the monthly mortgage payment does not sur-
    pass a third of your monthly income. On the other hand, if you opt for
    a variable-rate mortgage, you should take into account that it will be
    subject to change over the years.
–   What does a variable-rate mortgage mean?
–   Mortgages can be fixed-rate mortgages, in which the rate of interest
    does not change over the life of the loan; or hybrid mortgages, which
    means that they start with an unchanging interest rate during the early
    years, before switching over to an adjustable rate, becoming variable-
    rate mortgages. In the latter case, the interest rate is calculated by add-
    ing the differential you agreed with the bank to the index the mortgage
    is tied to. The rate normally adjusts every six or twelve months, so the
    monthly payment may go up or down.
–   So, when I go to the bank, will I have to decide which type of mortgage
    suits me more?
–   Yes. Also it is important to compare the different financial institu-
    tions and negotiate with them for the maximum discount on their
    commissions.

(Anguera et al. 2010a: 47)

With all the information and the specialized vocabulary presented in the
previous example, it seems that the textbook authors expect to prepare and
encourage learners to take out a mortgage. The textbook does not end its
activities related to real estate here. Following this listening exercise, in a
matching activity, students are to answer whether statements such as the
following are true or false: "Hybrid mortgages are best because the rate of
interest does not change during the period of the payment of the mortgage"
(Anguera et al. 2010a: 47). Later in the book, there is a text adapted from a

The world of housing 153

document authored by the Catalan government in which the administration sets out its views as to who can take on a mortgage: "It is necessary to have money for the downpayment, and work and life stability in the future to meet the financial commitments that have been agreed on" (Anguera et al. 2010a: 51). The year this series was published, labor stability was already a problem, with around five million unemployed in Spain and many examples of families being evicted from their houses because they were unable to pay their mortgage. The many risks behind this capitalist practice, especially with the housing boom and bust in Spain, are not mentioned in textbooks. Instead, taking out a mortgage is generally treated as a given, a practice which is normal, natural and inevitable.

The banking sector as the main actor

Private financial institutions are among the main stakeholders of the majority of the biggest Spanish companies such as the oil company *Repsol*, the natural gas company *Gas Natural Fenosa*, the telecommunications firm *Telefónica*, the energy provider *Endesa*, the airport operator *AENA* or the *Abertis* motorway concession company. In recent years, banks have also become the main agents in the neoliberal organization of the Spanish housing sector, not only because they have specialized in providing mortgages for families and loans to construct buildings, but also because banks are the largest real estate agents in Spain since the housing bubble burst (Cuesta and Velloso 2015). In content related to housing, and especially in that dedicated to mortgages, banks feature prominently in the textbook material, and always appear in a positive light. There is no reference to the controversial role played by the banks that led to the 2008 financial crash, by inflating the giant bubble of easy credit and using it to fund their own speculative gambling in what was known as 'casino capitalism' (Sinn 2010). Obviously, there is no reference either to the massive amounts of public money injected into the Spanish financial system to rescue its failing banks, which resulted in a further reduction in public spending, because the 100 billion Euro Spanish bailout was passed in 2012, when the textbooks from the corpus had already been or were in the process of being published.

A paradigmatic example of the chief role of banks in Catalan textbooks is the unit entitled "Let's get married to the mortgage" (Roig and Daranas 2011: 89–96). It belongs to the series *Passos*, the only one from the corpus that has immigrants as main characters and, in that way, is addressing the fact that the type of people most likely to be in Catalan language courses are recently arrived migrants. At the beginning, there is the only reference I found in all the textbooks to one of the Catalan social organizations that is demanding decent housing for everybody, with a quote that says that to have a proper home is "a basic and inalienable right for human dignity" (89). But beyond that, there is no further reference to this right or to any of the social movements that for many years have promoted this right, not even

154   *The world of housing*

to the popular Platform for those Affected by Mortgage, to which I referred in the first part of this chapter. The main character of the unit is Rosa from Ecuador. She came to Catalonia four years ago and has had many different jobs, especially in hotels and restaurants. After finding a more or less secure job taking care of elderly people, the first thing on Rosa's mind is apparently to buy a house. And the only way to do so is to get a mortgage from a bank, as the textbook will show. Before getting to the (more complicated) bank loan stage, the authors choose to explain more basic issues related to banking. Learners are asked for examples of which documents are necessary to open a bank account or what the difference is between a credit and a debit card. In another activity, students are invited to learn how to use ATMs.

Another way of introducing the banking system practices as something routine and necessary is the dialogue in the bank between two friends, Irene and Santi (Roig and Daranas 2011: 90). Both characters talk about various bank procedures to pay electricity and municipal taxes, and the differences between credit and debit cards. From their dialogue, students also learn that in order to buy a house and even clothes or textbooks for their children it is necessary to owe money to the bank because "it is impossible to do it in any other way", as one of the characters says. This assertion from Santi resembles the famous phrase of 'There is no alternative (TINA)' associated with Thatcher's government in Britain to justify that free-market capitalism is the only possible economic system. What we need to remember, and these textbooks do not help to raise awareness of this, is that TINA is an erroneous viewpoint, propagated by the same proponents of the capitalist system in its current neoliberal form (George 1999; Harvey 2005). Unfortunately, from these examples, we can conclude that these textbooks, similar to the mainstream media, perpetuate the no-alternative mantra. The previous dialogue also portrays the banks in a positive light when Santi explains that he received a very good deal for a car loan from them.

After the dialogue in the bank, the unit continues with a fictional text taken from the Catalan writer Quim Monzó about the Sultan of Brunei's visit to the New York Tiffany's store. Students learn about another aspect of the banking system from this text: that credit cards sometimes cannot be used without identification cards, at least in "the civilized world" (91). Therefore, this text associates the adjective 'civilized' with knowing about a financial practice characteristic of capitalist societies. In Monzó's story, the Sultan of Brunei, one of the wealthiest persons on earth, did not have an ID card on him when he wanted to buy diamonds. Unfortunately for him, in Monzó's story, he was unable to do so because he did not know about, or care to know about, a 'civilized' capitalist practice. What Monzó does not explain is that credit cards were at first reserved only for the wealthy. Few banks and companies offered credit cards to their clients unless they were well known by name and for their wealth. During the 1970s and the invention of magnetic tape, credit cards were introduced to the general public creating a boom in consumer spending throughout the Western world

The world of housing   155

(Kaplan 2006). So what Monzó unknowingly did was to create a parallel between the 'civilized world' and the neoliberal economic practice of constantly borrowing and owing money in order to buy whatever can be sold on the market, a practice previously reserved for the few and now offered to the vast majority of people living in capitalist societies. What this 'civilized' practice did not bring about, however, is a reduction in the gap between the rich and poor. This gap only continued to grow. The following activity in *Passos* includes four radio commercials all related to buying things on credit. The companies announcing their services all refer to special offers to attract customers. They are all invented companies and announcements, but their offers resemble authentic offers and marketing strategies used by banks, as can be seen in the following passage:

> *Li presentem la nova hipoteca mínima de Cat Banca. Li oferim els interessos més baixos del mercat, ens esperem si un mes no pot pagar, ens adaptem als imprevistos que pugui tenir. I per als joves, facilitats i comissió zero d'obertura als menors de trenta anys. Tu també pots tenir casa teva. Vine a veure'ns, segur que tenim una hipoteca mínima per a tu.*
>
> [We present you with Cat Banca's new small home loan. We offer you the lowest interest rates on the market, a one-month grace period, and we adapt to the circumstances that you may have. And for the young population, under the age of thirty, we offer better terms and no fees when taking out a home loan. You can have your home as well! Come to see us, and be sure that we have a small home loan for you.]
>
> (Roig and Daranas 2011: 91)

The advertisement above sounds too good to be true, but the capitalist system, especially in its most recent neoliberal form, has provided a variety of incentives to offer consumers more credit for all sorts of things and thereby keep the system going. Unfortunately, the system has failed, producing bubbles more often than not. The way that these Ponzi schemes work is, however, not mentioned to students, as indeed they are never explained to customers visiting banks. After listening to these advertisements, students are to imagine themselves as marketing executives designing a campaign for a bank, inventing slogans for a bank that wants to attract young mortgage customers. Before the final task (buying a house with a mortgage), learners are asked in a very lengthy exercise to rate and comment on the value of the apartment they now live in, which will apparently help them choose between buying a new apartment, renovating the one they own, or doing nothing. The survey for this activity is adapted from a document belonging from one of the major financial entities in Spain, the Catalan bank *La Caixa*.

The final task in the unit is called "We have to take on a mortgage: let's do the math" (95–6). Using the modal verb *haver de* ("have to"), the authors again highlight the necessity of this practice, as if there are no alternatives, in

156   *The world of housing*

line with neoliberal thinking. The task consists of helping Rosa from Ecuador and her boyfriend buy an apartment in a city near Barcelona on a mortgage. Students are asked to choose an apartment for the young couple and to calculate their monthly mortgage payment through a table that presents the interest rates and the years they have to pay off the mortgage. However, since the textbook does not include any discussion of Rosa's background, life choices, or the health of the housing market in Spain, the opportunity to get students to discuss the situation more critically is lost. For example, learners might discuss Rosa's decision to take on a mortgage since she has a profile very similar to the typical student learning Catalan as a second language. Furthermore, it would also be interesting to present and discuss the fact that a very high proportion of homeowners have lost their homes due to defaults on their mortgage since the start of the financial crisis. In addition, a high percentage of these 'failed' homeowners were immigrants with low-income jobs (Human Watch 2014), such as Rosa from Ecuador.

Some readers may ask why the great prominence of the banks in the textbooks should be problematized since nowadays virtually everyone uses banking services. Nevertheless, what I want to point out here is the ideological construction of the banking system in the housing-related content in the textbooks. As explained above, the textbooks tend to present banks and mortgages by showing only one side of the coin, without mentioning any of the very significant negative aspects of banking activity in the world of housing.

The rise of consumerism

Consumption related to housing does not end with buying an apartment or taking on a mortgage. Textbooks also include other consumer practices, such as renovating a house or buying items for the home. In *Nou Nivell Elemental*, after dedicating extensive space to mortgages, there are two pages focused on home renovation (Anguera et al. 2010a: 48–9), in which students are to compare the renovation budgets explained in a listening activity.

Fil per randa is the textbooks series that dedicates the most space proportionally to content related to housing. These textbooks present the entire housing industry and related services, from the efforts of looking for an apartment to rent or buy, to those who support those efforts: the real estate agencies as intermediaries and consultants, the banks that are responsible for credit or loans, and finally the construction companies and contractors in charge of home renovations. Last but not least, there is also the whole furnishings and appliances business that also profits from the buying, renting and home decoration. In one of the units, for example, after presenting several dialogues between real estate agents and customers, Martina writes in an e-mail to a friend that she has decided to take out a mortgage to buy a flat. Martina asks her friend for information about the mortgage process: "You took out a loan or a mortgage a year ago, didn't you? You told me

The world of housing   157

you were very happy with it! Which bank was it? How much commission did you pay? What were the interest rates?" (Vilà and Homs 2013b: 94). This e-mail, apart from including vocabulary related to the banking system ("loan", "mortgage", "commissions", "interest rate"), also presents the strong reliance on a friend's previous experience with mortgages that was positive in the past, and explains mortgages as a natural practice in which everyone engages. Later in the book, there are various advertisements that offer home renovation, furniture and home decorating products on which students should comment (Vilà and Homs 2013b: 165). After that, learners are asked to imagine that they want to renovate their kitchen and to write down all the things needed for the new kitchen (Vilà and Homs 2013b: 166). In another unit in the same textbook, students are to imagine their ideal home, list and describe the furniture and appliances, read advertisements for renting a place and then listen to dialogues between people that have just bought their houses or apartments (Vilà and Homs 2013b: 32–41). The unit ends with ideas to save energy in the home and a final task in which the students are to propose measures to save energy in the building in which they live. The necessity to save energy is aligned with the promotion of individual responsibility in late capitalist societies that frequently appears in mainstream media reports, corporate-backed science and in political discourses and documents. According to neoliberal logic, individuals increasingly must take responsibility for the common interests of society since public administrations are less and less engaged in them and have transferred such responsibilities to private companies. In the particular case of the energy sector in Spain, the government privatized it in the mid-1990s, with the argument that the change would promote competition among companies and the prices of electricity would go down. Since then, electricity companies have reaped a multimillion-euro profit, electricity bills have constantly risen, and hundreds of thousands of working-class families have enormous difficulties paying their monthly electricity bills (LibreRed 2015). Instead of commenting on this huge problem, *Fil per Randa* opted to focus on the individual's responsibility to save energy.

According to these textbooks, the only solution to finding decent housing seems to be requesting a loan from commercial banks, which tends to be presented as a positive practice, as discussed. However, it should also be mentioned that certain Catalan language teaching materials do present alternatives to taking out a mortgage, which will be discussed below.

Alternatives to a mortgage

Veus presents a series of four texts that discuss alternative lifestyles, or simply stories about people who live in impossible conditions and are happy about it (Mas and Vilagrassa 2008: 53–5). Thus, we have a text about Xavi who lives in a trailer, Andrea who lives in a 14-square-meter flat, the García family of five who live in a 40-square-meter flat, and an Argentinean named

158 *The world of housing*

Cristian who lives on a small boat in a Catalan coastal town. Their stories are as follows:

> Xavi, who decided to live in a trailer, was a circus employee and later decided to travel through Europe. The text with a drawing of a young man in shorts and t-shirt says that "Xavi considers himself a freedom lover, and he does not want to be tied down by a mortgage" (53). He is living in a camping site in Catalonia and seems very cheerful: "Here I have everything. [. . .] The space is small, but you can organize it as you like. I accept what I have, but this does not mean that I don't have ambitions" (53). What kind of "ambitions" Xavi is talking about? The readers are not told. It is assumed that these go beyond living in a trailer.

> Andrea, who is a translator, decided to move to a 14-square-meter flat in the center of Barcelona because she did not want to share apartments anymore. Her tiny room is not just her living space but also her work space. With regard to her circumstances, she says: "I spend a lot of hours between these four walls and it is very important to feel comfortable in the workplace" (54). Andrea also has high hopes for the future: "Once I earn more money, [. . .] I will move to a bigger flat, but at the moment I can't afford a different home."
>
> (54)

> The García family lives in a working-class neighborhood in Barcelona. Five members of the family of different ages live in a 40-square-meter flat. However, the father of the family does not see their living situation as impossible: "Considering how costly apartments are nowadays, it is not worthwhile to look for bigger one. We are already very used to the neighborhood and to the community."
>
> (54)

> Cristian, a 30-year-old man from Argentina, formerly lived on a boat moored near Barcelona. Previously he lived in a rented apartment, but he decided to look for alternatives "because I didn't want to pay without getting anything in return" (55). So, he bought an 8.5-meter-long boat where he had lived with his wife until their daughter was born. They temporarily moved to a rented apartment, but his dream is to buy a bigger boat and live in it. He says: "I don't know if we will ever live in an apartment again. At the moment, we don't desire it at all. My dream is to continue living on the sea and that mortgages do not sink me."
>
> (55)

What these stories offer, then, are various housing options. The alternatives presented are examples of small, even minuscule spaces that these people somehow manage to live in. In some cases, these are just temporary solutions

The world of housing   159

until better options are at hand. However, analyzing these stories in more depth, it is easy to see that three of the four cases are not about people who would normally have to live in substandard housing. Xavi, a young Catalan who used to work for a circus and has traveled around Europe, is obviously not the example of a typical poor person. Neither is Andrea who could live in a different kind of place if she had not chosen to live in Barcelona's city center. Similarly, Cristian's decision to live on a boat seems more motivated by personal preferences than by economic limitations. The García family is the only example of characters who are forced to live in a tiny apartment for financial reasons. Clearly, they are not completely satisfied with their housing conditions. Some of them say explicitly that they do not want to give money to the banks, but they are not really complaining about their choices. Furthermore, living in a trailer or on a boat is represented as a matter of personal decision, an imaginative and ingenious alternative lifestyle that fits perfectly into the neoliberal model of the individualization of housing options and into the entrepreneurial spirit in today's capitalist societies. It is not my intention here to enter into a discussion of the possible alternatives to the commodification of housing in capitalist societies. This may be an interesting point, but it would clearly go beyond the object of this study. What I do wish to highlight is that alternatives to mortgage do exist, even in neoliberal capitalist societies, and that some of the Catalan language textbooks in my corpus include them in their content.

Similar to the above examples of alternative lifestyles, the internet platform *Parla.cat* includes a text about a Catalan man who has a different lifestyle than the rest of the characters. His name is Xifré and he lives in a squat. He is a historian, volunteers in a geriatric center, and, in his daily life, in his own words, deals very much with "people who are very engaged in politics" (DGPL 2008: Elemental 3, Unit 2, 1.2). He gives talks on the situation in the Middle East and, on his blog, he appears in a photo with a Palestinian scarf on the front page. Xifré likes running, going to a bar for drinks, electronic music and Ken Loach's films, but he does not have a TV at home because he thinks that "television doesn't let people think" (DGPL 2008: Elemental 3, Unit 2, 1.3). Readers also know that Xifré is saving money so someday he can go on "a good trip" (DGPL 2008: Elemental 3, Unit 2, 1.4). To explain the reasons why he is living in a squat, Xifré only says: "I didn't want to pay the rent for an apartment, so I chose an alternative option" (DGPL 2008: Elemental 3, Unit 2, 1.3). Talking with his friend Neus, Xavi expresses his indignation about exploitation in the workplace and relates it to the high cost of buying a house and to mortgages: "It makes my blood boil when I see that some of my friends, scared they won't be able to meet mortgage payments, put up with anything at work" (DGPL 2008, Elemental 3, Unit 2, 2.11). This commentary describes a very frequent phenomenon in a neoliberal world, where people are more susceptible to labor exploitation due to fear of mortgage defaults or evictions (Glynn 2009). Later, Xifré finds an internet article called "Why don't young people leave their parents' home?"

160 *The world of housing*

and sends it to his friends by e-mail (DGPL 2008: Elemental 3, Unit 2, 3.14). The text written in 2007 admits that it is difficult for young people to get a well-paid job but presents a positive outcome: "Although there are lots of difficulties to overcome, the majority of them, in the end, find a job". It is also said that "in theory to have a house is a right", and that "to have a proper house has become a luxury or an impossible dream", but without explaining the reasons that led to this anomalous situation. Instead, the text concludes: "those who are luckier manage to buy a house, very often with the help of their families, but they have to pay the mortgage all their lives". Although the text mentions the deploring fact that people "have to pay the mortgage all their lives", taking on a mortgage is presented again as natural and a practice reserved for 'the lucky ones'. The explanation for the reason why these people have to pay a mortgage all their lives, without it being said how much interest they are paying to the banks, is quite naive: "The prices to buy a flat have increased considerably, and therefore mortgages are planned for 30 and 40 years".

With Xifré's case, *Parla.cat* seems to approach the topic of housing (and also of work) differently from other series. The neoliberal economy is not presented from such a positive and optimistic perspective. However, the example of a young Catalan squatter who has a more 'radical' view on the global order seems to be only a question of lifestyle, that of certain young and modern city dwellers that have a university degree and their upper-middle class family's support for the life they lead. Xifré is by no means an example of the victims of the housing crisis that have been forced to occupy abandoned properties after suffering years of unemployment or been evicted from their homes by the banks, as for example those of the Spanish '*corrala*' movement, who have occupied empty buildings in Seville since 2012 (Candón 2013). Neither is Xifré a leftist libertarian squatter of the type found in European cities since the late 1960s (Martínez 2013). In brief, although in *Parla.cat* not everything is presented in a positive way, this material also fails to open a serious debate about issues concerning labor exploitation or the commodification of housing that are real and severe in the era of neoliberalism.

Conclusion

This chapter has shown that a large proportion of housing-related content in textbooks emphasizes consumer-centered issues like buying, selling or renting a house, renovating a home or buying various home products. The increasing commodification of housing appears as a natural phenomenon and is presented, generally speaking, in a positive light. In some textbooks, the banks have a central role, especially in content related to taking out a mortgage. Through a variety of language learning activities, textbooks expose students to expert knowledge about the world of finance and the real estate sector, without any mention of the consequences of the Spanish property bubble, the collapse of which affected hundreds of thousands of people from working-class and middle-class backgrounds. In this way, materials often prepare students for roles as consumers and bank clients in Catalan society. To sum up, Catalan textbooks emerge as disseminators of a neoliberal fairytale, presenting the topic of housing mainly from a positive perspective and concealing the negative impact of neoliberal housing policies on working-class and middle-class citizens and residents.

In the next chapter, by way of conclusion, I will attempt to answer the question of why the content of Catalan language textbooks is presented in the way the results of this study have shown. In other words, why do Catalan language materials present an idealized neoliberal world, free of social conflicts and problems, which closely resembles images that appear in commercials or in lifestyle and entertainment magazines? The final chapter will also address the similarities between the content of textbooks for a minor language without international pretensions, such as Catalan, and that of global English textbooks as shown by other critical authors (Gray 2010b; Gray and Block 2014; Copley 2017), against the backdrop of neoliberalism as the ruling ideology and political economy of our times.

Notes

1 As is well known, the proposals of Engels and his comrade Marx were implemented first in the former Soviet Union after the Bolshevik Revolution in 1917, and later in other countries organized under a socialist system.
2 Banks initiated more than 400,000 mortgage foreclosures in Spain between 2008 and 2012, among which almost 80,000 were in Catalonia (De Weerdt and Garcia 2016: 274).

9 Conclusions

Following a Marxist view of society, this book started with the proposition that language textbooks are conditioned by the particular economic, political and social context within which they come into being. I have been especially interested in examining in which ways textbooks contain the ideological underpinnings of neoliberalism, the current stage of capitalism, doing so from a critical perspective that focuses on political economy. In particular, I have analyzed the dimensions of social class that appear in textbooks and the content related to the worlds of work and housing. This approach fills a gap in the field of critical studies of language textbooks that in recent decades has focused on identity politics, but has neglected issues related to social class and the economic bases of society (see Chapter 3). One of the aims of my study is to awaken awareness among the educational and academic communities about the necessity to look critically at textbooks from a political and economic perspective.

As seen in the three previous chapters, the content proposed for teaching and learning Catalan as a second language in textbooks presents an idealized neoliberal world that arguably clashes with the social life of economic migrants, who represent the majority of actual and potential learners of Catalan as a second language. The results show that the neoliberal content of Catalan textbooks is quite similar to that of global English textbooks (Chun 2009; Gray 2010b; Gray and Block 2014; Copley 2017). And, as suggested by Block and Gray (2018), it is the kind of content that we are likely to find, very most probably, in the great majority of contemporary language textbooks in the age of neoliberalism, at least in those coming from Western countries. In this last chapter, I will first briefly comment on the results of the content analysis. I will then discuss why textbooks for the teaching of a medium-sized European language like Catalan, that are not distributed internationally, have similar content to that of global English textbooks. Finally, I will propose some suggestions to challenge neoliberalism in language textbooks and in education in general.

Neoliberal content

The results of my study suggest that Catalan language textbooks, in the same vein as mainstream education textbooks (Luke 1988; Apple1990; Apple and Christian Smith 1991), opt to transmit so-called official knowledge, that which is also disseminated by the mass media and the capitalist class. In that way, textbooks naturalize and reinforce the current economic, social and political organization of society. As with the cultural products (TV, radio, movies, pop songs) studied by the Frankfurt School more than a half century ago, current language textbooks can also be made tools for the reproduction and legitimation of the capitalist system (Bori and Petanović 2016). They promote the conformism or even the alienation of individuals, in endowing them with a 'happy consciousness' (Marcuse 1964), the pressing need to consume (Debord 1970) and the 'instrumental reason' to achieve only utilitarian purposes (Horkheimer and Adorno 2002 [1944]). In this regard, however, it is worth recognizing that all this may be contested and subverted by students and teachers in class.

On the other hand, language materials sidestep and hide the violence and the socioeconomic inequalities generated by capitalism, in a very similar way to that described by Frankfurt scholars in the case of the cultural products they analyzed (Taylor and Harris 2008). Louis Althusser, another Marxist thinker whose work was contemporaneous with that of Frankfurt school theorists, argues that in order for the capitalist relations of production to be maintained, the reproduction of labor skills is necessary. However, he adds that, "at the same time, a reproduction of its submission to the rules of the established order, i.e. a reproduction of submission to the ruling ideology for the workers" (Althusser 1971: 132–3) is necessary. As I have shown in this study, by promoting the roles of consumers and entrepreneurs among learners, Catalan language textbooks also give resources to learners about how to obey the ruling ideology, and very often may contribute to shaping submissive roles for students.

Furthermore, what Catalan textbooks almost always show are the voices of the economically well off. They can be women and men, LGBT (in a lesser extent but steadily gaining ground) or heterosexual; they can be African, Asian and Caucasian, atheist, Christian or Muslim. The only thing that people in the texts cannot be is poor, or at least not in any great numbers. The textbooks for Catalan will do everything they can to get the poor to at least aspire to become wealthy – using all the mechanisms of neoliberal capitalist management, gurus, self-help, self-responsibilization technicians, celebrities, alternative lifestyle, yoga and meditation coaches. To put it bluntly, they will use every tool they can to alienate people, turning away from making humans more human and less zombie.

In that vein, Catalan textbooks, following a communicative task-based approach to learning languages, provide students with resources to learn a

164 *Conclusions*

narrow version of the language, namely a utilitarian one to resolve everyday situations and especially economic transactions. Therefore, the language taught in textbooks is only a communication tool for individuals to survive in a neoliberal environment. There is not a single example of activity or text that stimulates a social awareness of the injustices in the world of which we are part. Furthermore, with their obsession with an instrumental language, textbooks also tend to marginalize a richer version of the language, such as we find in literary texts, which might stimulate critical understanding among learners, and help them to grow intellectually. Literature could also be a way to introduce history into language education, since in current language textbooks everything happens today, as if the past does not matter at all.

In brief, one key phenomenon that this book highlights is the impact of neoliberalism on the content presented in language textbooks and how this content is presented in an idealized way, as in a fairytale. Another important phenomenon is the similarity between the content of global English textbooks and that which appears in textbooks for a smaller language. This is somewhat surprising because the situation of the Catalan language is diametrically opposed to that of the new global *lingua franca*. The reasons for these similarities will be discussed in the next section.

Global vs. smaller language textbooks

The current sociolinguistic situation of the Catalan language has little, if anything, to do with that of English as a global language. Catalan is considered a 'medium-sized' language, but it is in the tricky situation of being in conflict with Spanish, and it is not even an official language in the institutions of the European Union. However, the different circumstances of Catalan and English languages cannot be appreciated in language textbooks. The main particularities of the content of the Catalan textbooks of my corpus in relation to that of global English textbooks are limited to certain specific aspects of Catalan culture and geography. Catalan textbooks include references to customs, fairs, festivals, popular sayings, food and drinks, or mass media, which tend to have a local accent. On the other hand, global English textbooks often emphasize international cultural traditions, together with Anglo-American ones. The local accent can also be noticed in references to Catalan geographical locations, emblematic places in Catalonia, local celebrities and, more rarely, to Catalan literary works and artists. In addition, Catalan textbooks provide practical information to foreigners living in Catalonia, related for example to local medical services, public transport, libraries or post offices. Yet, in essence, both global language and 'smaller' language textbooks today tend to present very similar approaches and content, as both promote the construction of an entrepreneurial and consumer identity, of the so-called neoliberal citizen (Block 2018a).

As we come to the end of this book, I would like to address what I consider the core of the matter, that is, why the content of contemporary language textbooks presents neoliberal practices and values from a positive perspective. The first answer, I think, can be found in neoliberalism as the dominant ideology of our times, which emerges from a particular political economic organization of society based on free trade, the reduction of public spending and the privatization and flexibilization of work, which, in turn, has led to increasing inequality in the distribution of wealth. As stated by Littlejohn 25 years ago, language textbooks "constitute part of a struggle for hegemony in which (ruling class) ideologies are represented as 'natural' and 'commonsensical'" (1992: 256). More recently, Gray (2010b), Littlejohn (2012) and Copley (2017) agreed that the dominant neoliberal ideology should be taken into account to understand the ways in which the neoliberal culture is naturalized in global English textbooks. Gray (2010a, 2010b, 2012a) also stressed economic profit as a key factor, since publishers have the perception that the apparently 'aspirational content' will be motivating for students and result in high sales for the multi-billionaire dollar industry that ELT is in the age of neoliberal globalization. However, it also may happen that on occasion, especially in the case of textbooks for smaller languages whose primary aim is not to make great profits, authors may still choose to present uncritically a neoliberal world in language textbooks. These authors certainly do not belong to the ruling class and indeed very often work under precarious labor conditions. To understand this last phenomenon, we should probably refer to neoliberalism in a Foucauldian way, that is, as the rationality of contemporary capitalism, which has penetrated the behavior of every human being in a way that "tends to organize and structure not only the action of the rulers but also the conduct of the ruled" (Dardot and Laval 2013: 9).

Regarding the particular case of Catalan language textbooks, there are at least three additional reasons why their content is the way it is. The first one is the impact of the global English Language Teaching (ELT) industry on the teaching and learning of all modern languages today. The British Council, the University of Cambridge with its examination systems and British publishing houses with their global product distribution, all have the ability to shape the approaches to and content of foreign language teaching and learning around the world (Brinning 2015: 37).

A second key reason why the content of Catalan textbooks is neoliberal in nature is the great impact of the policy of the Council of Europe over the last four decades. As I illustrated with the example of Catalan as a second language in Chapter 5, the recommendations of the Council of Europe is an imposition from above regarding the ways language education should be. The experts from the Council of Europe have promoted a wide range of reforms in foreign language teaching, which has led to greater homogeneity and control of much of language education practices, language materials and tests across the European continent and beyond. These reforms have imposed the communicative teaching of an instrumental language, aligned with the interests of the economically powerful sectors of society (see

166 *Conclusions*

Chapter 2). The policies of the Council of Europe thus have fallen within the neoliberal reforms of broader education in recent decades based on concepts such as 'skills', 'employability', 'lifelong learning', 'competitiveness' or 'entrepreneurialism'. The rapid spread of the proposals of the Council of Europe has been possible thanks not only to the prestige that this institution has within academic and political spheres, but also the economic and human resources invested by this institution and other political bodies in disseminating and popularizing the Council of Europe's language projects.

Finally, a third reason for the uncritical implementation of the trends of the global ELT industry and especially of the recommendations of the Council of Europe without meaningful local variations in the case of the teaching of smaller languages such as Catalan is a kind of insecurity or lack of self-confidence in the contexts in which such languages both exist and are taught. The fact that these languages in many cases have a limited political, economic and cultural power favors the interest to adopt a defensive or even a self-conscious strategy. In other words, following the approaches of English, the most learned foreign language in the world, or the proposals of an international organization such as the Council of Europe, is safer and far more comfortable than exploring alternative ways to teach the languages of smaller cultures without a high international impact.

What can be done?

In recent years, there has been a partial revolt against neoliberalism as its socially polarizing effects have become more obvious. Some of the most famous protest movements have been the Spanish *Indignados* ('the Outraged') and the Occupy Wall Street phenomenon, but there have also been protests against neoliberal policies and for social justice all around the capitalist world. More recently, despite all their contradictions, the victories of the Brexit and of Donald Trump in the US presidential elections in 2016 may also be understood as a protest against the status quo. These developments may seem to undermine the acceptance of widespread neoliberal values. However, at the moment it is difficult to claim that neoliberalism is in danger of being overturned.

My book grew out of the desire to help develop a better awareness of the false neutrality of foreign language education, and particularly of language textbooks. By exposing the political, economic and social implications of teaching and learning languages, I aim to contribute, albeit only to a limited extent, to constructing a more egalitarian, fair and ethical education, and, ultimately, a better world. In my view, language materials should not be tools for the reproduction of the status quo, but pedagogic tools that encourage critical thinking in students and help them to grow intellectually. For this reason, we should find or create alternative language materials which do not work for the maintenance of the social relations of power and domination in the era of neoliberalism.

As an example of alternative material, Gray and Block (2014) mention the ELT textbook *Problem-Posing at Work: English for Action* (Auerbach and Wallerstein 2004). It is a book addressed to immigrants living in North America, based in the Freirean concept of 'critical consciousness' (*conscientização*, in Portuguese), which refers to an understanding of the world that recognizes the existing political and social contradictions and allows for fighting against factors that oppress the vulnerable groups of society (Freire 1970). The textbook proposes to examine and share students' experiences, to teach a kind of language and knowledge that allow learners to gain control of their circumstances in order to be able to transform them (Gray and Block 2014: 66–7). In a similar vein, 25 years earlier, *TESOL Quarterly* reviewed a total of 14 ELT materials with alternative approaches for adults in North America published in the 1980s. What all these nontraditional materials had in common was that they reflected the real experiences of immigrants and refugees and encouraged them to actively participate in the process of language learning (Auerbach 1989).

On the other hand, it is also very important that teachers participate in the language learning process as active subjects who do not passively accept the proposals of textbooks and who are aware that textbooks (as all language teaching processes) are shaped by a greater socioeconomic context. This might be achieved by making critical pedagogy the foundation of future language teachers' curriculums. Any language material may help in learning a new language and, even, in recognizing the structure of power and domination, as long as teachers and learners are critically aware citizens. In fact, there are many teachers who feel uncomfortable with these kinds of neoliberal textbooks. Some of them, as I have become aware through personal communication, challenge these textbooks with different approaches and content. They create their own materials or sometimes do not even use materials, as proposed by Dogme Language Teaching. Chun (2016) explains and implements a critical pedagogy approach in an English for academic purposes classroom that would be interesting to develop further. It consists of situating critical pedagogies at the center of the teaching process in order to empower students to go far beyond the presentations of language materials and to create their own alternative interpretations, based on their meaningful and real experiences, and in that way question the hegemonic discourses found in the language textbook (Chun 2016).

In summary, to challenge the dominant ideologies in existing textbooks, and especially neoliberalism, we need further work in two directions. The first consists of transforming current language materials and curricula in order to include alternative knowledge to that disseminated by the dominant classes of society. And the second, and probably the most important, involves encouraging education professionals to include critical awareness, reflection and dialogue in the classroom. In that way, following the tenets of critical pedagogy, teachers could ultimately become advocates for social justice.

168   *Conclusions*

Concluding thoughts

To conclude, I would like to add some additional final thoughts. In my view, it is necessary to challenge the current economic rationalism and the instrumental purposes of education in general, and also those of foreign language education. We should replace the managerial discourses in education, based on the mercantile logic of profit-making, short-term results and accountability, for a more humanist and ethical understanding of education. Against the dominant policy in neoliberal societies that business should indirectly or even directly control the goals of education, I am of the opinion that this should never be the case. The reason is very simple: businesses' main purpose is profit-making, which is oppositional to the highest goal of the education which should be social justice, as advocated by critical pedagogy. In this regard, education should help students to understand and compare, to analyze and discern, to refine their perception of reality and to form their own opinions. Education cannot be disconnected from the lived experiences of people and from the recognition of the power structures of the wider society. In conclusion, education should help people to transform themselves, as well as their relations with others for the purpose of constructing a fairer and more caring world. This task, however, is not an easy one. As John Gray (personal communication) reminds me, education under capitalism cannot be easily divorced from the need to produce citizens of the type required by the system at any given historical moment.

With regard to this last point, we must recall that practices promoted by the ruling class do not emerge exclusively in the content of textbooks and in education in general. They are dominant and are disseminated throughout society at large. Hence, in order to fight against existing injustices, inequalities and contradictions, it would be necessary to transform the economic, social and political structures in today's capitalist societies. I strongly agree with Block and Gray, whose works have guided my study, when they adopt a Marxist position regarding this matter:

> In Marxist terms, we need to deal with education as a superstructural phenomenon which is inextricably linked to the economic base of society and understand that profound changes in the former are difficult without profound changes in the latter. The economic base is at this point in history constituted by the model of capitalism (call it neoliberalism, call it 'late') in which we and everything we do are currently enmeshed.
>
> (Block and Gray 2016: 492)

Finally, I would like to mention, once again, that the current structure of society is not a natural one and consequently it is not inevitable. It is historically situated, as Marx might say. We should work further to persuade ourselves and our fellow citizens that there are many possible ways to organize society. As Fredric Jameson (1991: 263) noted more than 25 years ago, the neoliberal idea that the market is a part of human nature should always be challenged. In keeping with this ideological struggle, we may aim to fully dismantle the current hegemony of neoliberalism and make obvious to people the tremendous injustices that capitalism incarnates. Because, yes, another world is indeed possible.

References

Aaker, J. (1997) 'Dimensions of brand personality', *Journal of Marketing Research*, 34(3): 347–56.

Akin, O., Montalvo, J.G., Villar, J.G., Peydró, J.L. and Raya, J.M. (2014) 'The real estate and credit bubble: Evidence from Spain', *SERIEs*, 5: 223–43.

Albó, M., Gimeno, M., Pelegrí, I. and Porter, R. (1980) *Retalls: Textos i exercicis de l'aprenentatge del català*, Barcelona: Teide.

Alderson, J.C. (2007) 'The CEFR and the need for more research', *Modern Language Journal*, 91(4): 659–63.

Alderson, J.C., Figueras, N., Kuijper, H., Nold, G., Takala, S. and Tardieu, C. (2006) 'Analysing tests of reading and listening in relation to the common European framework of reference: The experience of the Dutch CEFR construct project', *Language Assessment Quarterly*, 3(1): 3–30.

Alptekin, C. (1993) 'Target-language culture in EFL materials', *ELT Journal*, 47(2): 136–43.

Althusser, L. (1971) 'Ideology and the ideological state apparatuses', in B. Brewster (ed.), *Lenin and philosophy and other essays* (pp. 127–88), London: New Left Books.

Amini, M. and Birjandi, P. (2012) 'Gender bias in the Iranian high school EFL textbooks', *English Language Teaching*, 5(2): 134–47.

Anguera, X., Roig, M., Tomàs, N. and Verdugo, M. (2010a) *Nou Nivell elemental 1*, Barcelona: Castellnou.

Anguera, X., Roig, M., Tomàs, N. and Verdugo, M. (2010b) *Nou Nivell elemental 2*, Barcelona: Castellnou.

Anguera, X., Roig, M., Tomàs, N. and Verdugo, M. (2010c) *Nou Nivell elemental 3*, Barcelona: Castellnou.

Apple, M.W. (1985) 'The culture and commerce of the textbook', *Journal of Curriculum Studies*, 17(2): 147–62.

Apple, M.W. (1990) *Ideology and curriculum*, 2nd edn, London: Routledge.

Apple, M.W. (1993) 'The politics of official knowledge: Does a national curriculum make sense?', *Teachers College Record*, 95(2): 222–41.

Apple, M.W., Ball, S.J. and Gandin, L.A. (eds.) (2010) *The Routledge international handbook of the sociology of education*, London: Routledge.

Apple, M.W. and Christian-Smith, L. (1991) 'The politics of the textbook', in M.W. Apple and L. Christian-Smith (eds.), *The politics of the textbook* (pp. 1–21), London: Routledge.

References   171

Argente, J.A., Castellanos, J., Jorba, M., Molas, J., Murgades, J., Nadal, J.M. and Sullà, E. (1979) 'Una nació sense estat, un poble sense llengua' [A nation without state, people without language], *Els Marges: revista de llengua i literatura*, 15: 3–13.

Auerbach, E. (1989) 'Nontraditional materials for adult ESL', *TESOL Quarterly*, 23(2): 321–35.

Auerbach, E. and Burgess, D. (1985) 'The hidden curriculum of survival ESL', *TESOL Quarterly*, 19: 475–95.

Auerbach, E. and Wallerstein, N. (2004) *Problem-posing at work: English for action*, Edmonton: Grass Roots Press.

Awasthi, J.R. (2006) 'Textbook and its evaluation', *Journal of NELTA*, 11(1–2): 1–10.

Baleghizadeh, S. and Motahed, M.J. (2010) 'An analysis of the ideological content of internationally-developed British and American ELT textbooks', *The Journal of Teaching Language Skills*, 2(2): 1–27.

Basabe, E.A. (2006) 'From de-anglicanization to internationalisation: Cultural representations of the UK and the USA in global, adapted and local ELT textbooks in Argentina', *Profile Issues in Teachers' Professional Development*, 7: 59–75.

Batteman, B. and Mattos, M. (2006) 'An analysis of the cultural content of six Portuguese textbooks', *Portuguese Language Journal*, 1: 23–36.

Bauman, Z. (2007) *Consuming life*, Cambridge: Polity Press.

Beacco, J.C. (2004) 'Influence du cadre sur les programmes et les dispositifs d'évaluation' [Influence of the framework on programmes and assessment instruments], *Le Français dans le Monde*, 336.

Beacco, J.C. and Byram, M. (2003) *Guide for the development of language education policies in Europe*, Strasbourg: Council of Europe.

Beacco, J.C., Byram, M., Cavalli, M., Coste, D., Cuenat, M.E., Goullier, F. and Panthier, J. (2010) *Guide for the development and implementation of curricula for plurilingual and intercultural education*, Strasbourg: Council of Europe.

Beck, U. (1992) *Risk society: Towards a new modernity*, London: SAGE.

Bernstein, B. (1971) *Class, codes and control, volume 1: Theoretical studies towards a sociology of language*, London: Routledge & Kegan Paul.

Bernstein, K.A., Hellmich, E.A., Katznelson, N., Shin, J. and Vinall, K. (2015) 'Introduction to special issue: Critical perspectives on neoliberalism in second/foreign language education', *L2 Journal*, 7(3): 3–14.

Bhabha, H. (1994) *The location of culture*, London: Routledge.

Biesta, G. (2006) 'What's the point of lifelong learning if lifelong learning has no point? On the democratic deficit of policies for lifelong learning', *European Educational Research Journal*, 5(3–4): 169–80.

Block, D. (2002) 'Negotiation for meaning as McCommunication: A problem in the frame', in D. Block and D. Cameron (eds.), *Globalization and language teaching* (pp. 117–33), London: Routledge.

Block, D. (2008) 'Language education and globalization', in S. May and N. Hornberger (eds.), *Encyclopedia of language and education, 2nd ed., Vol. 1: Language policy and political issues in education* (pp. 31–43), Dordrecht, The Netherlands: Springer Science+Business Media.

Block, D. (2010) 'Globalisation and language teaching', in N. Coupland (ed.), *Handbook of language and globalisation* (pp. 287–304), Oxford: Basil Blackwell.

172 References

Block, D. (2012a) 'Economic globalization and identity in applied linguistics in neoliberal times', in D. Block, J. Gray and M. Holborow (eds.), *Neoliberalism and applied linguistics* (pp. 68–85), London: Routledge.

Block, D. (2012b) 'Class and SLA: Making connections', *Language Teaching Research*,16(2): 188–205.

Block, D. (2014) *Social class in applied linguistics*, London: Routledge.

Block, D. (2015a) 'Social class in applied linguistics', *Annual Review of Applied Linguistics*, 35: 1–19.

Block, D. (2015b) 'Becoming a language teacher: Constraints and negotiation in the emergence of new identities', *Bellaterra Journal of Teaching & Learning Language & Literature*, 8(3): 9–26.

Block, D. (2016a) 'Social class in language and identity research', in S. Preece (ed.), *The Routledge handbook of language and identity* (pp. 241–54), London: Routledge.

Block, D. (2016b) 'The impact of globalisation, internationalisation and migration on the use and vitality of Catalan in secondary school and higher education settings', *Language, Culture and Curriculum*, 29(1): 107–16.

Block, D. (2017a) 'Political economy in applied linguistics research', *Language Teaching*, 50(1): 32–64.

Block, D. (2017b) 'Migration, language & social class', in S. Canagarajah (ed.), *Routledge handbook on migration and language*, London: Routledge.

Block, D. (2018a) *Political economy and sociolinguistics: Neoliberalism, inequality and social class*, London: Bloomsbury.

Block, D. (2018b) 'What is language commodification?', in S. Breidbach, L. Küster and B. Schmenk (eds.), *Sloganizations in language education discourse*, Bristol: Multilingual Matters.

Block, D. (2018c) 'Inequality and class in language policy and planning', in J. Tollefson and M. Pérez-Milans (eds.), *The Oxford handbook of language policy and planning*, Oxford: Oxford University Press.

Block, D. and Gray, J. (2016) ' "Just go away and do it and you get marks": The degradation of language teaching in neoliberal times', *Journal of Multilingual and Multicultural Development*, 37(5): 481–94.

Block, D. and Gray, J. (2018) 'French language textbooks as ideologically imbued cultural artefacts: Political economy, neoliberalism and (self) branding', in S. Coffey and U. Wingate (eds.), *New directions for language learning in the 21st century*, London: Routledge.

Block, D., Gray, J. and Holborow, M. (2012a) *Neoliberalism and applied linguistics*, London: Routledge.

Block, D., Gray, J. and Holborow, M. (2012b) 'Introduction', in D. Block, J. Gray and M. Holborow (eds.), *Neoliberalism and applied linguistics* (pp. 1–13), London: Routledge.

Boix-Fuster, E. and Farràs, J. (2012) 'Is Catalan a medium-sized language community too?', in F.X. Vila (ed.), *Survival and development of language communities: Prospects and challenges* (pp. 157–78), Bristol: Multilingual Matters.

Boltanski, L. and Chiapello, E. (2007) *The new spirit of capitalism*, London: Verso.

Bori, P. (2015) 'Anàlisi crítica de llibres de text català per a no catalanoparlants adults en temps de neoliberalisme' [Critical analysis of Catalan language textbooks for non-Catalan adult speakers in times of neoliberalism], unpublished thesis, Pompeu Fabra University in Barcelona. Online. Available HTTP: <www.tdx.cat/handle/10803/350798> (accessed 4 October 2016).

Bori, P. (2017) 'Evolució dels llibres de text de català per a no catalanoparlants adults des d'una perspectiva socioecòmica' [The development of Catalan as a

References   173

second language textbooks from a socioeconomic perspective], in V. Dickov (ed.), *Identidad, movilidad y perspectivas de los estudios de lengua, literatura y cultura* (pp. 263–82), Belgrade: University of Belgrade.

Bori, P. and Petanović, J. (2016) 'Constructing the entrepreneurial-self: How Catalan textbooks present the neoliberal worker to their students', *Journal for Critical Education Policy Studies*, 14(3): 154–74.

Bori, P. and Petanović, J. (2017) 'The representation of immigrant characters in Catalan as a second language textbooks: A critical discourse analysis', *Lengua y migración/Language and Migration*, 9(2): 61–75.

Boufoy-Bastick, B. (2015) 'Rescuing language education from the neoliberal disaster: Culturometric predictions and analyses of future policy', *Policy Futures in Education*, 13(4): 439–67.

Bourdieu, P. (1998) 'Utopia of endless exploitation: The essence of neoliberalism', *Le Monde diplomatique*, December. Available HTTP: <http://mondediplo.com/1998/12/08bourdieu> (accessed 12 March 2017).

Branchadell, A. (ed.) (2005) *La moralitat de la política lingüística* [The morality of the language policy], Barcelona: Institut d'Estudis Catalans.

Branchadell, A. (2015) 'Language education for adult migrants in Catalonia', in J. Simpson and A. Whiteside (eds.), *Adult language education and migration: Challenging agendas in policy and practice* (pp. 82–93), London: Routledge.

Breeze, R. (2011) 'Critical discourse analysis and its critics', *Pragmatics*, 21(4): 493–525.

Brenner, N., Peck, J. and Theodore, N. (2010) 'After neoliberalization?', *Globalizations*, 7(3): 327–45.

Brinning, D.J. (2015) 'The challenges faced by teachers of English as a foreign language to young learners in international contexts and their training and development needs and opportunities', unpublished thesis, University of New York. Online. Available HTTP: <https:// http://etheses.whiterose.ac.uk/13826/> (accessed 4 July 2017).

Brown, G. (1990) 'Cultural values: The interpretation of discourse', *ELT Journal*, 44(1): 11–17.

Butcher, J. and Smith, P. (2010) '"Making a difference": Volunteer tourism and development', *Tourism Recreation Research*, 35(1): 27–36.

Byram, M. (1997) *Teaching and assessing intercultural communicative competence*, Clevedon: Multilingual Matters.

Byram, M. and Parmenter, L. (eds.) (2012) *The common European framework of reference: The globalisation of language education policy*, Bristol: Multilingual matters.

Cabré, A. and Pujadas, I. (1984) 'Tendencias demográficas recientes en Cataluña y su repercusión territorial' [Recent demographic tendencies in Catalonia and their territorial impact], *Documents d'anàlisi geogràfica*, 5: 3–23.

Cachón, L. (2009) 'En la "España inmigrante": entre la fragilidad de los inmigrantes y las políticas de integración' [In "the immigrant Spain": Between the immigrants fragility and the politics of integration], *Papeles del CEIC*, 45: 1–35.

Callinicos, A. (1990) *Against postmodernism: A Marxist critique*, New York: St. Martin's Press.

Cameron, D. (2000) 'Styling the worker: Gender and the commodification of language in the globalized service economy', *Journal of Sociolinguistics*, 4(3): 323–47.

Cameron, D. (2002) 'Globalization and the teaching of "communication skills"', in D. Block and D. Cameron (eds.), *Globalization and language teaching* (pp. 67–82), London: Routledge.

Campoy, M., Esteban, J. and Sagrera, M. (2011) *Català elemental*, Barcelona: Teide.

Canagarajah, S. (1993) 'American textbooks and Tamil students: A clash of discourses in the ESL classroom', *Language, Culture and Curriculum*, 6(2): 143–56.

174 References

Canagarajah, S. (2005) 'Critical pedagogy', in E. Hinkel (ed.), *Handbook of research in second language learning and teaching* (pp. 931–50), Mahwah: Lawrence Erlbaum Associates.

Candón, J. (2013) 'Las luchas por la vivienda en Sevilla: De las okupas a las corralas y más allá' [The struggles for housing in Sevilla: From squats to corralas and beyond], *La Ciudad Viva*, 7: 36–43.

Carroll, D. and Kowitz, J. (1994) 'Using concordancing techniques to study gender stereotyping in ELT textbooks', in J. Sunderland (ed.), *Exploring gender* (pp. 73–82), London: Prentice Hall.

Castells, M. (2000) 'Materials for an exploratory theory of the network society', *The British Journal of Sociology*, 51(1): 5–24.

Choppin, A. (2000) 'Pasado y presente de los manuales escolares' [Present and past of school manuals], *Revista Educación y pedagogía*, 13(29–30): 207–29.

Chun, C. (2009) 'Contesting neoliberal discourses in EAP: Critical praxis in an IEP classroom', *Journal of English for Academic Purposes*, 8(2): 111–20.

Chun, C. (2016) 'Addressing racialized multicultural discourses in an EAP textbook: Working toward a critical pedagogies approach', *TESOL Quarterly*, 50(1): 109–31.

Chun, C. (2017) *The narratives of capitalism: Everyday economists and the production of public discourses*, London: Routledge.

CNLB (Barcelona Center for Linguistic Normalization) (2008a) *Curs de català bàsic B1*, Barcelona: CPNL and CNLB.

CNLB (Barcelona Center for Linguistic Normalization) (2008b) *Curs de català bàsic B2*, Barcelona: CPNL and CNLB.

CNLB (Barcelona Center for Linguistic Normalization) (2011) *Curs de català bàsic B3*, Barcelona: CPNL and CNLB.

Codó, E. and Patiño-Santos, A. (2014) 'Beyond language: Class, social categorisation and academic achievement in a Catalan high school', *Linguistics and Education*, 25: 51–63.

Coffey, S. (2013) 'Communicating constructions of Frenchness through language coursebooks: A comparison', in J. Gray (ed.), *Critical perspectives on language teaching materials* (pp. 137–60), Basingstoke: Palgrave.

Colectivo IOÉ (2012) *Impactos de la crisis sobre la población inmigrante* [Impacts of the crisis on the immigrant population], Madrid: Organización Internacional para las Migraciones. Online. Available HTTP: <www. colectivoioe. org/index. php/publicaciones_libros/show/id/101> (accessed 15 May 2017).

Cook, V. (2003) 'Materials for adult beginners from an L2 user perspective', in B. Tomlinson (ed.), *Developing materials for language teaching* (pp. 275–90), London: Continuum.

Copley, K. (2017) 'Neoliberalism and ELT coursebook content', *Critical Inquiry in Language Studies*, 2017: 1–20.

Corona, V. (2016) 'Latino trajectories in Barcelona: A longitudinal ethnographic study of Latin American adolescents in Catalonia', *Language, Culture and Curriculum*, 29(1): 93–106.

Corona, V., Moore, E. and Unamuno, V. (2008) 'Linguistic reception in Catalonia: Challenges and contradictions', in J. Erfurt (ed.), *Sprache, Mehrsprachigkeit und sozialer Wandel* (pp. 121–44), Berna: Peter Lang.

Cortazzi, M. and Jin, L. (1999) 'Cultural mirrors: Materials and methods in the EFL classroom', in E. Hinkel (ed.), *Culture in second language teaching and learning* (pp. 196–219), Cambridge: Cambridge University Press.

References 175

Council of Europe (2001) *Common European framework for languages: Learning, teaching, assessment*, Cambridge: Cambridge University Press.

CPNL (Consortium for Linguistic Normalization) (2012) 'Consorci per a la Normalització Lingüística. Memòria 2012'. Online. Available HTTP: <http://arxius.cpnl.cat/arxius/consadm/93/memoria2012_digital.pdf> (accessed 11 March 2016).

CPNL (Consortium for Linguistic Normalization) (2014) 'Consorci per a la Normalització Lingüística. Memòria 2014'. Online. Available HTTP: <http://arxius.cpnl.cat/edicions/cnl/memoria2014_doble.pdf> (accessed 11 June 2017).

Crookes, G. (2009) *Values, philosophies, and beliefs in TESOL: Making a statement*, Cambridge: Cambridge University Press.

Cuesta, M. and Velloso, M. (2015) 'La banca marca el ritmo de la nueva era inmobiliaria' [The bank sets the pace for the new real estate era], *ABC*, 4 May. Available HTTP: <www.abc.es/economia/20150504/abci-banca-marca-ritmo-nueva-201505031815.html> (accessed 11 November 2016).

Curdt-Christiansen, X.L. and Weninger, C. (eds.) (2015a) *Language, ideology and education: The politics of textbooks in language education*, London: Routledge.

Curdt-Christiansen, X.L. and Weninger, C. (2015b) 'Introduction: Ideology and the politics of language textbooks', in X.L. Curdt-Christiansen and C. Weninger (eds.), *Language, ideology and education: The politics of textbooks in language education* (pp. 1–7), London: Routledge.

Daly, S. and Zarco, J. (2015) 'The global economic crisis: Spain's housing bubble', *Expert Journal of Finance*, 3: 40–4.

Dant, T. (2003) *Critical social theory: Culture, society and critique*, London: SAGE.

Dardot, P. and Laval, C. (2013) *The new way of the world: On neoliberal society*, London: Verso Books.

De Angelis, M. (2007) *The beginning of history: Value struggles and global capital*, London: Pluto Press.

De Castell, S., Luke, A. and Luke, C. (1989) *Language, authority, and criticism*, London: Falmer.

De Weerdt, J. and Garcia, M. (2016) 'Housing crisis: The Platform of Mortgage Victims (PAH) movement in Barcelona and innovations in governance', *Journal of Housing and the Built Environment*, 31(3): 471–93.

Debord, G. (1970 [1967]) *Society of the spectacle*, Detroit: Radical America and Black & Red.

Del Percio, A. (2016) 'The governmentality of migration: Intercultural communication and the politics of (dis) placement in Southern Europe', *Language and Communication*, 51: 87–98.

Del Percio, A. (2017) 'Engineering commodifiable workers: Language, migration and the governmentality of the self', *Language Policy*: 1–21.

Del Percio, A., Flubacher, M.C. and Duchêne, A. (2017) 'Language and political economy', in O. García, N. Flores and M. Spotti (eds.), *The Oxford handbook of language and society* (pp. 55–75), Oxford: Oxford University Press.

Delgado, A. (2010) 'Política de vivienda en España: vivienda, mercado y actuaciones protegidas' [Housing policy in Spain: Housing, market and protected action], *Revista Pueblos*, 44: 52–3.

Dendrinos, B. (1992) *The EFL textbook and ideology*, Athens: N.C. Grivas.

DGPL (The General Directorate of Linguistic Policy) (2008) *Parla.cat*, Barcelona: Direcció General de Política Lingüística, with the collaboration of Institut Ramon Llull and CPNL. Online. Available HTTP: <www.parla.cat> (accessed 15 May 2016).

176 References

Di Bernardo, F. (2016) 'The impossibility of precarity', *Radical Philosophy*, 198: 7–14.

Di Paolo, A. and Raymond, J.L. (2012) 'Language knowledge and earnings in Catalonia', *Journal of Applied Economics*, 15(1): 89–118.

Duchêne, A. and Heller, M. (eds.) (2012) *Language in late capitalism: Pride and profit*, London: Routledge.

Eagleton, T. (1996) *The illusions of postmodernism*, Oxford: Basil Blackwell.

Ecclestone, K. and Hayes, D. (2009) *The dangerous rise of therapeutic education*, London: Routledge.

Editors.cat (2016) 'Creix el mercat del llibre en català' [The Catalan book market grows]', Associació d'Editors en Llengua Catalana, 30 August. Available at: <http://ccaa.elpais.com/ccaa/2016/08/31/catalunya/1472670419_227628.html> (accessed 11 November 2016).

Engels, F. (1970 [1872]) *The housing question*, Moscow: Progress Publishers.

Esteban, J. (2012a) *Català inicial*, Barcelona: Teide.

Esteban, J. (2012b) *Català bàsic*, Barcelona: Teide.

Etxezarreta, M. (1991) *La reestructuración del capitalismo en España, 1970–1990* [The reorganization of the capitalism in Spain, 1970–1990], Barcelona: Icaria.

Etxezarreta, M., Navarro, F., Ribera, R. and Soldevila, V. (2012) 'Boom and (deep) crisis in the Spanish economy: The role of the EU in its evolution', *Boletim de Ciencias Económicas*, 55: 1–56.

EU-OSHA (European Agency for Safety and Health at Work) (2013) *Occupational safety and health and education: A whole school approach*, Luxembourg: Publications Office of the European Union. Online. Available HTTP: <https://osha.europa.eu/en/tools-and-publications/publications/reports/occupational-safety-and-health-and-education-a-whole-school-approach> (accessed 4 October 2016).

European Commission (2012) 'Communication from the Commission to the European Parliament, the Council, the European Economic and Social Committee and the Committee of the Regions: Rethinking education – investing in skills for better socio-economic outcomes', Brussels: COM (2012) 669 final. Online. Available at: <http://eur-lex.europa.eu/legal-content/EN/TXT/PDF/?uri=CELEX:52012DC0669&from=EN (accessed 15 April 2017).

Fairclough, N. (1992) *Discourse and social change*, Cambridge: Polity press.

Fairclough, N. (1995) *Critical discourse analysis*, London: Longman.

Fairclough, N. (2002) 'Language in new capitalism', *Discourse & Society*, 13(2): 163–6.

Fellner, W. and Spash, C.L. (2014) *The ilusion of consumer sovereignty in economic and neoliberal thought*, Institute for the Environment and Regional Development, Vienna University of Economics and Business. Online. Available HTTP: <http://www-sre.wu.ac.at/sre-disc/sre-disc-2014_02.pdf> (accessed 15 October 2016).

Figueras, N. (2012) 'The impact of the CEFR', *ELT Journal*, 66(4): 477–85.

Fishman, J.A. (1991) *Reversing language shift*, Clevedon: Multilingual Matters.

Flecker, J., Fibich, T. and Kraemer, K. (2017) 'Socio-economic changes and the reorganization of work', in C. Korunka and B. Kubicek (eds.), *Job demands in a changing world of work* (pp. 7–24), Cham: Springer International Publishing.

Fleming, P. (2015) *The mythology of work: How capitalism persists despite itself*, London: Pluto Press.

Fletcher, R. (2008) 'Living on the edge: The appeal of risk sports for the professional middle class', *Sociology of Sport Journal*, 25(3): 310–30.

References   177

Flores, N. (2013) 'The unexamined relationship between neoliberalism and plurilingualism: A cautionary tale', *TESOL Quarterly*, 47(3): 500–20.

Fogde, M. (2007) 'How to write your CV: Advice, expert knowledge and job seeking skills', Paper presented at The Fifth Critical Management Studies Conference, Manchester, 11–13 July. Online. Available HTTP: <www.management.ac.nz/ejrot/cmsconference/2007/proceedings/managingtheself/fogde.pdf> (accessed 8 April 2016).

Foucault, M. (2008) *The birth of biopolitics: Lectures at the Collège de France, 1978–1979*, Basingstoke: Palgrave.

Foucault, M. (1993) 'About the Beginning of the Hermeneutics of the Self', *Political Theory*, 21(2): 198–227.

Fraser, N. (2003) 'Social justice in the age of identity politics: Redistribution, recognition, and participation', in N. Fraser and A. Honneth (eds.), *Redistribution or recognition? A political-philosophical exchange* (pp. 7–109), London: Verso.

Freire, P. (1970) *Pedagogy of the oppressed*, New York: Continuum.

Frekko, S. (2013) 'Legitimacy and social class in Catalan language education for adults', *International Journal of Bilingual Education and Bilingualism*, 16(2): 164–76.

Fulcher, G. (2004) 'Deluded by artifices? The common European framework and harmonization', *Language Assessment Quarterly: An International Journal*, 1(4): 253–66.

Fundación Foessa (2016) *Análisis y perspectivas 2016* [Analysis and perspectives 2016], Madrid: Cáritas Española. Online. Available HTTP: <http://estaticos.elmundo.es/documentos/2016/06/02/informe-caritas-2016.pdf> (accessed 15 June 2017).

Furedi, F. (2004) *Therapy culture: Cultivating vulnerability in an uncertain age*, London: Routledge.

Galceran, A. (1984) 'La Generalitat utilizará la televisión, la radio y la prensa para enseñar el catalán' [Catalan government will use television, radio and press to teach Catalan], *El País*, 9 October. Available at: <http://elpais.com/diario/1984/10/09/sociedad/466124403_850215.html> (accessed 11 March 2016).

Gao, A. (2014) 'Social-class identity and English learning: Studies of Chinese learners', *Journal of Language, Identity, and Education*, 13(2): 92–8.

Garrido, H.M. (2016) 'El drama de la precariedad: solo uno de cada 20 nuevos contratos son fijos y de jornada completa' [The drama of precarity: Only one in every 20 new contracts is fixed-termed and full-time], *20 minutos*, 22 February. Available at: <www.20minutos.es/noticia/2669447/0/precariedad-al-alza/temporalidad-tiempo-parcial/crece-desde-inicio-crisis/> (accessed 11 December 2016).

Garsten, C. and Jacobsson, K. (eds.) (2004) *Learning to be employable, new agendas on work, responsibility and learning in a globalizing world*, Basingstoke: Palgrave.

Garton, S. and Graves, K. (eds.) (2014) *International perspectives on materials*, Basingstoke: Palgrave.

Generalitat de Catalunya (2001) *Català inicial*, Barcelona: Generalitat de Catalunya, Departament de Cultura. Online. Available HTTP: <http://llengua.gencat.cat/ca/serveis/informacio_i_difusio/publicacions_en_linia/classific_temes/temes_materials_didactics/catala_inicial/> (accessed 4 October 2016).

Generalitat de Catalunya (2003a) *Programa de llengua catalana, nivell bàsic (versió revisada)*, Barcelona: Generalitat de Catalunya, Departament de Presidència. Online. Available HTTP: <http://llengua.gencat.cat/web/.content/documents/publicacions/programacions_ensenyament_adults/arxius/basic.pdf/> (accessed 4 October 2016).

178 *References*

Generalitat de Catalunya (2003b) *Programa de llengua catalana, nivell elemental (versió revisada)*, Barcelona: Generalitat de Catalunya, Departament de Presidència. Online. Available HTTP: <http://llengua.gencat.cat/web/.content/documents/publicacions/programacions_ensenyament_adults/arxius/basic.pdf> (accessed 4 October 2016).

Generalitat de Catalunya (2013a) 'Els usos lingüístics de la població de Catalunya' [Language use of the population of Catalonia]. Online. Available at: <http://llengua.gencat.cat/ca/serveis/dades_i_estudis/poblacio/eulp/2013/> (accessed 11 May 2017).

Generalitat de Catalunya (2013b) 'La Generalitat adjudica el contracte per a la Governança del nou model TIC a Deloitte i Capgemini' [Catalan government assigns the contract for the governance of the new model ICT to Deloitte and Capgemini], *Sala de premsa*, 14 January. Available at: <http://premsa.gencat.cat/pres_fsvp/AppJava/notapremsavw/176967/ca/generalitat-adjudica-contracte-governanca-model-tic-deloitte-capgemini-estalvi-dun-17-despesa-serveis-gestio.do> (accessed 11 November 2016).

Generalitat de Catalunya (2016) 'L'espai d'aprenentatge Parla.cat supera els 200.000 usuaris inscrits' [The learning space Parla.cat surpasses 200.000 registrations], *Sala de premsa*, 15 March. Available at: <http://premsa.gencat.cat/pres_fsvp/AppJava/notapremsavw/291482/ca/lespai-daprenentatge-parla-cat-supera-200-000-usuaris-inscrits.do> (accessed 11 November 2016).

Gentier, A. (2012) 'Spanish banks and the housing crisis: Worse than the subprime crisis?', *International Journal of Business*, 17(4): 342–51.

George, S. (1999) 'A short history of neo-liberalism: Twenty years of elite economics and emerging opportunities for structural change', Paper presented to Economic Sovereignty in a Globalising World, Bangkok, 24–26 March. Online. Available at: <www.tni.org/en/article/short-history-neoliberalism> (accessed 11 December 2016).

Gil-Alonso, F. and Vidal-Coso, E. (2015) 'Inmigrantes Extranjeros en el mercado de trabajo español: ¿más resilientes o más vulnerables al impacto de la crisis?' [Foreign immigrants in the Spanish labour market: Are they more resilient or more vulnerable to the economic crisis?], *Migraciones*, 37: 97–123.

Gimeno, M. (2012) 'La Direcció General de Política Lingüística i l'ensenyament de català per a adults. La perspectiva històrica, 1' [The General Directorate of Linguistic Policy and the teaching of Catalan for adults. The historical perspective, 1], *Llengua i ús: revista tècnica de política lingüística*, 51, 3–13.

Giroux, H. (1997) *Pedagogy and the politics of hope: Theory, culture and schooling*, Oxford: Westview Press.

Glynn, S. (2009) *Where the other half lives: Lower income housing in a neoliberal world*, New York: Pluto.

Gore, S. (2002) 'The Catalan language and immigrants from outside the European Union', *International Journal of Iberian Studies*, 15(2): 91–102.

Grady, K.(1997) 'Critically reading an ESL text', *TESOL Journal*, 6(4): 7–10.

Gramsci, A. (1971) *Selections from the prison notebooks*, New York: International Publishers.

Gray, G.C. (2009) 'The responsibilization strategy of health and safety neo-liberalism and the reconfiguration of individual responsibility for risk', *British Journal of Criminology*, 49(3): 326–42.

Gray, J. (2000) 'The ELT coursebook as cultural artefact: How teachers censor and adapt', *ELT Journal*, 54(3): 274–83.

References   179

Gray, J. (2002) 'The global coursebook in English language teaching', in D. Block and D. Cameron (eds.), *Globalization and language teaching* (pp. 151–67), London: Routledge.

Gray, J. (2010a) *The construction of English: Culture, consumerism and promotion in the ELT global coursebook*, Basingstoke: Palgrave.

Gray, J. (2010b) 'The branding of English and the culture of the new capitalism: Representations of the world of work in English language textbooks', *Applied Linguistics*, 31(5): 714–33.

Gray, J. (2012a) 'Neoliberalism, celebrity and "aspirational content" in English language teaching textbooks for the global market', in D. Block, J. Gray and M. Holborow (eds.), *Neoliberalism and applied linguistics* (pp. 86–113), London: Routledge.

Gray, J. (2012b) 'English the industry', in A. Hewings and C. Tagg (eds.), *The politics of English: Conflict, competition, and co-existence* (pp. 137–63), Milton Keynes: The Open University/Routledge.

Gray, J. (ed.) (2013a) *Critical perspectives on language teaching materials*, Basingstoke: Palgrave.

Gray, J. (2013b) 'Introduction', in J. Gray (ed.), *Critical perspectives on language teaching materials* (pp. 1–16), Basingstoke: Palgrave.

Gray, J. (2013c) 'LGBT invisibility and heteronormativity in ELT materials', in J. Gray (ed.), *Critical perspectives on language teaching materials* (pp. 40–63), Basingstoke: Palgrave.

Gray, J. (2015) 'ELT materials: Claims, critiques and controversies', in G. Hall (ed.), *Routledge handbook of English language teaching* (pp. 95–108), London: Routledge.

Gray, J. and Block, D. (2014) 'All middle class now? Evolving representations of the working class in the neoliberal era: The case of ELT textbooks', in N. Harwood (ed.), *English language teaching textbooks: Content, consumption, production* (pp. 45–71), Basingstoke: Palgrave.

Grup Koiné (2016) 'Per a un veritable procés de normalització lingüística a la Catalunya independent' [For a true process of linguistic normalization in an independent Catalonia]. Online. Available at: <http://llenguairepublica.cat/prodsite/wp-content/uploads/2016/04/ManifestParanimf.pdf> (accessed 4 May 2017).

Guerrero, I., Mercadal, T., Roig, M. and Rovira, M. (2010a) *Nou Nivell bàsic 1*, Barcelona: Castellnou.

Guerrero, I., Mercadal, T., Roig, M. and Rovira, M. (2010b) *Nou Nivell bàsic 2*, Barcelona: Castellnou.

Guerrero, I., Mercadal, T., Roig, M. and Rovira, M. (2010c) *Nou Nivell bàsic 3*, Barcelona: Castellnou.

Gulliver, T. (2010) 'Immigrant success stories in ESL textbooks', *TESOL Quarterly*, 44(4): 725–45.

Gümüşok, F. (2013) 'A quest for literature in ELT coursebooks', *Journal of History Culture and Art Research*, 2(2): 114–33.

Hall, M. (2014) 'Gender representation in current EFL textbooks in Iranian secondary schools', *Journal of Language Teaching & Research*, 5(2): 253–61.

Hall, S. and O'Shea, A. (2013) 'Common-sense neoliberalism', *Soundings: A Journal of Politics and Culture*, 55(1): 8–24.

Halliday, M.A.K. (1990) 'New ways of meaning: A challenge to applied linguistics', *Journal of Applied Linguistics*, 6: 7–36.

180 References

Hardt, M. and Negri, A. (2001) *Empire*, Cambridge: Harvard University Press.

Harman, C. (1986) 'Base and superstructure', *International Socialism*, 2(32): 3–44.

Harris, R.L. and Seid, M.J. (2000) 'Critical perspectives on globalization and neoliberalism in the developing countries', *Journal of Developing Societies*, 16(1): 1–26.

Hartman, P.L. and Judd, E.L. (1978) 'Sexism and TESOL materials', *TESOL Quarterly*, 12: 383–93.

Harvey, D. (1991) *The condition of postmodernity*, London: Wiley-Blackwell.

Harvey, D. (2005) *A brief history of neoliberalism*, Oxford: Oxford University Press.

Harwood, N. (ed.) (2014a) *English language teaching textbooks: Content, consumption, production*, Basingstoke: Palgrave.

Harwood, N. (2014b) 'Content, consumption, and production: Three levels of textbook research', in N. Harwood (ed.), *English language teaching textbooks: Content, consumption, production* (pp. 1–41), Basingstoke: Palgrave.

Hearn, A. (2008) 'Meat, mask, burden' probing the contours of the branded "self"', *Journal of Consumer Culture*, 8(2): 197–217.

Heidepriem, E. (2011) 'An overview of Catalan research into language policy and planning', in M. Strubell and E. Boix (eds.), *Democratic policies for language revitalisation: The case of Catalan* (pp. 224–46), New York: Palgrave.

Heller, M. (2002) 'Globalization and the commodification of bilingualism in Canada', in D. Block and D. Cameron (eds.), *Globalization and language teaching* (pp. 47–63), London: Routledge.

Heller, M. (2003) 'Globalization, the new economy and the commodification of language', *Journal of Sociolinguistics*, 7(4): 473–92.

Heller, M. (2010) 'The commodification of language', *Annual Review of Anthropology*, 39: 101–14.

Hickey, T. (2006) ' "Multitude" or "class": Constituencies of resistance, sources of hope', in M. Cole (ed.), *Education, equality and human rights* (pp. 180–201), London: Routledge.

Higgins-Desbiolles, F. (2010) 'The elusiveness of sustainability in tourism: The culture-ideology of consumerism and its implications', *Tourism and Hospitality Research*, 10(2): 116–29.

Hill, D. (2010) 'Class, capital, and education in this neoliberal and neoconservative period', in S. Macrine, P. McLaren and D. Hill (eds.), *Revolutionizing pedagogy* (pp. 119–43), Basingstoke: Palgrave.

Hill, D. and Kumar, R. (eds.) (2009) *Global neoliberalism and education and its consequences*, London: Routledge.

Hill, D., Greaves, N. and Maisuria, A. (2009) 'Education, inequality and neoliberal capitalism: A classical marxist analysis', in D. Hill and R. Kumar (eds.), *Global neoliberalism and education and its consequences* (pp. 102–26), London: Routledge.

Hinkel, E. (1999) *Culture in second language teaching and learning*, Cambridge: Cambridge University Press.

Hirtt, N. (2009) 'Markets and education in the era of globalized capitalism', in D. Hill and R. Kumar (eds.), *Neoliberalism and education and its consequences* (pp. 208–26), London: Routledge.

Holborow, M. (2007) 'Language, ideology and neoliberalism', *Journal of Language and Politics*, 6: 51–73.

Holborow, M. (2012a) 'What is neoliberalism? Discourse ideology and the real world', in D. Block, J. Gray and M. Holborow, *Neoliberalism and applied linguistics* (pp. 14–32), London: Routledge.

References 181

Holborow, M. (2012b) 'Neoliberal keywords and the contradictions of an ideology', in D. Block, J. Gray and M. Holborow, *Neoliberalism and applied linguistics* (pp. 33–55), London: Routledge.

Holborow, M. (2013) 'Applied linguistics in the neoliberal university: Ideological keywords and social agency', *Applied Linguistics Review*, 4(2): 229–57.

Holborow, M. (2015) *Language and neoliberalism*, London: Routledge.

Holliday, A. (1994) *Appropriate methodology and social context*, Cambrige: Cambridge University Press.

hooks, b. (2000) *Where We Stand: Class Matters*, London: Routledge.

Horkheimer, M. and Adorno, T.W. (2002 [1944]) *Dialectic of enlightenment: Philosophical fragments*, Stanford: Stanford University Press.

Howatt, A.P. (1984) *A history of English language teaching*, Oxford: Oxford University Press.

Howatt, A.P. and Smith, R. (2014) 'The history of teaching English as a foreign language, from a British and European perspective', *Language & History*, 57(1): 75–95.

Hu, A. (2012) 'Academic perspectives from Germany', in M. Byram and L. Parmenter (eds.), *The common European framework of reference: The globalisation of language education policy* (pp. 66–75), Bristol: Multilingual matters.

Hu, G. (2002) 'Potential cultural resistance to pedagogical imports: The case of CLT in China', *Language, Culture and Curriculum*, 15(2): 93–105.

Human Rights Watch (2014) *Shattered dreams: Impact of Spain's housing crisis on vulnerable groups*, Washington, DC: Human Rights Watch.

Hutchinson, T. and Torres, E. (1994) 'The textbook as an agent of change', *ELT Journal*, 48(4): 315–28.

Hymes, D.H. (1972) 'On communicative competence', in J.B. Pride and J. Holmes (eds.), *Sociolinguistics: Selected readings* (pp. 269–93), Harmondsworth: Penguin.

Idescat (Catalan Statistical Office) (2015a) 'Distribution by countries'. Online. Available HTTP: <www.idescat.cat/poblacioestrangera/?geo=cat&nac=a&b=12&lang=en> (accessed 11 March 2016).

Idescat (Catalan Statistical Office) (2015b) 'Total and foreign population series'. Online. Available HTTP: <www.idescat.cat/poblacioestrangera/?b=0&lang=en> (accessed 11 March 2016).

INE (Spanish Statistical Office) (2016a) 'Unemployed persons'. Online. Available HTTP: <www.ine.es/jaxiT3/Tabla.htm?t=4086&L=1> (accessed 11 March 2016).

INE (Spanish Statistical Office) (2016b) 'Long term unemployment rate (12 months or more) according to period'. Online. Available HTTP: <www.ine.es/jaxiT3/Datos.htm?t=11185> (accessed 15 May 2017).

Institut Ramon Llull (2016) 'University network of Catalan studies abroad'. Online. Available HTTP: <www.llull.cat/english/aprendre_catala/mapa_llengua.cfm> (accessed 4 October 2016).

Jameson, F. (1991) *Postmodernism or the cultural logic of late capitalism*, Durham: Duke University Press.

Jaworski, A. and Thurlow, C. (2010) *Tourism discourse: Language and global mobility*, Basingstoke: Palgrave.

Jones, G. (2005) *Multinationals and global capitalism: From the nineteenth to the twenty-first century*, Oxford: Oxford University Press.

Junyent, M.C. (1999) 'El català, una llengua en perill d'extinció?' [Catalan, an endangered language?], *Revista d'Igualada*, 1: 27–38.

Kalleberg, A.L. (2007) *The mismatched worker*, New York: WW Norton & Company.

182 References

Kaplan, L.E. (2006) *God bless you Joe Stalin: The man who saved capitalism*, New York: Algora Publishing.

Kaščák, O. and Pupala, B. (2011) 'Governmentality-neoliberalism-education: The risk perspective', *Journal of Pedagogy/Pedagogický casopis*, 2(2): 145–58.

Keshavarz, M.H. and Malek, L.A. (2009) 'Critical discourse analysis of ELT textbooks', *The Iranian EFL Journal*, 5: 6–19.

Kincheloe, J.L. and McLaren, P. (2002) 'Rethinking critical theory and qualitative research', in Y. Zou and E.T. Trueba (eds.), *Ethnography and schools: Qualitative approaches to the study of education* (pp. 87–138), Maryland: Rowman and Littlefield Publishers.

Kinginger, C. (2004) 'Alice doesn't live here anymore: Foreign language learning and identity reconstruction', in A. Pavlenko and A. Blackledge (eds.), *Neogotiation of identities in multilingual contexts* (pp. 219–42), Clevedon: Multilingual Matters.

Klein, N. (2007) *The shock doctrine: The rise of disaster capitalism*, New York: Metropolitan Books.

Kramsch, C. (1993) *Context and culture in language teaching*, Oxford: Oxford University Press.

Kramsch, C. (1998) *Language and culture*, Oxford: Oxford University Press.

Kramsch, C. (2000) 'Second language acquisition, applied linguistics, and the teaching of foreign languages', *The Modern Language Journal*, 84(3): 311–26.

Kramsch, C. (2005) 'Post 9/11: Foreign languages between knowledge and power', *Applied Linguistics*, 26(4): 545–67.

Kramsch, C. (2014) 'Teaching foreign languages in an era of globalization: Introduction', *The Modern Language Journal*, 98(1): 296–311.

Kramsch, C. and Vinall, K. (2015) 'The cultural politics of language textbooks in the era of globalization', in X.L. Curdt-Chrisitiansen and C. Weninger (eds.), *Language, ideology and education: The politics of textbooks in language education* (pp. 11–28), London: Routledge.

Kress, G. (2010) *Multimodality: A social semiotic approach to contemporary communication*, London: Routledge.

Kubota, R. (2006) 'Teaching second languages for national security purposes: A case of post-9/11 USA', in J. Edge (ed.), *(Re-) locating TESOL in an age of empire* (pp. 119–38), Basingstoke: Palgrave.

Kubota, R. (2011) 'Questioning linguistic instrumentalism: English, neoliberalism, and language tests in Japan', *Linguistics and Education*, 22(3): 248–60.

Kubota, R. (2013) 'Language is only a tool: Japanese expatriates working in China and implications for language teaching', *Multilingual Education*, 3(4). Online. Available HTTP: <https://multilingual-education.springeropen.com/articles/10.1186/2191-5059-3-4> (accessed 4 March 2017).

Kubota, R. (2014) 'The multi/plural turn, postcolonial theory, and neoliberal multiculturalism: Complicities and implications for applied linguistics', *Applied Linguistics*, 2014: 1–22.

Kubota, R. and Lin, A. (eds.) (2009) *Race, culture, and identities in second language education: Exploring critically engaged practice*, London: Routledge.

Kullman, J. (2013) 'Telling tales: Changing discourses of identity in the 'Global' UK-published English language coursebook', in J. Gray (ed.), *Critical perspectives on language teaching materials* (pp. 17–39), Basingstoke: Palgrave.

Kumar, R. and Hill, D. (2009) 'Introduction: Neoliberal capitalism and education', in D. Hill and R. Kumar (eds.), *Global neoliberalism and education and its consequences* (pp. 1–11), London: Routledge.

References   183

Kumaravadivelu, B. (2008) *Cultural globalization and language education*, New Haven: Yale University Press.

Kumaravadivelu, B. (2012) 'Individual identity, cultural globalization, and teaching English as an international language', in L. Alsagoff, S.L. McKay, G. Hu and W.A Renandya (eds.), *Principles and practices for teaching English as an international language* (pp. 9–27), New York: Routledge.

Kustati, M. (2013) 'The shifting paradigms in the implementation of CLT in southeast Asia countries', *Al-Ta lim Journal*, 20(1): 267–77.

Labov, W. (1966) *The social stratification of English in New York city*, Washington, DC: Center for Applied Linguistics.

Lambert, S.J. (2008) 'Passing the buck: Labor flexibility practices that transfer risk onto hourly workers', *Human Relations*, 61(9): 1203–27.

Levidow, L. (2007) 'Marketizing higher education: Neoliberal strategies and counter-strategies', in E.W. Ross and R. Gibson (eds.), *Neoliberalism and education reform* (pp. 237–56), New Jersey: Hampton Press.

LibreRed (2015) 'La privatización del sector energético en España, un negocio redondo para los empresarios' [The privatization of the energy sector in Spain, a great deal for the companies], *LibreRed*, 3 March: <www.librered.net/?p=37565> (accessed 11 December 2016).

Liddicoat, A.J. (2009) 'Sexual identity as linguistic failure: Trajectories of interaction in the heteronormative language classroom', *Journal of Language, Identity, and Education*, 8(2–3): 191–202.

Littlejohn, A. (1992) 'Why are English language teaching materials the way they are?', unpublished thesis, Lancaster University. Online. Available at: <www.AndrewLittlejohn.net> (accessed 4 October 2016).

Littlejohn, A. (2012) 'Language teaching materials and the (very) big picture', *Electronic Journal of Foreign Language Teaching*, 9(1): 283–97.

Littlejohn, A. (2013) 'The social location of language teaching: From zeitgeist to imperative', in A. Ahmed, M. Hanzala, F. Saleem and G. Cane (eds.), *ELT in a changing world* (pp. 3–16), Cambridge: Cambridge Scholars Publishing.

Llobera, M., Mas, M., Melcion, J., Rosanas, R. and Vergés, M.H. (1989) *Digui, digui . . . Curs de català per a no catalanoparlants adults 1. Llibre del professor*, 2nd ed., Montserrat/Barcelona: PAMSA and Enciclopèdia Catalana.

Long, M. (2014) *Second language acquisition and task-based language teaching*, Malden: Wiley-Blackwell.

López, D. (2015) 'Neoliberal discourses and the local policy implementation of an English literacy and civics education program', *L2 Journal*, 7(3): 97–122.

López, I. and Rodríguez, E. (2011) 'The Spanish model', *New Left Review*, 69(3): 5–29.

López-Gopar, M. and Sughrua, W. (2014) 'Social class in English language education in Oaxaca, Mexico', *Journal of Language, Identity and Education*, 13(2): 104–10.

Luke, A. (1988) *Literacy, textbooks and ideology*, London: Falmer.

Luke, A. (2002) 'Beyond science and ideology critique: Developments in critical discourse analysis', *Annual Review of Applied Linguistics*, 22: 96–110.

Luke, A. (2006) 'Teaching after the market', in L. Weis, C. McCarthy and G. Dimitriadis, *Ideology, curriculum, and the new sociology of education: Revisiting the work of Michael Apple* (pp. 115–44), New York: Routledge.

Luke, A., Luke, C. and Graham, P. (2007) 'Globalization, corporatism, and critical language education', *International Multilingual Research Journal*, 1(1): 1–13.

Macrine, S., McLaren, P. and Hill, D. (eds.) (2010) *Revolutionizing pedagogy: Education for social justice within and beyond global neo-liberalism*, Basingstoke: Palgrave.

184 References

Maley, A. (2001) 'Literature in the language classroom', in R. Carter and D. Nunan (eds.), *The Cambridge guide to teaching English to speakers of other languages* (pp. 180–85), Cambridge: Cambridge University Press.

Marcuse, H. (1964 [1954]) *One-dimensional man: Studies in the ideology of advanced industrial society*, Boston: Beacon Press.

Marcuse, P. (2008) 'Subprime housing crisis'. Online. Available HTTP: <http://www.hic-net.org/articles.php?pid=2281> (accessed 15 October 2016).

Marí, I. (1986) 'El consell d'Europa i l'aprenentatge de llengües modernes' [The Council of Europe and the learning of modern languages], *Butlletí de la Societat Catalana de Pedagogia*, 0–2: 95–104.

Martí Henneberg, J. (2005) 'Els Alpinistes i la muntanya: La literatura de muntanya a Suïssa Romanya i a Catalunya en el segle XIX' [The Mountaineers and the Mountain: The Mountain Literature in Swiss Romandy and in Catalonia in the nineteenth century], *Treballs de la Societat Catalana de Geografia*, 24: 65–73.

Martínez, M. (2013) 'The squatters' movement in Europe: A durable struggle for social autonomy in urban politics', *Antipode*, 45: 866–87.

Martyniuk, W. and Noijons, J. (2007) 'Executive summary of results of a survey on the use of the CEFR at national level in the Council of Europe Member States'. Online. Available at: <www.coe.int/t/dg4/linguistic/Publications_EN.asp> (accessed 4 March 2017).

Marx, K. (1904 [1859]) *A contribution to the critique of political economy*, Chicago: Charles H. Kerr.

Marx, K. (1976 [1867]) *Capital: A critique of political economy, Volume 1*, New York: Vintage Books.

Marx, K. and Engels, F. (1998 [1845]) *The German ideology*, New York: Prometheus Books.

Mas, M., Melcion, J., Rosanas, R. and Vergés, H. (1984) *Digui, digui . . . Curs de català per a no catalanoparlants adults. Primer nivell*, Montserrat/Barcelona: PAMSA/Enciclopèdia Catalana.

Mas, M., Melcion, J., Rosanas, R. and Vergés, H. (1985) *Digui, digui . . . Curs de català per a no catalanoparlants adults. Segon nivell*, Montserrat: PAMSA.

Mas, M. and Vilagrassa, A. (2005) *Veus 1. Llibre de l'alumne*, Barcelona: PAMSA.

Mas, M. and Vilagrassa, A. (2007) *Veus 2. Llibre de l'alumne*, Barcelona: PAMSA.

Mas, M. and Vilagrassa, A. (2008) *Veus 3. Llibre de l'alumne*, Barcelona: PAMSA.

Masuhara, H., Hann, N., Yi, Y. and Tomlinson, B. (2008) 'Survey review: Adult EFL courses', *ELT Journal*, 62(3): 294–312.

McGill, K. (2013) 'Political economy and language: A review of some recent literature', *Journal of Linguistic Anthropology*, 23(2): 196–213.

McGrath, I. (2013) *Teaching materials and the roles of EFL/ESL teachers: Practice and theory*, London: Bloomsbury.

McVeigh, P. (2005) 'Embedding neoliberalism in Spain: From Franquismo to neoliberalism', in S. Soederberg, G. Menz and P.G. Cerny (eds.), *Internalizing globalization* (pp. 90–105), Basingstoke: Palgrave.

MECR (2003) *Marc europeu comú de referència per a les llengües: aprendre, ensenyar, avaluar*, Barcelona: Generalitat de Catalunya, Govern d'Andorra and Govern de les Illes Balears. Online. Available HTTP: <http://llengua.gencat.cat/ca/serveis/informacio_i_difusio/publicacions_en_linia/classific_temes/temes_materials_didactics/marc_europeu_de_referencia_per_a_les_llengues> (accessed 11 March 2016).

References 185

Michaels, W.B. (2006) *The trouble with diversity: How we learned to love identity and ignore inequality*, New York: Metropolitan Press.

Minett, A.J. (2009) 'Reproduction, resistance, and supranational language management: A critical discourse analysis of the role of soros-funded English language programs in the building of open societies', unpublished thesis, Indiana University of Pennsylvania. Online. Available at: <http://knowledge.library.iup.edu/cgi/view content.cgi?article=1042&context=etd> (accessed 30 August 2017).

Mirowksi, P. (2013) *Never let a serious crisis go to waste: How neoliberalism survived the financial crisis*, New York: Verso.

Mitchell, K. (2006) 'Neoliberal governmentality in the European Union: Education, training, and technologies of citizenship', *Environment and Planning D: Society and Space*, 24(3): 389–407.

Montañés, J.A. (2016) 'El sector editorial catalán crece gracias a los libros de texto' [The Catalan publishing sector grows thanks to the textbooks], *El País*, 31 August. Available at: <http://ccaa.elpais.com/ccaa/2016/08/31/catalunya/14726 70419_227628.html> (accessed 11 November 2016).

Moran, M. (2014) *Identity and capitalism*, London: SAGE.

Morgan, M. (2013) 'The paradoxical perpetuation of neoliberalism: How ideologies are formed and dissolved', Heathwood Institute. Online. Available at: <www.heathwoodpress.com/the-paradoxical-perpetuation-of-neoliberalism-how-ideolo gies-are-formed-and-dissolved> (accessed 23 January 2017).

Morrow, K. (2004) 'Background to the CEF', in K. Morrow (ed.), *Insights from the common European framework* (pp. 3–11), Oxford: Oxford University Press.

Muñoz, R. (2015) 'European education policy: A historical and critical approach to understanding the impact of neoliberalism in Europe', *Journal for Critical Education Policy Studies*, 13(1): 19–42.

Naredo, J M. (2009) 'La cara oculta de la crisis: El fin del boom inmobiliario y sus consecuencias' [The hidden face of the crisis: The end of the real estate boom and its consequences], *Revista de economía crítica*, 7: 118–33.

Ndura, E. (2004) 'ESL and cultural bias: An analysis of elementary through high school textbooks in the Western United States of America', *Language, Culture and Curriculum*, 17: 143–53.

Nelson, C. (1999) 'Sexual identities in ESL: Queer theory and classroom inquiry', *TESOL Quarterly*, 33(3): 371–91.

Nelson, C. (2008) *Sexual identities in English language education: Classroom conversations*, London: Routledge.

North, B. (2000) *The development of a common framework scale of language proficiency*, New York: Peter lang.

Norton, B. (1995) 'Social identity, investment, and language learning', *TESOL Quarterly*, 29(1): 9–31.

Nóvoa, A. (2002) 'Ways of thinking about education in Europe', in A. Nóvoa and M. Lawn (eds.), *Fabricating Europe* (pp. 131–55), Dordrecht, The Netherlands: Kluwer.

Olssen, M. (2008) 'Understanding the mechanisms of neoliberal control', in A. Fejes and K. Nicoll (eds.), *Foucault and lifelong learning: Governing de subject* (pp. 34–47), London: Routledge.

Olssen, M. and Peters, M. (2005) 'Neoliberalism, higher education and the knowledge economy: From the free market to knowledge capitalism', *Journal of Education Policy*, 20(3): 313–45.

186 References

O'Neill, M. (1995) 'Introduction', in D. Carter and M. O'Neill, *International perspectives on educational reform and policy implementation* (pp. 1–11), Brighton: Falmer.

Otxoa, I. (2007) *El recorte de derechos en las reformas laborales* [Curtailing rights in the labor reforms], Bilbao: Manu Robles-Arangiz Institutua.

Oxfam (2016) 'An economy for the 1%'. Online. Available at: <http://policy-practice.oxfam.org.uk/publications/an-economy-for-the-1-how-privilege-and-power-in-the-economy-drive-extreme-inequ-592643> (accessed 1 February 2017).

Papageorgiu, S. (2006) 'The CEFR and language policy outside of Europe', Message posted to LTEST-L, 'Language Testing Research and Practice'.

Paramenter, L. (2014) 'Globalization in Japan: Education policy and curriculum', in N.P. Stromquist and K. Monkman (eds.), *Globalization and education: Integration and contestation across cultures* (pp. 201–15), Lanham: Rowman & Littlefield.

Paran, A. (2008) 'The role of literature in instructed foreign language learning and teaching: An evidence-based survey', *Language Teaching*, 41(4): 465–96.

Park, J.S.Y. (2011) 'The promise of English: Linguistic capital and the neoliberal worker in the South Korean job market', *International Journal of Bilingual Education and Bilingualism*, 14(4): 443–55.

Park, J.S.Y. (2016) 'Language as pure potential', *Journal of Multilingual and Multicultural Development*, 37(5): 453–66.

Park, J.S.Y. and Wee, L. (2012) *Markets of English: Linguistic capital and language policy in a globalizing world*, New York: Routledge.

Patrick, F. (2013) 'Neoliberalism, the knowledge economy, and the learner: Challenging the inevitability of the commodified self as an outcome of education', *International Scholarly Research Notices*, 1: 1–8.

Pattillo, M. (2013) 'Housing: Commodity versus right', *Annual Review of Sociology*, 39: 509–31.

Peck, J. and Tickell, A. (2002) 'Neoliberalizing space', *Antipode*, 34(3): 380–404.

Pennycook, A. (1994) *The Cultural Politics of English as an International Language*, London: Longman.

Pennycook, A. (1998) *English and the discourses of colonialism*, London: Routledge.

Pennycook, A. (2001) *Critical applied linguistics: A critical introduction*, London: Lawrence Erlbaum Associates.

Pennycook, A. (2010) 'Critical and alternative directions in applied linguistics', *Australian Review of Applied Linguistics*, 33(2): 16.1–16.16.

Pereda, C. (2013) 'Los desahucios y el negocio de la vivienda' [Evictions and the housing business], *Éxodo*, 117: 5–10.

Peters, M. (2001) 'Education, enterprise culture and the entrepreneurial self: A foucauldian perspective', *Journal of Educational Enquiry*, 2(2): 58–71.

Peters, M. (2005) 'Critical pedagogy and the futures of critical pedagogy', in I. Gur-Ze'ev (ed.), *Critical theory and critical pedagogy today* (pp. 35–48), Haifa: University of Haifa Press.

Peters, M. (2016) 'Homo economicus as "entrepreneur of himself"', in S. Springer, K. Birch and J. MacLeavy (eds.), *Handbook of neoliberalism* (pp. 297–307), London: Routledge.

Peters, T. (1997) 'The brand called you', Fast Company, 31 August. Available at: <www.fastcompany.com/28905/brand-called-you> (accessed 11 November 2016).

Peters, T. (2008) *The brand you 50: Fifty ways to transform yourself from an "employee" into a brand that shouts distinction, commitment, and passion!* New York: Alfred A. Knopf.

References   187

Phillipson, R. (1992) *Linguistic imperialism*, Oxford: Oxford University Press.

Phillipson, R. (1997) 'The politics of English language teaching', in R. Wodak and D. Corson (eds), *Encyclopedia of language and education, 1* (pp. 201–10), Dordrecht: Kluwer Academic Publishers.

Phillipson, R. (2009) 'English in globalisation, a Lingua Franca or a Lingua Frankensteinia?', *TESOL Quarterly*, 43: 335–39.

Plehwe, D. (2009) 'Introduction', in P. Mirowski and D. Plehwe (eds.), *The road from Mont Pelerin: The making of neoliberalism* (pp. 1–42), Cambridge: Harvard University Press.

Porreca, K.L. (1984) 'Sexism in current ESL textbooks', *TESOL Quarterly*, 18: 704–24.

Prados de la Escura, L., Rosés, J.R. and Sanz-Villaroya, I. (2011) 'Economic reforms and growth in Franco's Spain', *Revista de Historia Económica – Journal of Iberian and Latin American Economic History*, 30(1): 45–89.

Prats, M., Rafanell, A. and Rossich, A. (1990) *El futur de la llengua catalana* [The future of Catalan language], Barcelona: Empúries.

Preece, S. (ed.) (2016) *The Routledge handbook of language and identity*, London: Routledge.

Price, G. (2014) 'English for all? Neoliberalism, globalization, and language policy in Taiwan', *Language in Society*, 43(5): 567–89.

Prodnik, J.A. (2014) 'A seeping commodification: The long revolution in the proliferation of communication commodities', *Triple C: Communication, Capitalism & Critique. Journal for a Global Sustainable Information Society*, 12(1): 142–68.

Pujolar, J. (2007a) 'The future of Catalan: Language endangerment and nationalist discourses in Catalonia', in A. Duchene and M. Heller (eds.), *Discourses of endangerment: Ideology and interest in the defence of languages* (pp. 121–48), London: Continuum.

Pujolar, J. (2007b) 'African women in Catalan language courses: Struggles over class, gender and ethnicity in advanced liberalism', in B.S. Mcelhinny (ed.), *Words, worlds and material girls* (pp. 305–48), Berlin: Mouton de Gruyter.

Ramirez, A.G. and Hall, J.K. (1990) 'Language and culture in secondary level Spanish textbooks', *The Modern Language Journal*, 74(1): 48–65.

Rebelo, J. (2010) 'The big information and communication groups in the world', *Janus.net*, 1(1): 59–69.

Richards, J. (2001) *Curriculum development in language teaching*, Cambridge: Cambridge University Press.

Richards, J. and Rodgers, T. (2001) *Approaches and methods in language teaching*, 2nd edn, Cambridge: Cambridge University Press.

Richardson, H. (2014) 'Modern languages "recovery programme" urged by MPs', *BBC News*, 14 July. Available at: <www.bbc.com/news/education-28269496> (accessed 11 November 2016).

Rifkin, B. (1998) 'Gender representation in foreign language textbooks: A case study of textbooks of Russian', *The Modern Language Journal*, 82(2): 217–36.

Risager, K. (1991) 'Cultural references in European textbooks: An evaluation of recent tendencies', in D. Buttjes and M. Byram (eds.), *Mediating languages and cultures: Towards an intercultural theory of foreign language education* (pp. 180–92), Clevedon: Multilingual Matters.

Ritzer, G. (1996) *The McDonaldization of society*, revised edn, Thousand Oaks: Sage.

Rodriguez, E. (2011) 'Constructivism and the neoliberal agenda in the Spanish curriculum reform of the 1980s and 1990s', *Educational Philosophy and Theory*, 43(10): 1047–64.

188 References

Rodríguez, E. and López, I. (2011) 'Del auge al colapso' [From the rise to the breakdown], *Revista de economía crítica*, 12: 39–63.

Roig, N. and Daranas, M. (2011) *Passos 2. Llibre de classe. Nivell Elemental*, Barcelona: Octaedro.

Roig, N., Padrós, M. and Camps, S. (2011) *Passos 1. Llibre de classe. Nivell Bàsic*, Barcelona: Octaedro.

Rolnik, R. (2013) 'Late neoliberalism: The financialization of homeownership and housing rights', *International Journal of Urban and Regional Research*, 37(3): 1058–66.

Ronald, R. (2008) *The ideology of home ownership*, Basingstoke: Palgrave.

Ros i Solé, C. (2013) 'Spanish imagined: Political and subjective approaches to language textbooks', in J. Gray (ed.), *Critical perspectives on language teaching materials* (pp. 161–81), Basingstoke: Palgrave.

Rose, N. (1990) *Governing the soul: The shaping of the private self*, London: Routledge.

Rose, N. (1999) *Powers of freedom: Reframing political thought*, Cambridge: Cambridge University Press.

Ross, E.W. and Gibson, R.J. (eds.) (2007) *Neoliberalism and education reform*, New Jersey: Hampton press.

Ruiz, E. (2006) 'Las reformas laborales en España (1977–2002)' [Labor reforms in Spain (1977–2002)], *Filosofía, política y economía en el Laberinto*, 20: 7–22.

Sánchez, A. (1992) *Historia de la enseñanza del español como lengua extranjera* [History of Spanish as a foreing language teaching], Madrid: Sociedad general española de librería.

Santos, D. (2007) 'Reconceptualizing textbooks in culture teaching', *Academic Exchange Quarterly*, 11(1): 36–41.

Savignon, S.J. (1991) 'Communicative language teaching: State of the art', *TESOL Quarterly*, 25: 261–77.

Saville, N. (2005) 'An interview with John Trim at 80', *Language Assessment Quarterly*, 2(4): 263–88.

Selwyn, N. (2015) 'The discursive construction of education in the digital age', in R.H. Jones, A. Chik and C.A. Hafner (eds.), *Discourse and digital practices: Doing discourse analysis in the digital age* (pp. 226–40), New York: Routledge.

Sennett, R. (1998) *The corrosion of character: The personal consequences of work in the new capitalism*, New York: W.W. Norton.

Servage, L. (2009) 'The scholarship of teaching and learning and the neo-liberalization of higher education: Constructing the "Entrepreneurial Learner"', *The Canadian Journal of Higher Education*, 39(2): 25–44.

Shamir, R. (2008) 'Corporate social responsibility: Towards a new market-embedded morality?', *Theoretical Inquiries in Law*, 9(2): 371–94.

Shardakova, M. and Pavlenko, A. (2004) 'Identity options in Russian textbooks', *Journal of Language, Identity, and Education*, 3(1): 25–46.

Sheils, J. (1988) *Communication in the modern languages classroom*, Strasbourg: Council of Europe.

Sheldon, L.E. (1988) 'Evaluating ELT textbooks and materials', *ELT Journal*, 42(4): 237–46.

Shin, H. (2016) 'Language "skills" and the neoliberal English education industry', *Journal of Multilingual and Multicultural Development*, 37(5): 509–22.

Shin, H. and Park, J.S.Y. (2016) 'Researching language and neoliberalism', *Journal of Multilingual and Multicultural Development*, 37(5): 443–52.

References   189

Silva, J. (2010) 'Becoming a neoliberal subject: Working-class selfhood in an age of uncertainty', Unpublished manuscript, Harvard Online. Available at: <http://blogs.sciences-po.fr/recherche-inegalites/files/2011/05/Jennifer-Silva-POLINE-2011-11.pdf> (accessed 4 May 2017).

Sinn, H.W. (2010) *Casino capitalism: How the financial crisis came about and what needs to be done now*, Oxford: Oxford University Press.

Skela, J. (2014) 'The quest for literature in EFL textbooks – a quest for Camelot?', *ELOPE: English Language Overseas Perspectives and Enquiries*, 11(1): 113–36.

Sklair, L. (1998) 'Transnational practices and the analysis of the global system', Seminar delivered for the Transnational Communities Programme Seminar Series, 22 May. Online. Available at: <http://163.1.0.34/working%20papers/sklair.pdf> (accessed 4 December 2016).

Sklair, L. (2002) *Globalization, capitalism and its alternatives*, Oxford: Oxford University Press.

Sola, J. (2014) 'El legado histórico franquista y el mercado de trabajo en España' [The francoist historic legacy and the labor market in Spain], *Revista Española de Sociología*, 21: 99–128.

Springer, S. (2012) 'Neoliberalism as discourse: Between Foucauldian political economy and Marxian poststructuralism', *Critical Discourse Studies*, 9(2): 133–47.

Springer, S., Birch, K. and MacLeavy, J. (2016) 'An introduction to neoliberalism', in S. Springer, K. Birch and J. MacLeavy (eds.), *The handbook of neoliberalism* (pp. 1–14), London: Routledge.

Standing, G. (2011) *The precariat: The new dangerous class*, London: Bloomsbury.

Stern, H. (1991) *Fundamental concepts of language teaching* (7th impression), Oxford: Oxford University Press.

Strubell, M. (1996) 'Language planning and bilingual education in Catalonia', *Journal of Multilingual and Multicultural Development*, 17(2–4): 262–75.

Strubell, M. and Boix-Fuster, E. (eds.) (2011) *Democratic policies for language revitalisation: The case of Catalan*, New York: Palgrave.

Sugarman, J. (2015) 'Neoliberalism and psychological ethics', *Journal of Theoretical and Philosophical Psychology*, 35(2): 103–16.

Sunderland, J. (2000) 'New understandings of gender and language classroom research: Texts, teacher talk and student talk', *Language Teaching Research*, 4: 149–73.

Takahashi, K. (2015) 'Literary texts as authentic materials for language learning: The current situation in Japan', in M. Teranishi, Y. Saito and K. Wales (eds.), *Literature and language learning in the EFL classroom* (pp. 26–40), Basingstoke: Palgrave.

Taki, S. (2008) 'International and local curricula: The question of ideology', *Language Teaching Research*, 12(1): 127–42.

Talmy, S. (2010) 'Critical research in applied linguistics', in B. Paltridge and A. Phakiti (eds.), *Continuum companion to research methods in applied linguistics* (pp. 127–42), London: Continuum.

Tan, P. and Rubdy, R. (eds.) (2008) *Language as commodity: Global structure, local marketplaces*, London: Continuum.

Taylor, P. and Harris, J. (2008) *Critical theories of mass media: Then and now*, New York: McGraw-Hill Education.

Taylor-Mendes, C. (2009) 'Construction of racial stereotypes in English as a Foreign Language (EFL) textbooks: Images as discourse', in R. Kubota and A. Lin (eds.),

190 References

Race, culture, and identities in second language education: Exploring critically engaged practice (pp. 64–80), London: Routledge.

Thomas, P. (2017) 'The portrayal of non-westerners in EFL textbooks in Norway', *Cogent Education*, 4(1): 1–12.

Thornbury, S. (2000) 'A dogma for EFL', *IATEFL Issues*, 153: 2.

Thornbury, S. (2009) 'Dogme: Nothing if not critical', *Teaching English*. Online. Available at: <www.teachingenglish.org.uk/article/dogme-nothing-if-not-critical> (accessed 4 October 2016).

Thornbury, S. (2013) 'Resisting coursebooks', in J. Gray (ed.), *Critical perspectives on language teaching materials* (pp. 204–23), Basingstoke: Palgrave.

Thornbury, S. (2015) 'English language teaching textbooks: Content, consumption, production' [Book review], *ELT Journal*, 69(1): 100–2.

Thornbury, S. (2016) 'Communicative language teaching in theory and practice', in G. Hall (ed.), *The Routledge handbook of English language teaching* (pp. 224–37), London: Routledge.

Tomlinson, B. (2003) *Developing materials for language learning and teaching*, New York: Continuum.

Tomlinson, B. (2012) 'Materials development for language learning and teaching', *Language Teaching*, 45(2): 143–79.

Tomlinson, B. (2013) *Applied linguistics and materials development*, London: Bloomsbury.

Tomlinson, B., Dat, B., Masuhara, H. and Rubdy, R. (2001) 'EFL courses for adults', *ELT Journal*, 55(1): 80–101.

Torres, C.A (2011) 'Public universities and the neoliberal common sense: Seven iconoclastic theses', *International Studies in Sociology of Education*, 21(3): 177–97.

Trim, J.L.M. (1992) 'El català amb relació a Europa' [Catalan language in relation to Europe], in *Ponències, comunicacions i conclusions; Segon simposi sobre l'ensenyament del català a no catalano-parlants. Vic. 4, 5 i 6 setembre 1991* (pp. 39–51), Vic: Eumo.

Trim, J.L.M. (ed.) (2003) *Common European framework of reference for languages: Learning, teaching, assessment. A guide for users*, Strasbourg: Council of Europe.

Trim, J.L.M. (2005) 'The place of the common European framework of reference for languages in teacher education and training', in *Project Y2- report of central workshop 4/2005*, Appendix 1 (pp. 13–27), Graz: European Centre for Modern Languages.

Trim, J.L.M. (2007) *Modern languages in the Council of Europe 1954–1997*, Straousburg: Council of Europe.

Troike, R.C. (1977) 'The future of English. Editorial', *The Linguistic Reporter*, 19(8): 2.

Trudgill, P. (1974) *The social differentiation of English in Norwich*, Cambridge: Cambridge University Press.

Tuschling, A. and Engemann, C. (2006) 'From education to lifelong learning: The emerging regime of learning in the European Union', *Educational Philosophy and Theory*, 38(4): 451–69.

Uljens, M. (2007) 'The hidden curriculum of PISA – the promotion of neoliberal policy by educational assessment', in S. Hopman, G. Brinek and M. Retzl (eds.), *PISA according to PISA: Does PISA keep what it promises?* (pp. 265–94), Wien: LIT.

Ullah, H. and Skelton, C. (2013) 'Gender representation in the public sector schools textbooks of Pakistan', *Educational Studies*, 39(2): 183–94.

References 191

Urciuoli, B. (2008) 'Skills and selves in the new workplace', *American Ethnologist*, 35(2): 211–28.

Urciuoli, B. (2010) 'Neoliberal education: Preparing the student for the new workplace', in C. Greenhouse (ed.), *Ethnographies of neoliberalism* (pp. 162–76), Philadelphia: University of Pennsylvania Press.

Valax, P. (2011) 'The common European framework of reference for languages: A critical analysis of its impact on a sample of teachers and curricula within and beyond Europe', unpublished thesis, University of Waikato, Australia. Online. Available at: <http://researchcommons.waikato.ac.nz/handle/10289/5546> (accessed 4 March 2017).

Vallverdú, F. (1984) 'A sociolinguistic history of Catalan', *International Journal of the Sociology of Language*, 47: 13–28.

Van Dijk, T.A. (2000) 'Ideology and discourse: A multidisciplinary introduction'. Online. Available at: <www.discourses.org/UnpublishedArticles/Ideology and discourse.pdf> (accessed 4 October 2016).

van Ek, J.A. (1975) *The threshold level*, Strasbourg: Council of Europe.

van Ek, J.A. and Alexander, L.G. (1980) *Threshold level English*, Oxford: Pergamon.

van Ek, J.A., Alexander, L.G. and Fitzpatrick, M.A. (1980) *Waystage English*, Oxford: Pergamon.

van Ek, J.A. and Trim, J.L.M. (1991) *Threshold level 1990*, Cambridge: Cambridge University Press.

van Ek, J.A. and Trim, J.L.M. (1998) *Threshold level 1990*, 2nd edn, Cambridge: Cambridge University Press.

van Ek, J.A. and Trim, J.L.M. (2001) *Vantage: Council of Europe*, Cambridge: Cambridge University Press.

Vilà, C. and Homs, L. (2013a) *Fil per randa Bàsic. Llibre de l'alumne*, Barcelona: Barcanova.

Vilà, C. and Homs, L. (2013b) *Fil per randa Elemental. Llibre de l'alumne*, Barcelona: Barcanova.

Vila, F.X. (ed.) (2012) *Survival and development of language communities: Prospects and challenges*, Bristol: Multilingual Matters.

Vila, F.X and Bretxa, V. (2012) 'The analysis of medium-sized language communities', in F.X. Vila (ed.), *Survival and development of language communities: Prospects and challenges* (pp. 1–17), Bristol: Multilingual Matters.

Vilar, M. (2012) '¿De aquellas arenas estos lodos? El mercado de trabajo en España desde una perspectiva histórica' [From that sand to this sludge? Labour market in Spain from a historical perspective], *Revista Galega de Economía*, 21(1): 1–32.

Virno, P. (2004) *A grammar of the multitude*, Los Angeles: Semiotext(e).

Warriner, D.S. (2016) ' "Here, without English, you are dead": Ideologies of language and discourses of neoliberalism in adult English language learning', *Journal of Multilingual and Multicultural Development*, 37(5): 495–508.

Warschauer, M. (2000) 'The changing global economy and the future of English teaching', *TESOL Quarterly*, 34(3): 511–35.

Webber, J. and Strubell, M. (1991) *The Catalan language: Progress towards normalisation*, Barcelona: The Anglo-Catalan Society.

Wilkins, D.A. (1976) *Notional syllabuses: A taxonomy and its relevance to foreign language curriculum development*, Oxford: Oxford University Press.

Williams, R. (1985) *Keywords: A vocabulary of culture and society*, New York: Oxford University Press.

192 References

Williamson, J. (1990) 'What Washington means by policy reform', in J. Williamson (ed.), *Latin American adjustment: How much has happened?* (pp. 5–20), Washington DC: Institute of International Economics.

Wisniewski, K. (2013) 'The empirical validity of the CEFR Fluency Scale: The A2 level description', in E. Galaczi and C. Weir (eds.), *Exploring language frameworks: Proceedings of the ALTE Kraków conference, July 2011. Vol. 36* (pp. 251–70), Cambridge: Cambridge University Press.

Woolard, K.A. (1989) *Double talk: Bilingualism and the politics of ethnicity in Catalonia*, Stanford: Stanford University Press.

Woolard, K.A. (2003) 'We don't speak Catalan because we are marginalized: Ethnic and class connotations of language in Barcelona', In R. Blot (ed.), *Language and social identity* (pp. 85–103), Westport: Praeger.

Woolard, K.A. (2009) 'Linguistic consciousness among adolescents in Catalonia: A case study from the Barcelona urban area in longitudinal perspective', *Zeitschrift für Katalanistik*, 22: 125–49.

Woolard, K.A. (2016) *Singular and plural: Ideologies of linguistic authority in 21st century Catalonia*, New York: Oxford University Press.

Zacchi, J. (2016) 'Neoliberalism, applied linguistics and the PNLD', *Ilha do Desterro*, 69(1): 161–72.

Zimmerman, J. (2008) 'From brew town to cool town: Neoliberalism and the creative city development strategy in Milwaukee', *Cities*, 25(4): 230–42.

Index

Aaker, Jennifer 62
Adorno, Theodor 4, 163
Alderson, Charles 31
Althusser, Louis 163
Apple, Michael 5, 74, 116, 163
Army Specialized Training Program
  (ASTP) 21
Arrese, José Luís 149
audiolingualism 21–2
audio-visual method 22
Auerbach, Elsa 54, 167
austerity 8

banking sector 79, 153–6
Barcelona 85–7, 143, 158
Baroness Coussins 34
Basabe, Enrique 49
Bauman, Zygmunt 79
Bernstein, Katie 16
bilingualism 84
Block, David 3, 11–12, 42–3, 55–6,
  58, 117, 132, 140, 168
Bologna process 30–1
Boltanski, Luc and Chiapello, Eve 76
Boufoy-Bastick, Béatrice 33
Bourdieu, Pierre 6
Brexit 11, 166
British Council 26, 165
Brown, Gillian 57
Burgess, Denise 54
Byram, Michael 48

call centers 13
Cameron, Deborah 12, 35
Cannagarajah, Suresh 48, 63
Capgemini 99
capitalism 3, 159, 165; capitalist class
  3, 14; casino capitalism 153; *see also*
  neoliberalism

Caritas 121
Catalan independence 86
Catalan language: *see also* bilingualism;
  social usage 84–6, 88; speaking
  community 83; teaching in schools
  84–5; teaching to non-Catalan adult
  speakers 90–1, 96–7
CEFR (Common European Framework
  of Reference) 27–31, 69, 96–7;
  critics of the 31–4
Chicago School of Economics 6–7
Christian-Smith, Linda 5
Chun, Christian 9, 60–1, 167
class erasure 114–17
Codó, Eva and Patiño-Santos,
  Adriana 85
Coffey, Simon 49, 59
Colau, Ada 143
commodification of housing 78, 144–5,
  147, 150
commodification of language 15–16
*Communication in the Modern
  Languages Classroom* (Sheils) 27–8
communicative language teaching
  22–3, 90
Consortium for Linguistic
  Normalization (CPNL) 96, 110
consumerism 79, 110–13, 156–7
Cook, Vivian 55
Copley, Keith 56
Corbin, Jeremy 11
Corona, Víctor 85
corrala 160
Cortazzi, Martin and Jin, Lixian 48
cosmopolitanism 53, 58
Council of Europe 23–4, 90–1,
  120, 165; *see also* CEFR; *see also*
  Threshold Level; *see also* Trim, John
critical discourse analysis 41, 74, 81

194 *Index*

critical pedagogy 4–5, 74, 167
culture: in language textbooks research 48–50
Curdt-Christiansen, Xiao Lan and Weninger, Csilla 43

Dardot, Pierre and Laval, Christian 10, 81, 133, 165
De Angelis, Massimo 65
Debord, Guy 163
Del Percio, Alfonso 15, 53, 138
Dendrinos, Bessie 54
Dialectic of Enlightenment (Horkheimer and Adorno) 4
Di Bernardo, Francesco 121
digital learning resources 98–9
Digui, digui 91–3, 103
Di Paolo, Antonio and Raymond, Josep Lluís 88
diversity 51–2
Dogme language teaching 64

economy: economic crises 8, 11, 89, 96, 107, 128, 140, 142–3; knowledge-based economy 12, 15, 98; *see also* political economy; postindustrial economy 7, 76; *see also* Spanish economy
El Corte Inglés 99
El País 92
Engels, Friedrich 82, 142
English as a *lingua franca* 21,35, 41
English language teaching (ELT) 14–15, 21, 26, 28, 37–8, 165
English language textbooks 44, 48–51, 54–61, 63, 139, 162, 165, 167
entrepreneurship 60–2, 77, 132–3; and education 139–40
Etxezarreta, Miren 90–1, 100, 143
European Agency for Safety and Health 135
European Commission 34, 139–40
European Union 28, 53; *see also* European Commission
evictions 143, 159
expert knowledge 78, 135–7, 147

Fairclough, Norman 13, 74
Fellner, Wolfgang and Spash, Clive 116
Figueras, Neus 30–1
Fletcher, Robert 113
flexibility 76, 122–4
flexicurity 121

Flores, Nelson 52–3
Follow Me 26, 91
Ford foundation 21
Foucault, Michel 10, 76, 132
Franco, Francisco 84, 87, 90, 149
Frankfurt School 4, 163
Fraser, Nancy 42
free market 6–7, 9–10, 34, 60, 112, 146–7; ideology 12, 36, 147, 154, 169; *see also* privatization
Freire, Paulo 4–5, 167
Friedman, Milton 7
Furedi, Frank 47

gender: in language textbooks research 44–6
German Ideology, The (Marx and Engels) 2
Giroux, Henry 4–5
globalization: and neoliberalism 7, 95–6
Grady, Karen 55
Gramsci, Antonio 3–4,
Gray, Garry 133–4
Gray, John 11, 43, 45, 55–9, 61–4, 117, 127, 165, 168
Gulliver, Trevor 51

Hachette Livre 98
Halliday, Michael 52
Hardt, Michael and Negri, Antonio 12
Harvey, David 6–9, 95–6
Harwood, Nigel 42, 57
Hayek, Friedrich 6
hegemony 3–4; neoliberalism as 9, 13, 169
Heller, Monica 13, 15
Hickey, Tom 53
Hill, Dave 14, 36–7, 52
Hirtt, Nico 36–7
Holborow, Marnie 4, 6, 8, 9, 11, 36–7
home ownership 78, 148–50
homo economicus 136
hooks, bell 52
Horkheimer, Max 4, 163

I, Daniel Blake (Loach) 8
identity: in language learning 46; in language textbooks research 47–8; entrepreneurial identity 132, 139, 164; politics 12, 42–3
ideology 2–3, 5–6; and textbooks 5–6, 43, 55, 58, 107, 163; Marxist

interpretation of 5; neoliberalism as 1, 8–9, 11, 15, 38, 56, 62, 165
Ideology and Curriculum (Apple) 5
immigration to Catalonia 87–8, 96, 107
indignados 166
individualism 14, 81, 113
instrumentalism 35, 118, 163
intercultural competence 48
International Monetary Fund 7, 87, 95, 121

Jameson, Fredric 169
Jaworski, Adam and Thurlow, Crispin 59
Jones, Geoffrey 20

Kincheloe, Joe 74
Kinginger, Celeste 55
Klein, Naomi 7
Kramsch, Claire 21–2, 48, 59–60
Kubota, Ryuko 33, 35, 37–8, 53
Kullman, John 47

labor exploitation 81, 159
labor precariousness 96, 121
La Caixa 155
Lagardère 98
language education 16; and neoliberalism 37–9; centralization of 32, 35, 93; *see also* English language teaching (ELT); *see also* marketization of education; standardization of 32–3, 35, 93
Language Learning for European Citizenship 28
language textbooks 1–2; aspirational content in 58, 60, 165; boom of Catalan 97–8; cultural artifacts 2, 41; critical research on 41–4, 64–5, 70; *see also* ELT textbooks; literature in 93–5; publishing companies 97–8; reception by teachers and learners 62–4
Levidow, Les 99
LGBT 45–6
lifelong learning 77, 128–30
Littlejohn, Andrew 2, 165
Loach, Ken 8
López, Dina 38
Luke, Allan 5, 13, 36, 74, 163

Marcuse, Herbert 4, 163
Marcuse, Peter 78

marketization of education 36–7, 139–40, 166
Marx, Karl 2–3, 82, 121
Marxist theory: base and superstructure 2–3, 161; of social class 3; of society 162; of capitalism 3; of ideology 5; of neoliberalism 8–9
material development 42
McCommunication 12–13
McDonaldization 12
McLaren, Peter 4, 74
McVeigh, Paul 90
medium-sized languages 83–4
method(s) 20–2
Michaels, Walter Benn 52
Mirowski, Philip 117
mismatched workers 124
mobility 77, 125–6, 131
Monzó, Quim 154–5
Moran, Mario 46
Morgan, Matthew 9
mortgage 79, 150–3, 155, 157, 159; *see also* banking sector
multiculturalism 52–3
Muñoz, Rubén 31, 37

NATO 83
Ndura, Elavie 50
neoliberalism 6–11, 95–6; applied linguistics studies of 11–16; as common sense 1, 3, 9, 65, 147; as ideology 1, 8–9, 11, 15, 38, 56, 62, 165; as economic theory 6–7, 165; as rationality 10, 53, 133, 165; political crisis of 10–11, 16, 166
North American supremacy 21
Norton, Bonnie 46
notional-functional syllabus 26

Occupy Wall Street 166
Olssen, Mark 37, 77
Open Society Foundation 28
Organization for Economic Cooperation and Development (OECD) 13, 36, 87
Oxfam 8

PAH (Plataforma d'Afectats per la Hipoteca) 143
Park, Joseph Sung-Yul 14–5
Parla.cat 67, 99
Pavlenko, Aneta 46–7
Pedagogy of the Oppressed (Freire) 4–5

196 *Index*

Pennycook, Alastair 19, 41
Petanović, Jelena 51
Peters, Michael 5, 36, 78, 134, 138
Peters, Tom 77, 81–2
Phillipson, Robert 21, 23, 54
Pinochet, Augusto 7
plurilingualism: and neoliberalism 53–4
political economy: in applied
    linguistics research 11–16,
    52,79–80; in Spain 87, 89–90,
    95–6, 120–1, 143, 145, 149, 157;
    neoliberalism as 6–7, 165
Porreca, Karen 44
postmodernism 46
precariat 14, 131–2
privatization 7, 95, 157
Prodnik, Jernej 98
Programme for International Student
    Assessment (PISA) 36
Pujolar, Joan 88
Punset, Eduard 127

race: in language textbooks research
    50–1
Ramirez, Arnulfo and Hall, Joan Kelly
    48–9
Reagan, Ronald 7
real estate bubble 143, 145, 147,
    148, 150
recognition paradigm 42–3, 46, 48
redistribution paradigm 42
Richards, Jack 20–1, 57
Risager, Karen 54
risk management 77–8, 133–4
risk society 125
Ritzer, George 12
Rockefeller foundation 21
Rodgers, Theodore 20–1
Rolnik, Raquel 78
Ronald, Richard 78
Rose, Nikolas 135–6
Ros i Solé, Cristina 50, 59

self-branding 77, 81, 130–1
self-responsibility 77, 133, 135, 157
Selwyn, Neil 99
Sennet, Robert 122
Servage, Laura 77
Shardakova, Marya 46–7
Sheils, Joe 27–8
Shin, Hyunjung 38
situational language teaching 22

Sklair, Leslie 79
social class 13–15, 54–6, 75–6, 85–6,
    106–14; *see also* class erasure
socialism 7
Soros, George 28
Spanish economy 87, 89–90, 95–6,
    120–1, 143, 145, 149, 157
Spanish language: in Catalonia 84–8;
    textbooks 48–9, 50, 59–60
Springer, Simon 8–9
squat 159–60
Standing, Guy 14, 131
subjectivity 136–7
Sugarman, Jeff 47–8
Sultan of Brunei 154
Sunderland, Jane 44

Taki, Saeed 60
task-based approach 35, 69
Taylor-Mendes, Cosete 63
technologization of discourse 13
telework 131–2
TESOL Quarterly 167
textual genres 117–18
Thatcher, Margaret 7, 154
therapy culture 47
Thomas, Paul 51
Thornbury, Scott 22, 36, 64
Threshold Level 24–27, 71, 90
TINA (there is no alternative) 154
Tomlinson, Brian 42, 57
Torres, Carlos Alberto 1
transnational corporations 76, 95, 98
Trim, John 23–30
Troika 121
Trump, Donald 11, 166

Uljens, Michael 36
unemployment 81, 89, 121, 126, 128

Valax, Philippe 31–2
Van Dijk, T. 50–1
Van Ek, Jan Ate 24–7
Vinall, Kimberly 59–60

Warriner, Doris 38
Washington consensus 7
Woolard, Kathryn 86
World Bank 7, 95

Zacchi, Vanderlei 60
zero drag 77, 126–9